THE GUN-REVIEW BOOK

MICHAEL McINTOSH

THE GUN REVIEW BOOK

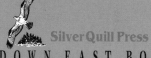

Silver Quill Press

DOWN EAST BOOKS CAMDEN·MAINE

COPYRIGHT © 1997 MICHAEL SCOTT MCINTOSH

ISBN 0-89272-405-6

DESIGNED BY LURELLE CHEVERIE

PRINTED AND BOUND AT THOMSON-SHORE, INC., DEXTER, MICHIGAN

2   4   5   3   1

DOWN EAST BOOKS
P.O. BOX 679 CAMDEN · MAINE 04843
BOOK ORDERS: 1-800-766-1670

LIBRARY OF CONGRESS CATALOGING-IN-PUBLICATION DATA
MCINTOSH, MICHAEL
        THE GUN-REVIEW BOOK / BY MICHAEL MCINTOSH.
        P.   CM.
        INCLUDES INDEX.
        ISBN 0-89272-405-6 (PBK.)
        1. FIREARMS.   I. TITLE.
TS5344.M287   1997
683.4—DC21
                                        97-10921
                                        CIP

TO THE READERS,

PAST, PRESENT, AND FUTURE –

WHERE WOULD I BE WITHOUT YOU ?

Contents

CONTENTS

Introduction

In the middle of 1988, *Shooting Sportsman* was still something of a fledgling magazine. The premiere issue had appeared the previous December, the brainchild of founder-publisher Steve Smith. Like most such things that have taken shape in Smitty's head, it was a sharply focused, well-defined concept, summed up nicely by the subtitle: *The Magazine of Wingshooting & Fine Guns.*

It was a hit right from the start, which was hardly surprising considering the subject matter and the fact that Smitty put together some serious talent for his staff of columnists—Gene Hill, John Falk, Rich Grozik, Tom Huggler, Carol Wary, Galen Winter. He and I had talked a bit about my taking on a column of some sort, but I still had a day job in 1987, and the time I had available for freelancing was both limited and largely already committed. So, I wrote feature stories for the first few issues and took pleasure in watching the magazine make an immediate impact in the sporting field.

Presently, two things happened that changed my relationship with *Shooting Sportsman.* For one, I made up my mind that I wanted to write full-time and gave my day-job employer several months' notice. For another, Gene Hill decided to retire as the gun-review columnist, and editor Dave Wonderlich offered the slot to me. The first one I wrote, on Arrieta, appeared in the issue of October/November 1988. The last one was in the July/August issue of 1996, when, feeling the need for a change of subject matter, I asked the editors if I could switch to the shooting column recently vacated by John Brindle's untimely death.

As sometimes happens to magazines, *Shooting Sportsman* went through a couple of changes in ownership during those years and endured some hardships in the process. By the time it landed in the Outdoor Group of Down East Enterprise in 1993, it needed a transfusion of both finances and promotional efforts.

This the magazine received, and as circulation doubled and then doubled again, I began to get more and more enquiries from new readers, asking if they could get copies of previous gun reviews and if there were plans to collect them all in one place.

There were no such plans initially, but as requests continued to mount, the notion of putting the reviews together in one volume seemed to make better and better sense, especially once I decided to close out my stint as the reviewer.

So that's how this little book came to be. All the pieces I wrote for the review column during those eight years are here, essentially. In a few instances, I had written on the same gun more than once, from different perspectives, and I've combined those into single chapters. I've rewritten all the rest to some extent, updating all the information to the present time. And I've written two new chapters, just for this; I had intended to devote columns to both the Parker and the Winchester Model 21 at some point, but though I never got around to writing them for the magazine, I decided they really ought to be in this book, to make it more complete.

As is inevitable given the span of time involved, some guns that were available new when I reviewed them are no longer in production. Even so, I think they belong here, too, because they're still available as used guns, and a discussion of them might come in handy if you're thinking of buying one.

Obviously, there's more than one way to review any product, and I decided in the beginning that the way to make these pieces most useful was to amplify my evaluations with detailed explanations of why I thought what I thought about any given gun. My intention has been to help readers develop their ability to make their own evaluations—by pointing out what to look at, what to look for, and what it all means to the quality of a gun. My only handle on measuring how successful I've been is that quite a few readers have told me they've felt more confident buying guns after reading my reviews for a year or two or three. If so, good; that's what I hoped for.

Given the nature of the task, a certain element of personal taste inevitably gets wound up in reviewing anything, and that's okay—so long as the distinction between taste and objective standards remains clear. Few things rankle me more than hearing someone say, in effect, "This is a bad [gun, book, car, whatever] because I don't like the way it looks or the subject or the color or whatever."

Now, I'm as strongly influenced by my own tastes as anyone, but I've tried to make clear in these reviews the difference between evaluations based on some objective standard and those that come from my particular prejudices. A conversation I had with a reader not long ago suggests that I've been at least partly able to pull it off.

"You don't think much of German guns, do you?" the man said.

"No, I don't, generally," I said. "But I sure like the craftsmanship that goes into a lot of them."

"Yeah," he said, "I can see that. So lemme tell you about my Merkel over/under . . ."

Nobody ever said that being a gun reviewer would be easy. Having been one, though, I can tell you there are worse ways to spend your time. What you're holding in your hands right now is the result of a lot of shooting and measuring and looking and thinking and writing. I hope it's as pleasant to read as it was to write. Above all, I hope you find it useful.

• • • •

That this book should exist owes a great deal of thanks to a relatively small number of people. Certainly to Steve Smith, for having the whole idea to begin with; to Dave Wonderlich, Bill

Buckley, Ralph Stuart, Vic Venters, and Silvio Calabi—in turn
or in concert, the editors who first saw these pieces into
print—and Tom Fernald, Karin Womer, and Chris Cornell of
Down East Books, for doing the same in their present form; to
my old friend Bill Headrick, to whose expertise and good taste
belong most of the illustrations; to the various gunmakers,
importers, dealers and others who provided the guns I worked
with; and to my dear friends the hands-on gunsmiths and
craftsmen who have taken the time to help me understand the
technical nature of their trade and whose graciousness has
never failed in the face of my sometimes dumb questions—
David Trevallion, Abe Chaber, David Brydon, Ken Hunt,
Marcus Hunt, Winston Churchill, the late John Realmuto, Bill
O'Brien, Russell Wilkin, Jack Rowe, James Flynn, Nick
Makinson, D'Arcy Echols, Steve Hughes, Adam Davies, Paul
Hodgins, Terry Smith, and Peter Finch.

MICHAEL MCINTOSH
Copper Creek Farm
Camdenton, Missouri
SEPTEMBER 1996

PART ONE

WHAT'S NEW

CHAPTER ONE

ARRIETA

As you might have noticed, the Spanish gun trade is making a definite run at the American market these days, and some of the guns represent a level of value that's hard to beat anywhere else. I won't belabor the point, except to say that a good-quality sidelock ejector gun built entirely to order for a price of less than five figures—in some cases, a lot less—is not a proposition to take lightly.

The very first gun review I wrote for *Shooting Sportsman*, in 1988, was on an Arrieta game gun built to specifications for Paul Jaeger, Inc., the gun department at Dunn's. Jaeger has since stopped handling them, and Orvis is using Arrieta as the maker for some of its proprietary guns built to company specs. Unlike that situation years ago, however, Arrieta now is approaching the American market on its own, through a consortium of four dealers, and that means it's more convenient than ever before to have one custom built.

What hasn't changed is that Arrieta is still one of the best gunmakers in Spain.

The company dates to 1916, when Avelino Arrieta set up as an outworker to the Spanish trade at the age of nineteen. Outworkers are the freelancers of the gun world, independent craftsmen who build guns or components for other makers, and they don't survive long without being very good at what they do. That King Alfonso XIII, a keen pigeon and game shot, was one of Sr. Arrieta's customers suggests a fair level of skill—particularly since the king also was a long-time customer of Purdey's. (And so good a patron that when he died in 1941, Tom Purdey closed his account in the Purdey ledgers with the comment: "The nicest man and best friend this firm has ever had.")

Sr. Arrieta taught his sons Victor and José the gunmaker's craft, and in 1940, with the turmoil of the Spanish Civil War finally over, the three set up shop in Elgoibar to build guns under the style Avelino Arrieta. Although the rest of the world was by then in a turmoil of its own, the domestic market in Spain, a neutral nation throughout World War II, provided more than enough work to keep them busy. In fact, they built guns almost exclusively for the Spanish market until 1970, when they reorganized as a limited company, becoming Manufacturas Arrieta. José Arrieta's son, Juan Carlos, became the third generation of the firm, and now that he has retired, Sr. Manolo Santos serves as managing director.

Like any shop that builds to order, Arrieta will make virtually any gun you want and decorate it in any style and to any extent that suits your taste and checkbook. Or you can browse the catalog and choose among thirteen different models available as standard fare. All are side-by-side sidelock ejector guns, and the differences among them are relatively slight, most a matter of decoration and such minor variations as a round-body frame or sideclips or self-opening in the Holland & Holland mode.

All thirteen come in all the bore sizes from 12 to .410, with chopper-lump barrels, Holland-style action and lockwork, and such niceties as automatic safety and articulated front trigger. Most of the options—self-opener, single trigger, Churchill rib, pistol grip and beavertail forend, choice of frame finish, hand-detachable locks, and so on—are available for most models. Barrel length, chokes, weight, balance, trigger-pulls, and stock dimensions are entirely the customer's choice.

You can get all these things from any number of gunmakers in various parts of Europe, but not at anything close to the prices the Spanish makers charge.

Of the dealers selling Arrietas these days, Jack Jansma of Wingshooting Adventures in Grand Rapids, Michigan, turns the highest volume. I've spent a few days every year shooting pheasants in Hungary with Jack for quite some time now, and on one trip in the early '90s, he brought along a splendid pair of self-openers. Being a thoughtful chap, he lent me one to shoot in a couple of drives. Although we are by no means of similar build, the stock fit wasn't too far off. (Jack's roughly the size of a grizzly bear; I'm basically Joe Average, but I like a fairly long stock.) We do have similar views on balance and trigger-pull, though, so I found his Arrieta a pleasure to shoot.

At the lodge that evening, soaking in the various warmths of the big ceramic-tiled woodstove and a glass of cognac, I asked if I could get hold of an Arrieta for a test and review. It showed up two weeks later, a Model 557 28-gauge fresh in from Spain.

The 557 is the lowest of the Arrieta grades and sells at a price comparable to the lowest grades from AyA and Garbi. You could say much the same for the quality.

ARRIETA MODEL 557
MICHAEL McINTOSH

The barrels are well-made, struck without unnecessary waves and ripples, and fitted with a Churchill rib. Filing and actioning are quite good. The wood is handsome, butt and forend well matched, all closely fitted, properly shaped, well checkered, and oil-finished. The frame is color-hardened, the rest of the metal nicely blacked and blued. For just under $3000, I really can't see anything major to quarrel with, but there's more than a little to be impressed by. This, of course, is the question of value, and it's where the Spanish are making their greatest headway in the world market at present.

For shooting, I must say this one comes closer to meeting my criteria for a good-handling gun than most of the 28-bores I see. Even though everything is scaled down to 28-gauge size, it still has some heft, with a total weight of about an ounce over 6 pounds on my scale. Together the 27-inch barrels and splinter forend account for just a smidgen less than half the weight, and that helps overcome the wispy, hard-to-control feel a lot of smallbores have. The balance point is essentially on the hinge, $1^1/_2$ inches ahead of the breech face. To my thinking, this gun beats hell out of the usual short-nosed wand that's as whippy as a willow switch. Even so, when I eventually ordered an Arrieta 28-bore of my own—a round-body Model 871—I asked for 29-inch barrels and a point of balance even farther forward.

The test gun has a bit of slack in the front trigger—about $1/_{16}$-inch—but none at all in the back one, and both pulls are beautifully light and smooth. By my gauge, the right sear breaks at $3^1/_4$ pounds, the left at $3^1/_2$, just about right for a 6-pound gun.

The ejectors, which are of the Southgate design, do their jobs equally well, although there's one little quirk. When both barrels are fired, the left ejector consistently pitches the empty case three or four feet farther than the right one. But if you fire and eject one at a time, they're identical. In fact, with a little body English you can drop the second hull onto the first. I suppose something in there is off by a thou or two, or else the springs aren't quite identical. I'm sure a good ejector man could put it all right, but for practical purposes it's not something worth being concerned about.

Like most Arrietas, the Model 557 comes with hand-detachable locks, which is always a treat for someone as perennially curious about lockwork as I am. These locks are nicely polished and the plates jeweled. You can see a few faint filing marks. As is fairly common among Continental guns, the locks differ somewhat from the traditional English design in that the sear and interceptor springs are coil rather than leaf-type. The interceptor spring and its tiny plunger nestle in a blind hole drilled into the side of the bridle—nestle there, that is, until you remove the interceptor itself, and then they ping off into the Land of the Lost; if you ever have occasion to disassemble a lock of this sort, drape a cloth over your hands to catch such flying parts, else you might never see them again.

The sear spring is of the same arrangement, but there the coil and plunger are mounted to the sear and bear against the bridle. It's a clever design, despite the potentially fugitive pieces. The springs are quite strong, so they ensure positive contact between the sears and their respective notches, and they'll go on working at least well enough to keep the gun in service even if a coil should break.

Other than this, Arrieta guns are as mechanically classic as a three-button navy-blue blazer, from the checkered butt to the Holland-style action, Purdey-type fastener, and Anson forend latch—all the features and designs that have been so thoroughly tested by time. Still, Arrieta does offer variations that some of the more conservative Spanish makers do not. You can, for instance, choose between two different round-body styles, a model with only some line engraving, or a gun with frame and lockplates deeply blacked and the contours highlighted by inlaid gold wire.

Moreover, you can order all sorts of extras and accessories—extra sets of barrels, single trigger, spare springs, leather cases, and such. And you can have your initials engraved on a stock oval or inlaid in gold on the trigger guard, and even have your gun's serial number inlaid in gold. All these things naturally represent additional cost.

With a workforce of nine craftsmen and an output of about four hundred guns per year, there's naturally a bit of a wait if you order one, but it isn't much. Typical delivery time is five or six months, which is about as close to instant gratification as you can get in the custom-gun world, particularly since a lot of makers' terms sound like a felony conviction—several years and many thousands of dollars.

A custom-made gun is the pinnacle of shooting, and for a very long time, custom-made guns have been available only to those with the deepest pockets. Anyone fortunate enough to have megabucks to spare can still have fabulous guns built in London and Edinburgh, St. Étienne and Liège, Brescia, and other places. But now the rest of us, people of more modest means, have the opportunity as well. At the moment, no one offers that opportunity to a greater extent than the gunmakers in Spain, and among those you'll find only a few that can match the quality and the value you get from the house that Avelino Arrieta built.

CHAPTER TWO

THE RENAISSANCE OF
AGUIRRE Y ARANZABAL

They always caught my eye in the full- and sometimes double-page ads that Klein's used to run in the sporting and gun magazines years ago—sleek boxlock side-by-sides styled something like the Winchester Model 21 and decidedly more graceful than anything else available in the hundred-dollar price range (this was, remember, a long time ago).

The name appealed to me, too: Matador by AyA. It was a gun I badly wanted to own. Which I did, eventually, and thereby learned several things. One was that "AyA" is a set of initials, short for Aguirre y Aranzabal, surnames of the founders. I also learned what some others had already figured out—that guns by AyA offered a whopping value for the money they cost.

That, unfortunately, was not the general view of Spanish guns on the American market at the time. In the 1950s and '60s, most of the guns brought into this country from Spain were cheaply built, cheaply sold, and their principal virtues lay in providing work for American gunsmiths. Parts that should have been hard were soft; parts that should have been tough were brittle; and guns that should have worked all too often didn't.

The Matador suffered none of those ills. It was well-built, graceful of form, reliable in function, altogether a good gun to have. What it did suffer, however, was a measure of undeserved prejudice simply because it was a Spanish gun, even though some of the most influential writers of the time spoke highly of it. Colonel Askins, in particular, always steadfastly championed AyA. Even so, sales never were as good as they should have been, and the Matador wasn't imported after about 1969.

If relatively few American shooters discovered what a good piece the Matador was, hardly anyone here realized that AyA also built high-quality sidelocks on the pattern of best English guns. It was a big operation in the 1960s, probably the largest gunmaker in Eibar, but by the early 1980s, shifting tides of the world gun trade had begun to erode Spain's share of the market. About 1986, sore beset by competition from Japan and Italy, AyA, Arizaga, and eighteen other Eibar makers joined together, built a new, highly mechanized factory in Itziar, and set out to do business as Diarm S.A. Toward the end of 1987, the whole thing went bust.

Of the marques that went down the Diarm drain, none was mourned more keenly than AyA, particularly in England, which ironically was the world's largest market for AyA guns, and to a lesser extent in America, where best-quality Spanish guns were only just becoming known and appreciated. Those who'd been aware of AyA's quality all along saw it as the passing of yet one more of the world's truly good guns.

Happily, the passing wasn't for good. With a staff of a dozen craftsmen who had been Diarm foremen and supervisors, Imanol Aranzabal restarted AyA as a small shop specializing in guns made to order. You can distinguish pre- and post-Diarm guns by serial number, for the later ones began at No. 600000.

In the winter of 1990–91, I tested an AyA No. 2 sidelock ejector in 28-gauge, and after a few weeks of shooting targets and game it was clear to me that AyA still offered a whopping value for the money.

The No. 2 is the second lowest grade of AyA sidelock, available in all bores from 12 through .410, including 16. Like most AyA sidelocks, it's built in the Holland & Holland mold, with hand-detachable, Holland-type bar-action locks and the classic Purdey-style double-bite fastener. Chopper-lump barrels are standard, and in the test gun the solder joint between the half-lumps is all but invisible. The locks, which are nicely filed and polished inside, are made with intercepting sears. Firing pins are bushed and the fences are ported to divert escaping gas from a pierced primer or ruptured case head. Details like these are part of what makes this gun an excellent value.

The other part, of course, is the quality of materials and craftsmanship, both of which seem to me generally better than you find on most guns of comparable price. Only time and use render the final judgment on how well the working parts are heat-treated, but the test gun digested about two cases of cartridges, both factory Winchester AA skeet loads and my hand-loads, without a glitch or a twitch. Look around a bit and you can find older AyAs that have gone through shells by the carload and are ready for many carloads more. And in fact, I later set out to create an AyA No. 2 for myself, but more on that presently.

The test-gun's barrels, 26 inches long, have a good ring to them and are smoothly struck, bored, polished, and blacked. The frame, which is made to true 28-gauge scale, is well filed and all metal parts closely fitted. The lockplates are properly chamfered where they meet the wood; if they weren't, the stock likely would crack. More to the point on that score, though, wood-to-metal fit at the stock head could scarcely be better. With the locks removed, flaws in the heading-up are often easy to spot, but I can't find any here.

Besides offering a good opportunity to examine the interior woodwork, the hand-detachable plates have also made it easy to see how well the lock parts are fitted. In a quality lock, the parts shouldn't rub against the plate, and since AyA engine-turns the inner surfaces of the plates, rub marks are easy to detect. After roughly five hundred cartridges through each barrel and a fair amount of dry-firing with snap caps, I see only two faint rubs, at the top of the tumbler on one lock and where the mainspring hooks to the tumbler-swivel on the other. Whoever made these knew what he was doing.

Intercepting sears are meant to block the tumbler if the main sear is tripped by something other than the trigger blade—if the gun is dropped, for instance, or if a sear is so worn or damaged that recoil from the other barrel trips it. Both barrels going off at once is always a nuisance, sometimes a painful nuisance, and a gun with a bad sear is dangerous besides.

The AyA showed no inclination to double, and I certainly didn't bash it around trying to make a sear jar off. But with the locks dismounted, you can test the system by manually tripping the main sear without touching the interceptor. These work just as they should.

Tripping locks the conventional way, by pulling the triggers, produced uneven results. Both sears are crisp enough, but the front trigger is too heavy for a $5\frac{1}{2}$-pound gun; it will almost but not quite bear the weight of the gun before it goes. The left lock, on the other hand, lets off at 3.8 pounds' pressure, and that's just about right.

Though I do plenty of grousing about triggers in these re-

AyA No. 2
WILLIAM W. HEADRICK

ports, you should understand that hard pulls are not necessarily a sign of inferior workmanship. They can also be a sign of good sense on the part of gunmakers who don't want to find themselves defendants in product-liability suits in America, where such matters have long since ascended to almost sublime levels of absurdity. To hold a manufacturer responsible for someone's lack of judgment or sheer stupidity borders, in my view, on the surreal. But there it is, and no gunmaker who aims to do business in this country can afford to ignore the reality.

If a sear is correctly fitted, a light trigger is every bit as safe as a heavy one, but it's delicate work and it takes time, and in a relatively inexpensive gun, leaving trigger pulls heavy is more economical. Which isn't to say you'll necessarily need any after-market trigger work, because if you order a new AyA you can, within reason, specify trigger pulls.

You can specify stock dimensions, too, on the same basis. The test gun's wood is every bit as well shaped as it is well fitted. The drop points are nicely carved, though somewhat more elongated than English stockers make them, and the diamond-hand wrist is comfortable to hold. Checkering, cut at 24 lines per inch, is a bit better on the hand than on the forend and butt, but overall it's quite good.

The wood itself is European walnut, close-grained, handsomely figured, and finished with oil. The test gun could use a couple more coats than it was given, but any oil-finished stock will benefit from a drop of linseed now and then. Given the amount of figure it has, I suspect this stock qualifies as what the catalog calls "special-grade" wood, which adds some money to the base price.

I was able to shoot the gun about as well as I can shoot any piece that's this light and balances about halfway between the trigger guard and the hinge—which is to say, none too well. Not that I humiliated myself—not permanently, anyway—but light-nosed guns make crossing shots difficult, so shooting quail and grouse with the AyA wasn't an entirely successful exercise. I did find it a splendid little woodcock gun, though, mainly because being able to instantly change the direction of your swing is sometimes an advantage.

My own shortcomings aside, the gun did its part in a perfectly satisfactory way—with two exceptions. The forend latch, of the Anson type, needs a few more strokes of the file where its hook engages the barrel loop. Push and pull as I might, I couldn't detach the forend without using some sort of tool for additional leverage. It's not really a functional problem, nor one that's difficult to remedy, but it is a bother.

The ejectors also showed a small hitch. In design, they are the classic Southgate type, used by gunmakers the world over. They're relatively simple and extremely reliable if properly regulated, but the test gun's left one was slightly mistimed. When I fired only the left barrel, the ejector wouldn't trip unless I opened the action with a smart yank. Everything worked fine with the right barrel alone or when both barrels were fired.

Ejector work can be a fairly simple job or a nightmare, depending on what's wrong. Since the test gun was brand-new, a bit of adjustment probably would do the trick, but it shouldn't be necessary; the ejectors should have been checked and any problems corrected before the gun left the factory.

So, the test specimen is not perfect. I've never seen a gun of this price range that was, and I don't expect I ever will. What I do see in the AyA No. 2 is an extremely good gun available for a remarkably small amount of money. You can have one built to order with your choice of barrel length and boring, stocked and balanced to your prescription, add in a half or full-pistol grip, a beavertail forend, single trigger, self-opener, or extra set of barrels, and still spend less than five figures.

All of which suggested to me that the new AyAs are a lot like the old ones—good guns that represent excellent value. I was happy to see them back.

Happy enough, in fact, that Aguirre y Aranzabal was the first maker to cross my mind about a year later, when I had a rare Good Idea. That led to an AyA No. 2 of my own.

One of the nicest things about doing what I do—as opposed to being independently wealthy or having a "real" job—is being able to shoot all over the world. Traveling to shoot combines two of the great passions in my life. The down side is that travel and guns are not always wholly compatible. Though there are some things you can do to minimize the risk, putting guns through any commercial transportation is a form of surrendering a hostage to fortune. Then once you get where you're going, there's the matter of ammunition. Getting your sweet, expensive fowling piece to the wilds of East Bunghole is one thing; getting there and finding that the only available cartridges are a half-inch longer than its chambers and loaded with something close to dynamite is another matter.

I went through this for a few years with an English gun that took the better part of my net worth to buy, and it was a frazzling experience, a constant worry. So in 1991 I decided to get a travel gun, one that I could take anywhere and shoot almost any cartridge through; one that was reliable, that handled well, that looked good; one I could afford to replace without mortgaging my soul if the worst should happen.

I asked AyA to build a duplicate of the English gun I love so well—a 6¼-pound, 12-bore ejector stocked to my dimensions, with 29-inch barrels, with trigger pulls and balance just so. As to the quality of fit and finish, AyA's standard No. 2 suited my purposes perfectly.

The gun that showed up four months later exceeded almost every expectation. The chopper-lump barrels are as good as in anything I've seen short of a top-quality English or Italian gun. They're beautifully bored and polished, their outsides are struck glassy-smooth, and they're deeply blacked. I asked for no choke at all in the right barrel and .015-inch in the left, which is just what my bore gauge says I got.

The stock is a handsome piece of European walnut, made exactly to the dimensions I requested. The diamond hand is AyA's standard, and it feels great.

AyA builds 12-gauge guns to essentially two weights. The

heavy version runs about 7½ pounds, the light one about a pound less. Mine is a lightweight that scales 6½ pounds on the dot.

I asked that the trigger pulls be adjusted to 3½ pounds in the right and a half-pound more in the left. That's just what I got. I also asked that the gun be balanced 2⅞ inches ahead of the breech face, and I got that, too. Light as it is, the gun's as quick as a snake to get moving, and the slightly muzzle-heavy balance makes the momentum smooth and steady.

Just after I placed the order I went through some transitions in stock dimensions to finally accommodate the changes in physique that come with age. So even though the maker did exactly as I asked, I was using more length of pull and slightly different dimensions of pitch and cast by the time the gun arrived. That was okay, because I'd screwed up anyway in asking for a plain checkered butt, not having taken into account that this was a gun I'd be using for such high-volume shooting as doves in South America and driven game in Europe.

So, off it went to stocker David Trevallion for some trimming and one of his leather-covered Decelerator pads to give it more length and a different pitch. A few hours in his setting bench added ⅛-inch more cast at the heel and ¼-inch more at the toe. When the gun came back, the dimensions exactly duplicated the stock David had made for my English gun a couple of months before, and after a few rounds of sporting clays I found I couldn't tell any real difference between the two in the way they handled and fit.

The AyA's maiden voyage amounted to ten days and about three thousand cartridges and doves and clays in Colorado, all with no malfunctions. Grouse in Minnesota, driven pheasants in Hungary, bobwhites in Mexico, and other excursions accounted for another three or four thousand rounds over the next four months. By spring I was beginning to think I'd come up with something special. A couple of my friends had ordered similar AyAs to use as travel guns; they were shooting theirs as much as I was shooting mine, and our collective total of hitches, glitches, breakdowns, and misfunctions stood at zero.

The next fall and winter brought more of the same. Ten shots in a day or five hundred, it was all the same. The gun never failed. The trigger pulls stayed at exactly the same weight, the ejectors remained perfectly timed, and the springs were just as springy as ever.

By the time we arrived in Argentina for a dove shoot, the gun had digested about twenty thousand cartridges, and the next seven days accounted for almost five thousand more— including one stint when I decided to find out how it feels to shoot two cases in a single day. (For the record, it feels like hell. A thousand rounds in one day in a break-action gun that you're loading yourself is exhausting; after so many repetitions of opening, closing, and lifting, I could scarcely raise my arms that night.)

Toward the end of the trip, something finally went wrong: The right barrel started misfiring about once in every three or four shots. It's the sign of a broken firing pin, and it can happen to any gun. I'd asked for a spare set of mainsprings and a top-lever spring when I placed the order—but of course I had not thought to get extra strikers. I have a set now, which, if things go as usual, I'll probably never need.

Actually, I have a notion that the striker broke quite some time before the symptoms showed up, judging from how heavily peened the two pieces were when I took them out.

I've lost track of how many cartridges I've put through this gun in the three years since, but as it's been back to Mexico twice, to Hungary three more times, to Spain for partridges, and in more parts of the United States than I can remember, I reckon the bottom line is somewhere near fifty thousand. Nothing else has gone even slightly wrong with it, which is not a bad track record.

There is a problem, though: I got my AyA in the first place to subject it to the risks of travel. But it's served me so well and become such a favorite that now I'm starting to worry about it, too.

CHAPTER THREE

BERETTA ASE 90

Some would have it that the only certainties are death and taxes. This is late-twentieth-century angst. Being fond of the notion, popular in Elizabethan England, that the human condition is shaped by tensional duality, I'd suggest as equal certainties the love of a dog and the likelihood of getting a good gun from Armi Pietro Beretta.

If canine devotion isn't quite as old as death, it certainly predates taxes. Armi Beretta is the latecomer in the equation, but not by much, and after 460-odd years in business, it's hardly surprising that their products should be reliable. Even so, being able to supply a high-quality gun to serve any purpose from game to targets and at any price from a few hundred to many thousands of dollars is a remarkable achievement. Whatever your taste, intentions, or budget, you simply cannot go wrong in choosing a Beretta; I'd be hard-pressed to think of any other single maker of whom to say the same.

Thanks mainly to sporting clays, target shooting represents the high-growth segment of the shotgun market these days. Within the past few years almost every manufacturer has brought out guns tailored to the target games. None has done so more actively than Beretta, offering skeet, trap, and clays guns in a variety of styles, all well designed and well built. But even in such good company, the ASE 90 stands out.

From the standpoint of leading-edge design, it is the premier target gun in the Beretta line. I haven't thought to ask the company what the initials stand for, but having spent some time on the target fields with a test gun, I'm inclined to think it could very well be Absolutely Superb Engineering. At a retail price of just over $8,000, it's not cheap, but this is one instance when you get everything you pay for and then some.

Designwise, the ASE 90 shows features both old and new, at least so far as Beretta is concerned. The fastening system, for instance, is the flat, Greener-type cross-bolt that Beretta has used for years in its Premium Grade sidelock over/unders— and in rifles as well as shotguns, so there's no question of its time-proven durability. On the other hand, this is the first Beretta gun with lockwork built on the trigger-plate system.

The notion of mounting lock parts to the trigger plate rather than on sideplates or inside a box frame is not new. English makers George Gibbs, Thomas Pitt, and Edwinson Green built hammerless guns on this concept in the 1860s and '70s. James MacNaughton, of Edinburgh, patented a similar design in 1879. German gunmakers liked the idea, too, and came up with a number of variations on what in Europe is typically called the Blitz action. Between 1880 and 1887, John Dickson the Younger entered a series of patents on yet another trigger-plate lock system, which thereafter became the famous Dickson round-action and which is still available today from Dickson's and from Scottish maker David McKay Brown.

In a side-by-side gun, trigger-plate locks allow the frame to be unusually small and therefore contribute to light weight. Pick up a 12-bore Dickson or McKay Brown and you'll be pleasantly impressed. In an over/under, the breech-end of the lower barrel has to fit inside the frame, so it isn't really possible to significantly reduce the weight by altering the lock design, but the trigger-plate system still offers some advantage, especially in its most modern incarnations.

So far as I know, it was Daniele Perazzi who came up with the idea of making the trigger-plate system hand-detachable. In a best-quality Perazzi target gun, you can simply push the safety button forward and drop out the whole trigger and lock assembly. It's a quick and painless way to get at the mechanism for cleaning or to replace it with a spare in the event of a broken spring or sear. It's also a handy way to switch around if you prefer a release trigger for some target events and a standard system for others. Serious competition shooters took to the arrangement straight away, and it helped place Perazzi in the forefront of the target-gun market.

Although the ASE 90 lock design is different from Perazzi's, the detachment system works the same way, using the safety button as the latch. The Beretta locks are powered by horizontally mounted V-springs that act directly on the tumblers, so it's all somewhat simpler than Perazzi's design. It's also a nicely compact assembly, beautifully machined and polished.

The ASE 90 comes in four versions—skeet, trap, sporting, and pigeon—all 12-bores. The one I tested is a skeet gun, which I find equally well suited for sporting clays. The main differences among them seem to be barrel length (28 inches in skeet, pigeon, and sporting, 30 inches in sporting and trap) and chokes (tubes in the trap and sporting guns, fixed chokes in skeet and pigeon). Otherwise, every ASE 90 is the same.

With its frame sculpted on the same pattern as the Pre-

BERETTA ASE 90
MICHAEL McINTOSH

mium Grade sidelocks, it's a handsome piece. But in a target gun beauty is as beauty does, and in the ASE 90 performance clearly is the prime objective, both in how it's built and what it's made of.

As in the Premium Grades, the barrels are Boehler steel, assembled on the standard Beretta monobloc system with trunnion action. Boring is highly precise; both of the test gun's bores measure .723-inch, with no more than a thousandth-inch variation. Chamber depth is nominally 2¾ inches, but my gauge drops in to a full 2⅞ inches, which I take to be a function of long, well-tapering forcing cones. The choke cones are also quite long, about 4¼ inches, and they flare out to about .020-inch larger than bore size. Patterns are consistent and show no tendency toward gaps or clumps with any of the cartridges I've used.

The barrel walls at the standard measuring points are about .033-inch—plenty thick enough to be safe and durable yet thin enough to promote good weight and handling. In fact, the barrels alone weigh only 2 pounds, 14 ounces, which in an 8-pound gun makes the handling lively without being whippy.

The rib is 10 millimeters wide and straight, which suits me better than the wider ribs you'll find on a lot of target guns nowadays. The side ribs are vented as well, and I don't notice any change of impact as the barrels heat up.

The best barrels in the world aren't much good unless they're combined with fast locks and a good trigger. I have no way of measuring the lock-time, but in terms of shooter perception, ASE 90 locks seem every bit as quick as those of every other top-quality gun.

I *can* measure trigger pulls, however, even though in this case I did so only as a matter of academic interest and thorough reporting. You don't need a scale to tell you that the ASE 90 has one sweet trigger. The first sear trips at a consistent 3¾ pounds, the second at just a hair under 4¼ pounds. Both are wonderfully crisp and clean.

Mechanically, it's a perfectly simple, non-selective affair

that uses an inertia block to shift from one sear to the other. I like the non-selective arrangement immensely. I don't think much of selective triggers; they're essentially useless, even in theory, and in practice offer nothing more than house-room for gremlins. Given my druthers, I prefer a mechanical shift over one that operates from recoil, but that's purely a personal quirk and more important to me in a game gun than in a target piece. The way I shoot, a dud cartridge is distracting enough that even if I can get to the second barrel I'll most likely miss anyway.

Like some other well-refined target guns, the ASE 90 trigger blade is adjustable for position, over a total distance of about $5/16$-inch. I've mentioned this before, but don't buy any nonsense you might hear about an adjustable trigger being a means of changing the length of pull. With a pistol-grip stock, the grip, not the trigger, determines hand position; a sliding trigger only accommodates the length of your finger—but for fine-tuning the way a gun feels, that's advantage enough.

With the trigger fully forward, the factory dimensions come out to $14^3/4$ inches in basic length, with enough additional length to the toe for a couple of inches of down-pitch. Bend is $1^1/2$ inches at the comb and two inches at the heel, with what appears to be about a $1/4$-inch cast-off.

The wood itself is good quality, nicely figured, and well-shaped. As with a lot of target over/unders, the buttstock is a chunky rascal, so your stockmaker will have plenty to work with if you need some alteration. Similarly, it's made with a palm-swell on the right side. The forend is extremely comfortable—slender, nicely rounded at the tip, and made with a full-length finger-groove on each side. Checkering is about 26 lines to the inch, well-executed though not perfectly so, and there's enough of it to be useful. The finish is an oil-type of some sort, rubbed to a fairly dull patina. A bit more rubbing wouldn't do any harm.

The only serious beef I have, in terms of appearance, is with the buttpad, which is soft rubber. It feels fine, but if there's an uglier specimen than a ventilated pad with a white spacer, I don't know what it might be. A solid-sided pad would be just as comfortable and look a lot better.

But as I said, beauty is as beauty does, and what the ASE 90 does is beautiful indeed. Everything functions exactly as it should, and on the rare occasions when I do, too, this gun will smoke targets with the best.

Which comes as no surprise, as it *is* one of the best.

CHAPTER FOUR

BERETTA 687EL
GOLD PIGEON FIELD

Just because the good five-cent cigar is out of the question doesn't mean there are not still some things this country needs—like good factory-made 28-gauge over/unders built on true 28-gauge frames.

Among those qualifications, the latter has long been the sticker. We have had several good factory-built 28-bore over/unders, among them the Winchester 101, the Browning Superposed, and the Japanese-built Superposed knockoff sold under the Charles Daly name. Some good ones are still offered by Browning, Weatherby, SKB, Perazzi, and others. But they're all hybrids—28-gauge barrels on 20-gauge frames.

This is not to suggest that any manufacturer has been out to shortchange us deliberately. The 28-bore has been an economic weak sister ever since Parker turned out the first American hammerless breechloading 28-gauge gun in 1905. It underwhelmed the market immediately and went on doing so for about eighty-five years, never popular enough to justify the expense of tooling up a factory production line for milling frames and lockworks in scale with the size of the barrels. Until recent years, in fact, the little gun scarcely justified its existence in any form, and were it not for skeet shooters and a small cadre of die-hard eccentrics, it would have gone extinct a generation ago.

That would have been a pity, because it's the sweetest of the smallbores, the one that can steal your heart and shatter the firmest resolve not to buy another gun. Going 28-gauge crazy isn't terminal, but it isn't really curable, either. The mal-

ady has not yet reached epidemic proportions, though it's
spreading. More new 28-bore guns and loads have come on the
market in the past few years than in the preceding fifty.
Clearly, more shooters are discovering that besides being a
wonderfully efficient bird gun, the 28 is no real handicap on
virtually any sporting clays course in the country.

Fans of the side-by-side have fared best in all this. Perfectly
scaled 28-gauge guns are available from Spain and Italy, beautifully proportioned, made-to-order sidelocks whose prices begin around $3,500 and go up to Scary Plus. You can get an
equally well-scaled over/under from Italy or England, but
those prices tend to *start* somewhere near Scary Plus. And that
brings me back where I started: The gunning world needs good
over/unders built to true 28-gauge scale, selling for something
less than the proverbial arm and leg.

For all practical purposes, this means factory-production
guns, because with few exceptions the big factories are the best
sources of high quality at relatively low prices. True, the Spanish trade turns out beautifully built, largely handmade side-by-
sides at astonishingly low prices—it's the only gun trade in the
world that seems able to do so—but the best Spanish makers
either don't build over/unders at all or don't sell them as in-
expensively. Compared with the rest of the world, the Basque
gunmakers are the exception, not the rule.

Among the big factories, Pietro Beretta is something of an
exception, too—the world's oldest gunmaker, one of the largest,
and certainly one of the most aggressive in devising new models and forms to fill a variety of niches. It is therefore no great
surprise that Beretta was the one to introduce the world's first
production over/under in true 28-gauge scale. A couple of
years later, in 1995, Ruger introduced a 28-bore version of its
Red Label over/under, but when I field-tested the Beretta in
'94, it was the only gun of its kind.

In the often-bewildering litany of Beretta model names, it's
officially known as the 687EL Gold Pigeon Field; for simplicity's sake, I'll just call it Gold Pigeon here. So far as I can tell,

it's the only Beretta model outside the Premium Grade series that's built on four different frames—12, 20, 28, and .410. (The latter is a charmingly tiny gun, and if you dig .410s, you'll find it a dandy.)

The action is Beretta's standard production over/under, the one the company uses for the series 682, 686, 687, and Onyx guns—slim and nicely sculpted, hinged on trunnions, and fastened by double pins in the standing breech. It's a design well-tested by time and use, as is the monobloc system, in which the barrels are sleeved into a breech milled from a single block of steel. This, too, is standard Beretta fare.

The Gold Pigeon 28 offers only two choices of barrels: 26 or 28 inches. The test gun was one of the shorter ones—too short for my taste, but as it was all Beretta U.S.A. had available in loaners, I decided I'd rather see the gun than be picky and wait longer. Actually, the barrels measure about 26¼ inches and are fitted with a low-set, field-style ventilated rib 6 millimeters wide.

They are good barrels, indeed—well-bored and nicely polished inside and out. At .546-inch, the bores are slightly smaller than the 28-gauge nominal standard of .550-inch, but I don't find as much as a thousandth-inch of variation anywhere, which is remarkable consistency in a production gun. The stampings indicate 2¾-inch chambers, but my gauges say they're really ¹/₁₆-inch deeper.

The gun came with three choke tubes, marked improved-cylinder, modified, and full. In actual diameter, the first two measured .536- and .528-inch, respectively—which, compared with the bores, mean Skeet 2 at .010-inch and an improved-modified of .018-inch. My pattern plate agreed. I can't tell you much about the full-choke tube, except that it's full-choke and then some. My bore gauge wouldn't go in far enough to get a measurement, and at twenty-five yards it printed a pattern the size of a dinner plate. Personally, I'd swap that one for another skeet 2, or a true cylinder if I could get one.

As I said earlier, the frame is standard Beretta boxlock design and, like Beretta's other EL and EELL models, it's fitted with sideplates to lend a sidelock appearance. What makes this frame unique is its size. My vernier caliper shows the maximum depth, measured from the top of the standing breech, to be 2⁵/₆₄ inches—which is ⁷/₆₄-inch shallower than a standard Beretta 20-bore frame. Differences in width are less pronounced: The 28-gauge frame is ¹/₁₆-inch narrower than the 20 at the rear and ¹/₃₂-inch narrower at the knuckle.

Considering that a 28-gauge bore is smaller than a 20 by only .065-inch, or just a hair over ¹/₁₆-inch, a reduction in depth of almost ¹/₈-inch is a substantial amount. Consider, too, that Beretta frames are among the shallowest of any factory over/under to begin with, and you start to get a sense of just how sleek and slender the Gold Pigeon 28 really is. You can recognize it instantly with the gun in hand, even if you can't tell by eye exactly how much smaller it is. All the proportions just look right.

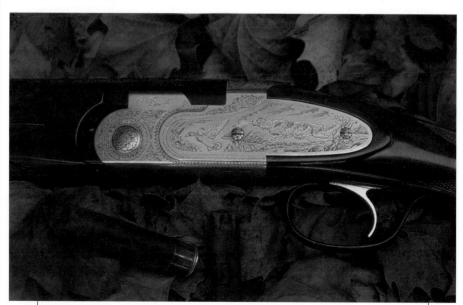

BERETTA 687EL GOLD PIGEON
MICHAEL McINTOSH

There are some good reasons why the reduction in width isn't greater. One has to do with the nature of the Beretta fastening system. The bolts themselves are round pins that slide forward out of the standing breech to engage recesses on either side of the monobloc; the size of the pins and the amount of steel that must surround the recesses in order to create a reliable, durable fastener dictate a certain minimum width. Moreover, chamber pressure created by the cartridge tends to increase as bore size decreases, so chamber walls need to be proportionally thicker; this, too, affects the width of an over/under frame.

It also affects the weight, so a Gold Pigeon 28 may actually be a few ounces heavier than a similar 20. The test gun tipped my scales at $6^{1}/_{4}$ pounds—which I consider close to the minimum weight for a gun that a shooter of average build can handle smoothly and consistently. A gun much lighter than that is jumpy and jerky and profoundly easy to stop in mid-swing—or it is in my hands, anyway.

Besides, this gun feels light, thanks to a balance point just at the forward edge of the hinge—or, in hard stats, $2^{1}/_{8}$ inches forward of the standing breech. If this were my gun, I'd move it forward just a skosh more, but not much.

The wood is, for the most part, as handsome as it ought to be for such a trim little piece. The forend is slim, rounded in the field style, and shaped with finger grooves that feel good in the hand. The stock is a bit thicker than it needs to be, but the shaping is good, especially in the pistol grip, which has a fairly long, shallow radius, somewhere between a standard pistol and half-hand. The checkering is 26 lines per inch and exceptionally good for a factory gun, especially on the forend. The diamonds line up like a crack drill team, and the grooves are almost perfectly cut for uniform depth. The grip panels aren't quite so well done, but you have to look closely to notice.

To round out the details, there's a silver oval inlet in the belly of the stock about 3 inches from the toe, where Italian makers seem to like placing such things. The buttplate is wood, made from a thin slab of figured walnut and laterally grooved like the old hard-rubber plates most American makers used years ago. The unblued Phillips-head screws don't contribute much to an elegant look, but it's a clever way of providing the beauty of a wooden butt while offering some protection to the toe of the stock, which is where plain-butt guns most often suffer chips and splits.

Dimensionally, the length of pull is $14^{5}/_{8}$ inches, drop at comb $1^{1}/_{4}$ inches, and drop at heel 2 inches. The angle of the butt creates about the right amount of down-pitch to suit me, and the stock is made without cast.

Though the metal is very well struck and polished, the stock shows more ripples on its surface than a gun of this price ought to, and the unevenness unfortunately is accentuated by a high-gloss finish that I assume is some sort of urethane varnish. Not pretty stuff. If ever a sweet little gun deserved an oil finish, or just some hand rubbing to soften the glare, this is it.

Similarly, I don't find the decoration entirely pleasing. I understand the economics of machine "engraving" and have no quarrel with it if it's well done. As machine work, the Gold Pigeon's scroll and border flowers are extremely well done. But game scenes don't move me much, gold-plated scenes even less. The right-hand sideplate shows a crook-tailed pointer and a bird I take to be a partridge. On the other side is a setter pointing a flushing mallard (!), and a gold pheasant flushes on the bottom of the frame. Personally, I'd rather see nothing but scrollwork against a blue or case-colored frame, with the maker's name in gold, but that's just my particular taste.

Keeping in mind the production-line nature of the gun, I really can't find any functional axes to grind. The single trigger has one little quirk; set to fire the under barrel first, the sears trip at 4.5 and 4.37 pounds of pressure. Both are a titch heavy, but they're certainly crisp enough. With the selector position the other way around, the first pull is 4.1 pounds and the second 4.37. This actually isn't unusual among selective triggers, and it points up a case when choke tubes really do have a practical use. For reasons both mechanical and ergonomic, the second sear ought to be the heavier of the two, and for this particular trigger that means firing the top barrel first. This creates a problem with fixed chokes, but with tubes you can set the selector for the best sequence of pulls and put the open choke into whichever barrel goes first.

Beretta ejectors have some qualities I find truly endearing. They're simple, for one thing; for another, they work. Those in the test gun are perfectly timed, and the springs are sufficiently stout to pop the empties well clear. A 28-gauge case is quite long in proportion to its diameter, which creates a lot of drag against the chamber walls, and I've found some guns to be inconsistent in ejecting. This isn't one of them.

The Gold Pigeon is priced just under $3,300 per copy—not cheap, but not out of line for what you get. I don't imagine that annual production will amount to great numbers, so you may have to do some looking to find a dealer who has one in inventory. If you're a fan of the over/under and a lover of the 28-gauge, you'll find the search well worth the effort. If you haven't yet become enthralled by the 28, beware; once she gets hold of your heart, she doesn't let go. And this is just the gun to give anyone a good case of the 28-gauge crazies.

CHAPTER FIVE

BERNARDELLI ITALIA

Forty years ago, when the rosy glow on my cheeks came from the bloom of boyhood instead of sun, wind, and whiskey, my friends and I had some rather firm attitudes toward guns. We lived in the quail country of southern Iowa, and to us a proper gun was a repeater, a pump at least and an autoloader at best.

Those were the guns our fathers shot and therefore the guns we paid self-conscious lip service to in the presence of men. A few of us coveted doubles, but we did so as surreptitiously as we coveted certain issues of *National Geographic* and in a few years would covet *Playboy*. Double guns were widely considered old-fashioned, and for whatever else we hoped to be, we were by-God determined to think ourselves modern.

Double guns were bad enough. Double guns with *hammers*—"ear hammers," we called them—were impossible, the stuff of grandfather tales. Even most of our grandfathers thought they were archaic as dinosaurs. If any of us saw anything neat about hammer guns, we were almighty careful not to say so.

But I love hammer guns, always have, and I've finally realized that doesn't necessarily make me a reactionary old fart. Which I'm not, usually. And even if it does, I have some good company—my friend Hill, for instance. Gene and I cannot spend more than an hour together without one of us mentioning the most recent hammer gun he's seen and hopes to buy or trade for. Then we segue into the hammer guns we've owned and wish we hadn't sold or traded away, and then to the hammer guns we'd have built for us if we had the money . . . you get the picture.

It's not just that we both harbor secret fantasies of being Lord Ripon, necktied and tweedy, shooting high pheasants at Sandringham or Studley Royal with a brace of loaders and a trio of hammer Purdeys, or of wishing we were able, as Ripon was, to have six pheasants dead in the air at once. Romance is part of it, but so, too, is a feeling that fine hammer guns own a parcel of elegance and grace that others don't.

The problem, as least in my boyhood time and place, was that fine hammer guns were as hard to find as a poacher's conscience. There were plenty of hammer guns around, but they were mostly remnants from the turn-of-the-century spate of cheap Belgian and domestic contract guns—poorly built, barreled with the flimsiest twist, stocked to dog-leg proportions, and falling apart. Occasionally, you could turn up a nice old English or French or high-quality Belgian piece among all the pot-metal wonders, but unless it was nitro-proofed, you were looking at a rebarreling job that cost more than the gun itself.

The barrel problem still exists, but over the past twenty years a shift in interest from firepower to aesthetics has brought about a minor renaissance for the hammer gun, especially in the Italian trade. You can get lovely hammer pieces from Abbiatico & Salvinelli, Bertuzzi, and a few others—sophisticated, self-cocking ejector guns built and decorated to the highest levels of the craft. To do so, you will, of course, pay a substantial price, although the guns are well worth it if you can spare that much coin. If you can't, and can't stand not owning a good hammer gun as well, Vincenzo Bernardelli has just the piece.

Actually, Bernardelli offers hammer guns in three versions: Brescia, a plain, lightly engraved, no-frills model; Italia, which has more sculpting in the frame and hammers, better wood, and scroll engraving; and Italia Extra, well-stocked, beautifully engraved and finished. The test gun was a 12-gauge Italia, which also is available in 16- and 20-bore.

Every new gun is fun to fool with, but this one was a special treat. I'll tell you why presently; for now, some comments on the nature of the piece.

The Italia's barrels measure 68 centimeters, roughly 26³/4 inches. They also come in lengths of 65, 71, and 75 centimeters—25¹/2 to 29¹/2 inches. They're of dovetail-lump construction, have chrome-plated bores, and respond with a sweet, clear tone when I ring them, which tells me all the joints and seams are properly soldered. According to the codes stamped underneath, the right side is bored improved-cylinder and the left improved-modified. My patterning plate essentially agrees. The rib is flat, level, and designed with enough pitch to place the standard two-thirds of the shot charge above the point of hold when you're looking straight from breech to bead.

The action fastens with a Purdey-type double underbolt augmented by a Greener cross-pin and an extra, fourth fastener at the back of the rib extension. Both sections of the barrel lump, moreover, extend through the bottom of the frame to act as recoil absorbers. The whole system arguably amounts to a degree of overkill, but there's no question that only an ungodly amount of abuse could bring the action off the face.

Bernardelli uses Greener-type back-action locks based on the rebounding principle invented in 1869 by the great English lockmaker John Stanton. When you trip the sear, the long limb of the mainspring drives the hammer down, and once it has struck the firing pin, the short limb springs it back about ³/16-inch to a safety notch. Works like a charm.

The Italia comes with two triggers and extractors, and if I read the factory catalog correctly, single triggers and ejectors aren't available for any of Bernardelli's hammer guns. Personally, I prefer two triggers on side-by-side guns anyway. I do miss the ejectors, though they'd add a pretty penny to the cost, and offering good value at a reasonable price is one of the Italia's important virtues.

Stockwork is done in traditional style—splinter forend with

BERNARDELLI ITALIA
MICHAEL McINTOSH

Anson fastener, straight hand, checkered butt—all well shaped. The finish appears to be urethane or something similar, rubbed to a handsome patina.

Unlike the Brescia model, which has a color-hardened frame, hammers, and lockplates, the Italia and Italia Extra are given what the Bernardelli catalog calls a "coin" finish, which is a sort of catch-all term that can mean anything from French gray to metal simply left white after the colors are polished off. On the Italia, the result is attractive and not overly prone to rust or discolor.

The engraving combines machine-cut bouquet-and-scroll with punchwork bordering. It's rather open, largely unshaded, and of uneven depth in some places. One could find much to criticize, but let's remember that first-rate hand engraving does not come cheap, and you aren't going to find it on a gun in this price range.

I might say as much for the Italia's wood, which is plain, straight-grained stuff; for the file marks that aren't completely polished out; or for the diamonds that didn't get pointed up at the edges of the checkering. These are details you should expect to find better handled in a gun costing two or three or five times more, but at less than $3,000, the Italia is a lot of gun for the money.

I've seen many more expensive guns with barrels not nearly so well struck as these, nor as deeply blacked. The fit, both metal to metal and wood to metal, isn't perfect, but there are no serious gaps anywhere. The wood's a bit proud in places, but you'll find that in most guns. The hammers and fences are gracefully sculpted, and the whole piece shows the elegant lines that make good hammer guns the elegant things they are.

But what, the unconverted might wonder, does one do with a hammer gun? Simply put, one shoots it—and has a hell of a good time in the process. My intention was to use the Italia mainly for sporting clays; then I figured it'd be fun for doves; and from there the whole thing snowballed to the point where

I ended up using it through the entire bird season. At worst, the results were mixed; at best, splendid.

Like all but the most innovative of current specimens, the Italia has no tang safety. Even if it did, that wouldn't be any substitute for proper gun handling, and the fact is, a hammer gun is no more liable to accident than any other. The Italia's locks do not have intercepting sears, so it will fire if the hammer is somehow jarred out of the full-cock notch, but that's true of most hammerless boxlocks and a few sidelocks as well.

The tumblers do have safety notches that keep the hammers from moving forward from the rebound position unless you hold the triggers back. The only thing that can cause an accidental discharge with the hammer down, therefore, is a blow directly to the hammer, hard enough to break the notch—conceivable but not likely.

Hammer guns do take some getting used to. On a clays course, you simply don't cock it till you're ready to shoot. You can do the same on a dove pass—or carry it cocked with the action open, but in that case you must be absolutely certain the barrels are pointed safely when you close it, in case shutting the action should jar off a sear.

You uncock a hammer gun by easing the hammers down one at a time, holding them with your thumb, but *always* with the action open. That way there's no harm done if one should happen to slip.

All told, the Italia performed like a champ. The triggers are quite stiff, harder than 5 pounds, which is as high as my trigger-scale goes. I certainly noticed the hard pulls shooting clays, but they didn't trouble me much at game.

Similarly, the improved-cylinder and improved-modified chokes are an excellent combination for game, but the left barrel is pretty tight for targets as oncoming pairs. If you prefer longer barrels and more open chokes, as I do, you'd want to special-order your Italia either with the chokes you want or without the chrome-lined bores. All the longer standard-length barrels are tightly choked, and chromed bores are difficult to ream out.

At $14^1/2$ inches, the Italia's stock is a bit short for me, but a pad would easily solve that. The standard $1^1/2$ inches bend at the comb and $2^3/8$ inches at the heel should fit most shooters fairly well. Total weight is just a smidgen under 7 pounds, and it's distributed well for good dynamics.

I took the gun to Minnesota, where I spend some time every fall communing with woodcock and grouse, and I have to say that in the uplands, a hammer gun can be damnably awkward. It's no problem to cock one as you walk in on a point, and this one worked great at woodcock. But grouse? Well, your dog probably has a better nose than mine, but not all the grouse I shoot are over points, so I spent most of the time carrying the gun cocked and open. It was a comedy of errors, and my friend Bill Habein, usually circum- spect as a judge, finally broke right down and laughed. With good reason.

When a bird flushed unexpectedly, I'd start to swing, re- member the gun was open, close it, run my thumb all over the tang after the nonexistent safety, look at the hammers to be sure they were cocked, start all over again, and fire an utterly aimless shot behind a bird that had disappeared quite some time before. The Italia finally claimed a couple of grouse, mostly from sheer determination, but I was glad it wasn't the only gun I had along.

A month later, though, it found its niche—in Arkansas, while I stood knee-deep in flooded timber, waiting for two zil- lion mallards to make up their minds to come in or go else- where.

Bernardelli certifies the barrels for steel shot—with, prop- erly, a caution that full chokes and steel shot do not keep good, long-term company. I suspect some thought I was borderline loony, bringing a hammer gun to a duck shoot on the eve of the millennium, but I can't think of a better place for it. You can see your shots coming, so there's more than enough time to cock the gun, and with green-timber shooting you need a gun that's quick to handle, which the Italia is.

Besides, taking my allotted daily brace of greenheads with a hammer gun felt good, felt connected with the days when huge flocks like those were the rule instead of the exception, felt like an idea long out of fashion that turns out to be right after all.

CHAPTER SIX

FRATELLI BERTUZZI

If you spend an hour or two reading gun barrels in a shop whose inventory includes the world's finest of both past and present, you'll notice a curious thing. The old jewels, trim and elegant under a patina of graceful age, will be marked *London* and *Edinburgh* and *Birmingham*. The names will be familiar ones—Purdey and Boss and Holland and Woodward and Dickson and Scott and others like them. The new jewels, equally trim and elegant, will say *Gardone, V.T.*; almost every name will contain a doubled consonant and end in a vowel.

I have more than once ventured the opinion that the Italian trade now occupies the position formerly held by the British—the position, simply put, of building the finest guns in the world. Which is not to say the English no longer build top-quality guns, or that you can't find a ration of junk stamped "Made in Italy." But it is to say that as the British trade has shrunken to a shadow of what it once was, the Italian trade has remained robust and has pushed the envelope of quality to levels that cannot be exceeded anywhere else.

Case in point: Armi Fratelli Bertuzzi—or, in English, Bertuzzi Brothers Gun Works. The brothers in question are Remigio and Elio, grandsons of a Val Trompian *maestro cannoniere*, master barrelmaker, and they pronounce their family name "Bear-TOOT-see." They are reported to have set up in business in Gardone as Fratelli Bertuzzi in 1976, and their output amounts to about three dozen guns per year—side-by-sides in the classic London mold, with Holland-style actions, Purdey-type fasteners, and some twists that are uniquely Italian.

I had two Bertuzzis as test guns, a 12-bore and a 28, both

sidelocks built with chopper-lump barrels; swamped, file-matted ribs; splinter forends with Anson latches; straight-hand stocks with checkered butts; ejectors; and non-selective single triggers. The quality and figure of the wood is excellent—in the 28-gauge, exceptional—with stocks and forends nicely matched and treated to well-cut fine-line, borderless checkering.

Metalwork is similar on both guns, in shape as well as decoration. Filing and barrel-striking leave nothing to quarrel with, and the fit is astonishing. It takes a jeweler's loupe to find even the slightest gap between wood and metal, and gaps between metal and metal simply aren't there at all. If they didn't have slots, you wouldn't be able to find the screw heads in the top levers, the hinge pins, the trigger guard tangs, or the trigger plates. The trigger plates themselves are so closely fitted to the frames that the outlines are invisible to the unaided eye, hard to find at 8X magnification, and don't show up all that clearly under a 12-power glass. This, I promise you, is no exaggeration.

Both guns are engraved in boldly cut, incised, Italianate floral scroll against a stippled background, and both are decorated with gold-inlaid birds in *bulino*-cut scenery. The 12-gauge shows a pointer and two flushing partridge on the left lock plate, three Canada geese on the right, and on the trigger plate a retriever with a duck. The 28-bore has four gold quail on the left plate, three ruffed grouse on the right, and a fourth grouse on the bottom. Bertuzzi crests, worked in gold, are inlaid in the forends. Both guns were done by the same engraver.

The 12-gauge, at 7 pounds, has a good, lively feel. The barrels are 71 centimeters, or a fraction over 28 inches, and the balance point is slightly forward of the hinge. I've spent some good time with it on the clays course. With the rib set below the muzzle and only 1 3/8 inches of drop at the comb, it's dandy for rising and incoming targets and predictably troublesome on falling-away shots.

The trigger is a bit heavier than it ought to be, but it has no slack and breaks crisply. The shift from one sear to the other is mechanical rather than inertia-dependent, so the left barrel is always available no matter what happens with the right. The non-selective configuration is fine with me; the advantages of selective triggers are more theoretical than real anyway, and the disadvantages are a royal pain in the butt.

Neither the engraving style nor the gold inlay particularly appeals to my taste, but the frame filing certainly does. In the 12-bore, both frame and lockplates are slightly rounded in cross section, slightly curved from top to bottom—not as a true round-body but rather something between that and a conventional Holland-style frame.

Handsome as it is, the 12-bore can't hold a candle to the 28 for sheer sex appeal, because a 28-gauge self-cocking hammer gun is a hard act to follow. This little thing is an eye-catcher and a heart-stealer.

It weighs 5 pounds, 6 ounces. The barrels are 68.5 centimeters long, a hair over 27 inches, and everything is in per-

FRATELLI BERTUZZI
WILLIAM W. HEADRICK

fect proportion to both the length and the diameter of these graceful tubes. It looks like a sword and handles like one, too. Everyone who's seen it has wanted a closer look, and everyone who's handled it has seemed reluctant to hand it back. I know the feeling.

Modern hammer guns have become something of a minor signature of the Italian trade, ever since Abbiatico & Salvinelli started making them in the 1970s. Making them self-cocking is no great trick—simply a matter of combining external hammers with Anson & Deeley cocking levers—but it adds an element to an already captivating style of gun.

They cock the same way hammerless guns do, just by opening the action, and, fitted with a tang safety, they're as safe to carry cocked as any other gun. With rebounding locks and intercepting sears, both of which Bertuzzi uses, they're also quite safe with the hammers down. And as you can uncock them manually, you don't have to fool with snap caps in order to relieve tension from the mainsprings.

Because the tumblers are smaller than those of a hammerless lock, a hammer-gun's frame can be smaller and slimmer, and that's where the smallbores truly shine. The Bertuzzi 28-gauge frame measures only $1^3/8$ inches at the widest point, just behind the hinge, and it's a shade less than $1^1/4$ inches wide at the rear. The lockplates reach a maximum height of scarcely more than an inch, and the whole frame is only $1^7/8$ inches tall at the top of the standing breech.

Here, too, the Bertuzzi actioner did some lovely work, on the frame, the hammers, and particularly in filing the fences. Photos can give you a sense of the overall effect, but without the gun actually in hand it's hard to fully appreciate how complex and delicate and graceful the file work really is. The craftsmanship of some guns becomes less impressive the closer you look; with these Bertuzzis it's the other way around.

Like the 12-bore, the little 28 handles and shoots beautifully. It, too, is balanced slightly forward, which is exactly how I like light guns set up; it gives me better control over the bar-

rels and a much smoother swing. Even though the gun was not
made for anyone in particular, the stock dimensions are almost
exactly to my prescription. Which is not an altogether happy
accident, because it gives me yet one more nudge toward
falling in love with a gun I can't afford. Love, they say, is blind,
but my accountant isn't.

Nevertheless, Heaven help me, I do love shooting this gun.
The trigger, which trips the right lock at about 4 pounds' pressure and the left at a couple of ounces more, is a joy. The locks
are extremely quick, and seeing the hammers in peripheral vision doesn't bother me at all. Lord Ripon, the great English
game shot who continued using hammer guns long after con-
cealed-hammer locks became the world standard, argued that
the hammer spurs helped direct his vision down the rib. This,
of course, is the function of a properly fitted stock, but His
Lordship knew that, too, so he may well have been right about
the subtle visual frame created by the hammers. In any case,
I don't now, nor ever will, shoot as well as he did, and while I
can't say I notice any advantage in the hammers, I certainly
can say they're no handicap.

Because most Bertuzzis are built to order, you can have any
choke boring you want, so I didn't bother computing pattern
percentages for the review guns. But I did fire both of them at
the patterning plate to see how the barrels distribute shot
charges—on the tight side, as it turned out, but also quite
evenly. The plate also showed that both barrels of both guns
shoot right where you look.

These are impressive guns, all in all. I'd have the 12-bore's
trigger lightened, if it were mine. One of the 28's ejectors is a
bit sticky and probably needs some wood shaved out of the
forend to free it up. The forend latches of both guns are stiffer
than they ought to be. I can put on my reading glasses and find
a few runovers and flat diamonds in the checkering.

Serious flaws, these? Not in the least. Neither gun has a serious flaw, nor in my estimation, any flaw at all that isn't easily corrected. They're that good. New jewels.

CHAPTER SEVEN

DARNE/PAUL BRUCHET

When Oliver Cromwell's army defeated the Scottish troops loyal to King Charles II in 1651, Charles fled Britain for the safety of exile in France. Had he not, he no doubt would have suffered the same fate as his father, who was beheaded in January 1649 by Cromwell's ruling Parliamentarian party. If Charles II had lost his head, both the game gun and the sport of wingshooting might well be very different from what we know today.

Even if Cromwell had lived longer, gunmaking and sport might have evolved along different lines. But the Lord Protector died in September 1658, and when his son Richard, heir to the title but not to his father's ability to dominate the British government, resigned shortly after, Parliament restored the monarchy and invited Charles home. Although it was later said of Charles that he never said a foolish thing nor ever did a wise one, he certainly was responsible for some auspicious beginnings. Among the things he brought to London in May 1660 were a couple of flintlock fowling pieces and a taste for shooting birds on the wing.

Both came from France, where the sport of *tir au vol*, or wingshooting, had found a place among the pastimes at the court of Louis XIV, along with hawking and coursing with horses and dogs. French guns were hardly efficient pieces by later standards, but they were better than the English guns of the period. They were lighter, balanced for good handling, and quicker to fire—all necessary qualities for hitting a moving target at any angle but straightaway.

What happened to the French fowling piece in England

during the hundred years after the Restoration is a long story and not really the one I'm concerned with here. Suffice it to say that under Charles's aegis, wingshooting became popular in England, too, and London gunmakers refined the game gun to such a level that their products became the standards by which guns everywhere were judged.

But they were muzzleloaders, and the British trade clung to them until the middle of the nineteenth century, when the demand for breechloaders became literally irresistible. Perhaps the English makers held out because they truly believed, as some of them said, that the breechloading principle was inherently inferior to the older style. Or perhaps, given the old nationalistic rivalry, they just didn't want to admit that there was merit in a French invention.

Samuel Johannes Pauly, a Swiss gunmaker who opened a shop in Paris in 1808, invented what amounts to the first modern breechloader. Pauly's action, which was patented in 1812, comprises a hinged breechblock with strikers inside. The barrels are fixed to the frame, and the breechblock pivots on trunnions at either side of the barrels, lifting from the rear and swinging forward to expose the breeches.

Pauly moved to London about 1814, but a number of other Parisian gunmakers, notably Roux, Pichereau, and Robert, continued working with Pauly's concept in several variations. Although the fixed-barrel design had no profound effect upon gunmaking till the advent of repeaters, it remained popular in France, even long after yet another Frenchman, Casimir Lefaucheux, gave the rest of the world the now-familiar hinge action.

Popular enough, in fact, that you can still buy a fixed-barrel, movable-breech gun built on a design descended in principle from Pauly's. It began with two brothers named Darne.

Regis and Pierre Darne set up shop together in 1881 in the old gunmaking city of St. Étienne and called their firm F. Darne Fils et l'Aîné. Regis was the designer, and his first gun was an odd but surprisingly efficient exposed-hammer action in which the entire frame rotates a quarter-turn away from the barrels and stock. It worked well enough, in any case, that a hammerless version, first produced in 1891, remained in production until the beginning of World War I.

The greatest of Regis Darne's designs, however, came on the scene in 1894. In this one, the breechblock slides rather than pivots, and it's brilliantly simple. All the shooter has to do is grasp the ears of a lever fitted to the top of the block and pull it backward. The lever, which is hinged at the rear, disengages the fastener, and the block slides back a few inches. The shooter then slips a cartridge into each chamber and pushes the lever forward; one motion closes and locks the action.

The Darne's simplicity is deceptive, because it represents a solution to some complex problems. In a movable-breech gun, the fastener is critical; it has to work easily but lock up firmly enough to withstand the full force of set-back and recoil. Bolt, pump, and autoloading actions do precisely that, but none of them is readily adaptable to a double gun. Darne chose a toggle-and-cam arrangement linked to the operating lever, so that the main bolt acts as a buttress between the block and the frame when the action is closed. As a secondary fastener, a notched extension projects from between the barrels and fits a hole in the breech face, where a second lug slides vertically into the notch as the main bolt drops into place.

Cocking, too, is a problem. The Anson and Deeley principle obviously can't be applied to a fixed-barrel, sliding-breech gun since there's no hinge to provide leverage, so the action lever itself is the logical choice. Like a well-designed bolt-action rifle, the Darne cocks on opening, when the action lever offers the greatest mechanical advantage and when the shooter's movements are least likely to be disturbed by resistance from the mainsprings. This, in turn, means that less effort is required to close the action.

French sportsmen took to the Darne immediately, and by 1928 they'd bought more than 100,000 of them. Other makers, both in France and Belgium, copied the design as the patents expired. Darne never made a great impression on the American market, but championed by such writers as Roger Barlow and John Amber, the guns weren't entirely unknown here, and those Americans who like them, liked them immensely.

A sluggish world economy in the late 1970s combined with ever-growing competition from Japan and Italy to send Établissements Darne into financial doldrums, and the company closed down in 1980. At that point, Paul Bruchet, who for some years had managed one of the Darne workshops, bought the machinery and production rights. By 1984, Bruchet, his son, and several other former Darne craftsmen were installed in new shops at 25 Rue des Armuriers in St. Étienne, building guns under the Darne mold under the style P. Bruchet. The style remained so for several years, until Bruchet eventually purchased the Darne name as well. And the Bruchet name was on the 28-gauge gun I tested and reviewed in 1989.

It was a model Bruchet called the No. 2, one of three or four standard grades whose engraving patterns ran the gamut from English scroll to *bulino*, in varying degrees of coverage.

The No. 2 is decorated in floral scroll that the French call *rosace*. All of the exposed metalwork—frame, breechblock, trigger guard and tang—is fully engraved and finished in French gray. There also is a bit of engraving on the rib and at the breech-end of the barrels. All of it is beautifully cut—and beautifully shaded, which in this style spells the difference between art and butchery. The bolder the scroll, the flatter it can look if it isn't properly shaded; look at almost any old No. 4 or No. 5 Ithaca for a case in point. The gun I tested is signed "Ripamonti," who I'm told is Bruchet's master engraver. Seeing his work, I can well believe it.

In terms of materials and workmanship, the test gun is impressive. The wood is dense, handsomely figured, and nicely shaped. Inletting is tight where it counts and only slightly short of perfect overall. The checkering is skillfully cut although not as well pointed-up as it should be. Barrel work is excellent; the tubes are smoothly struck and almost perfectly polished inside and out. The gun is fitted with a deeply swamped rib—a *bande de visée plume,* as the French call it—and has no bottom rib, to keep the weight down. If you want a *bande de visée droit,* or flat rib, you can specify that instead.

Metal-to-metal fit is all but flawless, and the breechblock itself is a marvel of machining and filing. Appropriate internal parts are broached, which helps those surfaces retain lubricating oil, and there's even a bit of broaching at the muz-

DARNE/PAUL BRUCHET NO.2
WILLIAM W. HEADRICK

zles. There, it serves no purpose other than decoration, but it looks good.

The old Darne guns were famous for certain characteristics both of design and dynamics, and the new ones have them all. Light weight is something of a Darne signature. The test gun registers 5³/₄ pounds on my scale, but the weight distribution is such that it feels lighter than that. Which is either a blessing or a curse, depending upon your shooting style. The barrels, which are 64 centimeters long, weigh only 2 pounds, 5 ounces, and the breechblock alone weighs nearly a pound, which means that the majority of the weight is in the shooter's trigger hand. The balance point, in fact, is only about 2 inches ahead of the front trigger—great for carrying, not so great if you need some weight in your forward hand to smooth out your swing. I find I have to deliberately steer these wispy barrels through a crossing target to have any hope of success. It's easy to overpower this little gun, to slow the swing, or to stop altogether.

You might not find a Darne comfortable if you have small hands or short fingers. The slope of the breechblock and the stock wrist are such that you may be inclined to grip the wrist a bit farther back than you would a break-action piece. I have fairly long fingers, but even at that, if I hold the wrist at the most natural-feeling place, my fingertip barely reaches the front trigger.

That also may explain the curiously short-stocked feel this gun has. My tape-measure says the pull is 14¹/₂ inches, which is shorter than my guns, but it feels even shorter still, and I often find my nose in contact with my thumb when I shoulder it. Anyone ordering a Darne would be well-advised to ask for a stock at least a half-inch longer than he normally shoots; a full inch might not be too much, as stocks are easier to shorten than to stretch.

I don't consider any of these things to be flaws in the gun, only peculiarities that should be considered and accommodated if one is to get optimum performance from a Darne. But

I do have one serious bone to pick: The test gun's triggers are entirely too hard to pull. In a 5$\frac{1}{2}$-pound gun, especially one as muzzle-light as this, the front trigger ought to pull at no more than 3 pounds' pressure and the back one at no more than a half-pound more. I don't know how heavy the test gun's are. My scale is calibrated only up to about 5 pounds, and both triggers will hold the full weight of the gun. The sears obviously are well filed, because they break perfectly; it just takes too much muscle to get there. If you order one, be specific about the trigger pulls.

Durability is a fair question to pose for any gun, and the old axiom that you get what you pay for isn't always absolute. In Darne's case, you may get a bit more than you pay for. I haven't fired the test gun nearly enough to make any sound judgment on durability over the long haul, but I have handled some Darnes that have digested many thousands of cartridges and have never seen one with a loose action. Neither the fastening bolts nor the surfaces they bear against are subject to much friction—somewhat less, I suspect, than those of a break-action gun—so there simply isn't much opportunity for wear.

Nonetheless, Regis Darne took pains to account for every detail, and that, in turn, accounts for some interesting features in the guns. Since a double gun's barrels are fastened together at a converging angle, cartridges in the chambers do not rest at precise right angles to the breech face. On the Darne breech are two flanged steel discs where the cartridge heads rest; they're called obturator discs, and their inner faces are milled at a slight angle so that each cartridge head is held exactly parallel with the breechblock.

Almost everyone who has written about Darne has made a great fuss about these, pointing out that the flanges enclose the cartridge rims as protection against escaping gas if a rim should crack. They also effuse over low recoil because the shell cases don't rap the breech face, marveling at how you don't hear cartridges rattle when the gun is closed and generally taking such a gee-whiz attitude that you begin to wonder why every gun doesn't have obturator discs.

Actually, no gun needs them, not even a Darne.

A cracked cartridge rim is no great disaster. It happens fairly often to shells made without integral base wads, especially if they've been reloaded a couple of times. If his gun is properly on-face, the shooter isn't likely to know it's happened until he sees the empty hull.

To insist that a Darne recoils less because of the obturator discs is princess-and-the-pea nonsense. A fixed- or locked-breech gun recoils just as much as any other, and a lightweight gun recoils more than a heavy one. There is some additional set-back if the cartridge is able to move in the chamber, but when there's more than a few-thousandths of extra headspace, the strikers won't crush the primers and the gun won't go off at all. In any event, a case that moves a few thousandths of an inch cannot create secondary set-back to a degree that any shooter can feel.

Which isn't to say that obturator discs serve no purpose. They do, and one of them really does have something to do with recoil. Regis Darne clearly understood all the potential weaknesses in a sliding-breech design and added the discs as a way of ensuring the most even distribution of recoil against as much of the gun's total mass as possible. Even though set-back isn't a serious factor, it does represent a small additional stress on the fastening system, so Darne gave his gun slightly less headspace than usual. There's no room for even thin-rimmed cartridges to move in the chambers, and the toggle-linkage in the fastener has sufficient camming force that a thick rim simply gets compressed slightly. Darne's concern for recoil was on behalf of the gun, not the shooter.

Despite the breathless claims you might read or hear, you may be assured that a Darne recoils just as much as any other gun, and that a heavy load in a light gun will rap you smartly. It's a law of physics that has not yet been repealed.

The obturator discs' flanges also serve a good purpose, but not one that has much to do with fairy-tale horror stories of cracked cartridge rims. If the flanges weren't there, the extractors wouldn't work very well.

Although the factory catalog describes the Darne system as *ejecteurs automatique*, they are neither *ejecteurs* nor *automatique* in the same sense as we usually think of such things. The Darne does have a small lugger mortised into the barrels, but it serves only to push cases about $^1/_8$-inch out from the chambers. Everything else is accomplished by two small hooks underneath the obturator discs. Mechanically, they operate the same way that extractor hooks operate in repeaters and simply pull fired cases fully out of the chambers. In the Darne, they're selective, only gripping a cartridge rim if the lock for that barrel has been tripped; otherwise, the lugger, always under spring tension, presents unfired cartridges to be slid out with a fingertip or a tilt of the gun.

The Darne ejector system works because the flanges around the obturator discs keep the shell cases from slipping away from the extractor hooks. Once the breechblock is drawn fully backward, all you have to do is roll the gun sideways a bit, and the cases fall away. It's marvelously simple and perfectly efficient. The test gun never showed the slightest hitch in disposing of empties, not even during the timed-series sequences on the sporting clays course. You can't ask for better than that.

Compared with guns built in the conventional break-action mold, a Darne is decidedly unorthodox, especially to American shooters. It would be a grave mistake, however, to equate "unconventional" with "inferior," for the Darne certainly is not that. Whether you find the design appealing is a matter of personal taste, but an objective view could only conclude that these guns are built to a truly impressive level of quality.

Besides its intrinsic merit, a Darne holds historical significance as well. To shoot one is to handle a piece of history, to touch a pedigree that reaches back to where the modern breechloading gun began, to demonstrate the truth of that fine old French axiom: The more things change, the more they remain the same.

CHAPTER EIGHT

FERLIB

Like any industry, gunmaking traditionally has thrived where nature has placed the raw materials within easy reach. In northern Europe, great coal fields, often laced with nearby veins of iron ore, reach from Wales nearly a thousand miles east to Polish Silesia, and at places where resources and trade routes coincide, gunmaking has flourished for hundreds of years—at Birmingham, Liège, Antwerp, Augsburg, Nuremburg, Suhl. Farther south, one of the oldest gunmaking districts in the world lies in a narrow valley along the Mella River in northeastern Italy. It, too, is a place where nature bestowed lavish gifts.

The slopes of the Trompia Valley are marbled with veins of ore that yield a particularly high grade of iron carbonate, which in turns produces a tough, readily worked, lightweight metal. It was perfect stuff for gun barrels in the days before steel, and by the sixteenth century, Val Trompian barrels were prized by gun trades all across Europe and Asia.

Iron barrels are no longer much in vogue, but Val Trompia remains one of the world's great gunmaking centers. Brescia, at the southern end of the valley, and Gardone, a few miles north, are home to virtually the entire Italian gun trade, which is home to some of the finest gunmakers in the world.

In fact, the more of them I see, the more convinced I am that the finest guns built in the world today are built in Val Trompia—an opinion that often is received like a lighted match in a flour mill, especially among Anglophiles. I confess to being as Anglophilic as anyone, but there's no denying the hard evidence. There are craftsmen in Italy capable of building and finishing guns to a level of quality that could soften the heart of a dead shark, and more of those guns are showing up in this country every year.

Given the extent of its history, the Italian trade certainly is no recent phenomenon, although you wouldn't realize it from what's been available here. Until the early '80s, the only Italian makers active in the American market were either quite large, highly specialized, or dedicated to low-priced exports, so that American gunners' perspective on the Italian trade scarcely extended beyond Beretta, Antonio Zoli, Bernardelli, Franchi, Perazzi, and a few others. None of them, moreover, made much effort to sell their highest-grade guns here, so for all we knew, what we saw in *Gun Digest* was the best Italy had to offer—good guns but not great ones.

That, happily, is changing, thanks in part to a more cosmopolitan view and in part to a domestic economy grown healthy enough that more of us can afford to sample the wares. Best-quality Italian guns aren't cheap, but you don't have to mortgage your unborn heirs to own one, and they *are* best-quality guns, by any standards.

The Italian trade today is remarkably similar to what the English trade was a hundred years ago, a thriving community of craftsmen—lockmakers, stockers, barrelmakers, engravers, and others whose expert skills are available to the trade in general. As it once was in England, there are a few makers of great renown but also many smaller shops that turn out extraordinarily fine guns at the rate of a few hundred or a few dozen or simply a few each year, guns bearing such names as Fabbri, Piotti, Rizzini, Marocchi, Casartelli, Zanotti, Bertuzzi, and others.

In the summer of '89 I spent several weeks with two guns from FERLIB of Gardone. The style is a portmanteau word made up from the name of Libero Ferraglio. The firm has been in existence since the late 1940s, turns out fifty guns or fewer each year, and occupies a middle price range.

The two guns—a 20-bore sidelock and a 28-gauge boxlock—well represent FERLIB's particular specialties, for it's one of the very few Italian makers that build best-quality boxlocks. Other than form, however, these two are more alike than different, both fitted with double triggers, straight-hand stocks with checkered butts, splinter forends fastened with the Anson latch, and swamped, hollow ribs with file-cut matte finish. Both show high-quality materials fitted and finished with considerable skill.

The 20-bore weighs 6 pounds. The barrels, which are chopper-lump, are 66 centimeters, or a shade under 26 inches, bored with $2^{3}/_{4}$-inch chambers and no choke in either tube. Like high-quality sidelocks made nearly everywhere, the action is of Holland & Holland type, fastened with a Purdey double bolt.

In most respects, it's what you'd expect of a gun in the $10,000-odd price range—well-struck barrels, skillfully filed frame, and extremely close fit among all the various parts. The engraving is English small scroll, very well executed, and there's a thin gold border around the lockplates. The wood is very handsome, oil-finished European walnut, with matched figure in stock and forend. Overall, the woodwork is excellent: well shaped, drop points gracefully sculpted, fittings precisely inlet. Checkering is fine and generally well done, although the pointing-up could be a bit better at the edges. There is no border to the checkering, which is fashionable in some quarters; it looks unfinished to my eye, but that's strictly a matter of taste.

The triggers seem to me a major flaw. The sears break crisply enough, but the pulls in both locks are dreadfully hard. I first fired this gun on the skeet field, and for an instant I thought I'd forgotten to disengage the safety. The right barrel finally went off, but only after I pulled hard enough to shoot three feet under the high-house target at Station 1. I subsequently found that either trigger will support the entire weight of the gun without tripping the sears. More than 6 pounds of pull is entirely unacceptable, particularly in a gun of this price. But I must add that this is the only FERLIB gun I've shot that's had such a problem.

In other respects, it's a delight, properly balanced and dynamic in the hands. It has performed flawlessly on a diet of Lyalvale Express ³/₄-ounce loads, which are themselves a delight to shoot in a lightweight gun, and the FERLIB delivers them in wide, even patterns with little apparent stringing. The ejectors work perfectly, and are precisely timed and sprung strongly enough to pitch the empties about ten feet.

The boxlock 28-bore, which FERLIB calls the Model F.VII, shows most of the 20's virtues and none of its faults. It, too, is heir to the classical influence of English gunmaking, with an Anson & Deeley action and Purdey bolt. The dovetail-lump barrels are 68 centimeters, or about 26³/₄ inches. Chambers are 2³/₄ inches; chokes are cylinder and full—which is not a bad combination in a 28-bore game gun, although the left barrel can be mightily unforgiving. It's great for going-away pairs at sporting clays, but there's no slack at all for dealing with the second of an incoming pair; shoot them in the standard right/ left sequence, and the second one either vanishes in a tight blossom of smoke or sails on unscathed. A chipper, it ain't.

The 5 pounds 10 ounces of its weight are centered about a half-inch back from the hinge pin, which gives it a lively but decidedly nose-light feel. If the gun were mine, I'd have an ounce or two bored out of the stock to shift the balance to the other side of the hinge.

Good triggers are an absolute must, in my opinion, and the proper weight of pull depends upon the weight of the gun. The sheer mass of a heavy piece naturally dampens the few ounces of pressure needed to trip a stiffer sear; a heavier pull therefore feels right in a heavier gun, so long as the proportion is reasonable. The lighter the gun, however, the more critical the pull becomes, simply because the motion of a lightweight object is more easily disturbed. Try to pull a really heavy trigger in a 5- or 6-pound gun, and you'll find the muzzles bouncing

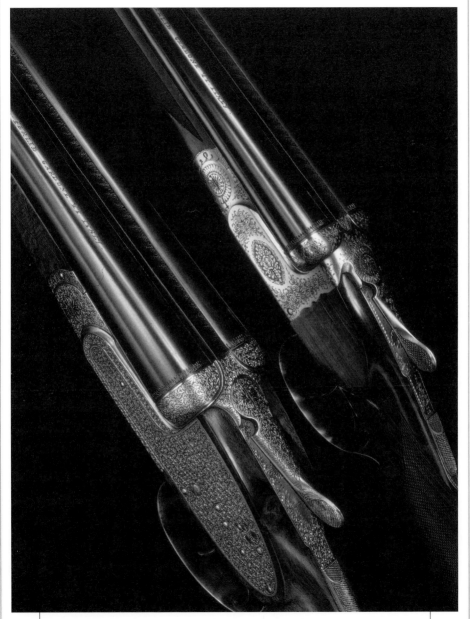

FERLIB
WILLIAM W. HEADRICK

madly up and down, crossing and recrossing the target's line of flight instead of tracking smoothly along it. The harder you pull, the more your trigger hand overpowers the one that's guiding the barrels, so your swing falls apart and you end up shooting well below and behind the target.

In contrast to the 20-bore, the little FERLIB 28's triggers are first-rate. Both sears break crisply at 4 pounds, which is just right for a game gun this size—light enough not to interfere with the handling and heavy enough not to jar off under recoil or from an accidental knock or a finger desensitized by cold weather. These are triggers adjusted the way triggers should be.

The Model F.VII sells for less than half the price of the sidelock, but it certainly is not less than half the gun. The wood is less richly figured, but it's handsome nonetheless. Wood-to-metal fit is extremely close, although the stock is left slightly proud. The stock panels are left plain and carved with good drop points. Checkering (also borderless) is only slightly coarser than that on the sidelock and every bit as well done.

The barrels are smoothly struck, leaving no ripples, and the frame is well filed and polished. Frames and furniture of both guns are finished in French gray; barrels are deeply blacked. The boxlock is engraved in English bouquet-and-scroll. The work isn't as extensive nor quite as painstakingly cut as the sidelock's, but it's done well.

Mechanically, the boxlock performs like a champ. The action is silky, the ejectors strong and properly timed. In short, everything about it works as it should.

The final consideration for any high-quality gun is durability. Beauty is one thing, reliable functioning quite another, and equal measures of both don't always come in the same package. FERLIB guns have been criticized in some circles—notably among Italian pigeon shooters—for breaking down more often than they should. Pigeon shooting, on the other hand, is brutally hard on guns, more so than almost any game shooting. I've put about a case of cartridges through each of the review guns, which certainly is no conclusive test of durability, but neither one has shown the slightest malfunction, either.

They are impressive guns, obviously built with skill and serious attention to detail. Standards of gunmaking quality have suffered somewhat over the past generation, but that has more to do with economic lunacy than from apathy on the gunmakers' part. History, in gunmaking as in everything else, tends to move in cycles, and while standards of excellence may be shifting geographically, they aren't likely to disappear. Superb craftsmanship is very much alive and well—and you'll find an abundance of it in the Trompia Valley.

CHAPTER NINE

THE NEW A.H. FOX

The Ph.D. advisors in graduate school used to tell us that whatever topic we chose for a dissertation should be one we were utterly mad about—because even at that we would despise the thought of it by the time the thing was finished.

As I ultimately chose a teaching job in lieu of the two more years of poverty that writing a dissertation would have involved, it was a long time before I put their notion to the test. But eventually I spent the better part of seven years researching the life of Ansley Fox and the production history of his guns. Then I wrote a six-hundred-page manuscript that ended up as a four-hundred-page book. Today, my response to the advisors would be, "Not necessarily." I'll confess I was not unhappy to reach the end of the project—but I was just as fascinated with Ansley Fox and as fond of Fox guns then as I'd been when I started.

It's not surprising, then, that I'm delighted to see Fox guns back in production once again, nor that I'm pleased to be able to write a new chapter in a history that went into eclipse almost fifty years ago.

The story of how the best gun ever built in America came to be reborn is simple enough. Tony Galazan is much the same sort of gutsy entrepreneur that Ansley Fox was—willing to take a risk and just as determined that whatever he makes will meet an extremely high standard of quality. In 1992 Galazan negotiated permission to use the Fox patents and trade names, which Savage Arms has owned since buying the A.H. Fox Gun Company in November 1929. Shortly thereafter, he organized the Connecticut Shotgun Manufacturing

Company in New Britain, Connecticut. Then Galazan began the long, enormously complicated job of outfitting a factory and getting production under way.

The old Foxes were built in three gauges and more than two dozen grades and models, which is something only a handful of gunmakers in the world can successfully carry off today. Sensibly, Galazan chose a much narrower approach and decided to build only 20-bore ejector guns in four grades—the standard Fox CE, XE, DE, and FE grades, plus an Exhibition Grade inspired by the special series of pieces Fox Gun Company built for display at the Panama-Pacific Exhibition in 1915.

Within those parameters, however, Connecticut Shotgun offered all the options the Fox Gun Company did and then some—pistol-grip, half- and straight-hand stock custom-built to customer prescriptions; cheekpiece or Monte Carlo comb; 26-, 28-, or 30-inch barrels choked to order; double triggers or the Fox-Kautzky single; splinter or beavertail forend; plate, pad, skeleton-steel butt or heel and toe clips; monograms, initials, or your signature on a stock oval or the trigger guard, the rib or the barrels; leather trunk case with accessories; even a choice of barrels made from the Chromox steel Fox began using in the 1910s or Krupp steel, which Fox used exclusively until about 1912 and then, at the onset of World War I, sparingly until the supply ran out.

The wood is all European walnut, Turkish-grown. You can handpick your own, and you should, if possible; there are blanks in Connecticut Shotgun's wood room that would make Ansley Fox salivate.

So would the technology Connecticut Shotgun brings to bear. The key word in the company name is *Manufacturing*, for these guns are made entirely in-house. The barrels come in as solid billets. Most of the parts start as investment castings, turned out at a Connecticut foundry in dies Galazan made in his own shop. The milling machines are computer-driven and capable of minute tolerance. The old Foxes were almost entirely machine-made, even the woodwork; the new ones are machine-made, too, up to a point, but the key is that all the parts are hand-fitted by a team of Austrian-trained gunsmiths. The new stocks are entirely handmade.

Ansley Fox would have done it exactly the same way. And

A.H. FOX MODEL XE
WILLIAM W. HEADRICK

in the beginning—from 1905 to 1907—he tried to, but his ambitions were too grand. The market was such that he couldn't afford to put as much handwork into the guns as he wanted; consequently, not many old Fox guns were as carefully and closely fitted as the new ones are.

Which brings me, finally, to the gun in question. I've had it since April '95, and I reckon it's fired about five thousand cartridges. That's only the start, though, because this one is mine.

It's an XE, aesthetically my favorite Fox grade—an engraving pattern that's a little showy, perhaps, but one that appeals to me in a boxlock gun.

The barrels are Chromox, 30 inches long, which reflects a certain prejudice of mine. Conventional wisdom wants small-bores to be almost as short as your arm, but they don't handle worth a damn for most shooters when they're made that way. Early on, I suggested that one of the company's display guns should have 30-inch tubes, and I stood for four days in the Fox booth at the '94 SHOT Show as the guns made their debut, watching people go back to that one time after time, remarking on how smoothly and gracefully it swung and yet how quick it was to handle. A few refused to believe the barrels were 30 inches until a tape measure proved it.

The chambers are 2³/₄ inches, as in all new Foxes. (These are meant to be lightweight bird guns, not instruments of torture, and the factory commendably refuses to bore 3-inch chambers.) At .614-inch, both bores are one thou smaller than the nominal 20-gauge standard, and there's no variation anywhere my bore gauge will reach.

The chokes are .007-inch constriction on the right side and .017-inch on the left, both a couple thou tighter than I wanted, but my patterning plate shows such lovely, even spreads with everything from three-quarters to a full ounce of shot that I'm not about to quibble. In practical terms I'll never notice the difference, and with these patterns the birds certainly won't, either.

Like the barrels, the rest of it expresses my particular

druthers in a side-by-side: two triggers, straight-hand stock with traditional Fox red rubber pad, and a splinter forend—the extra-long one that was a signature for the XE Grade, inlaid with a wedge of black buffalo horn at the tip and shaped to a tiny schnabel.

Stock and forend are from the same blank, which was seldom the case with old Foxes. It's a killer piece of wood and took me about an hour and a half to pick out. I confess to being a hopeless wood freak anyway, but the selection at Connecticut Shotgun really is that good.

The dimensions are mine, of course—$15^1/_4$-inch pull; $1^1/_2$-inch bend at the comb, $2^1/_8$-inch at the heel; $^1/_2$-inch cast-off at heel and $^5/_8$-inch at toe. (I need that much cast to compensate for my habit of mounting a gun farther out on my shoulder than most shooters do. It's not something I recommend; it's just the way I shoot.) At any rate, whoever made the stock got every dimension right on the dot, and when I mount the gun properly it points exactly where I'm looking.

Within reasonable limits, you can specify overall weight, and being no fan of ultralight smallbores, I asked that it scale about $6^1/_4$ pounds. In fact, it weighs 6 pounds, 5 ounces, which is a rather impressive achievement in building a 20 that's longer than average at both ends. You can also specify the balance point and the trigger pulls. I got just what I asked for in both cases. The triggers are especially nice; the right one breaks at $3^1/_2$ pounds, the left one at $3^3/_4$ pounds—dandy for a field gun of this weight.

The fit, finish, and decoration would turn Ansley Fox a deep shade of shamrock. The wood fits as if it grew around the steel, and steel meets steel without a hairline's gap anywhere. There are a few faint strike marks on the barrels, but the metal is otherwise extremely well polished. So is the wood—not a sanding mark left anywhere. The checkering has a few imperfections, but nearly all checkering does.

All in all, the fit and finish are noticeably better than I've seen in any but a small handful of old Foxes.

The same is true of decoration. I'd say I've seen about four old Foxes that are as well engraved as this one—or, for that matter, as well engraved as any of the new ones I've looked at.

As far as quality of engraving on American guns goes, Fox's was in the middle. It was generally better than Ithaca's or L.C. Smith's, but not as good as the best from Parker or Lefever. Virtually none of it could hold a candle to what Connecticut Shotgun is turning out. The engravers currently working on Fox guns are some of the best freelancers in the business—James DeMunck, Leo Schickl, Richard Boucher, Richard Roy, and Jim Blair. They all do lovely work. DeMunck engraved mine, cutting the oak-leaf XE pattern more cleanly, precisely, and delicately than anyone in the engraving shop at Fox ever did, including chief engraver William Gough. DeMunck's gold inlay—a thin band at the breech end of the rib, the word *SAFE* on the top strap, and my initials on the trigger guard—looks more as if it was done with a laser than a chisel. Only under a 10X glass does it show as freehand work, and it's impressive even then.

As in any process of manufacturing something as complicated as a fine gun, some bugs showed up in a few new Foxes—although the number is remarkably small and the problems have been minor.

As I said, I've fired about five thousand rounds through mine, and the total likely will be twice that by the time this appears in print. I started with game-farm pheasants and quail the day I got it; wild quail, woodcock, and grouse followed, along with a lot of clay targets and shots fired at the patterning plate. Apart from the occasional flinch, which comes from me and not the gun, the triggers have felt the same every shot. The ejectors have never failed, nor has their timing changed. And the handling is lovely, everything I'd hoped it would be. This gun is going to see a lot of use. Based on the way it's performed so far, I have every reason to expect that it will stand up beautifully.

In response to demands from the market, Connecticut Shotgun announced new gauges in 1996: 16, which like the old Fox, is built on the 20-gauge frame; and also 28- and .410-bore, built on a frame even smaller yet.

It's exciting enough to have the best of the American classics back and better than ever after all these years, but the new Foxes suggest something more—that the American gun trade is not as moribund as it has appeared to be, that quality in manufacturing has not been wholly usurped by the Europeans or the Japanese. Economic times, of course, have changed drastically since Fox guns were last in production. The last of the old price lists, issued in October 1946, shows the CE Grade at $236; a current CE, as of June 1996, costs $9,500. Comparatively, however, relative values aren't so different.

In another sense, though, value and price are entirely different, and in this case the value is something more than just the cost of a gun. The new Fox is something we haven't seen in quite some time—a genuine, top-quality American double gun. That's something to feel good about.

CHAPTER TEN

RENATO GAMBA OXFORD 90

Once beyond a certain age, people of every generation seem to make a hobby of arguing that the world has gone straight and thoroughly to hell since the days of their youth. It's a pastime guaranteed to bore the pants off each succeeding generation, forced into the role of audience.

I found it so, anyway, since I could never quite understand what was so good about the good old days, neither those of my grandparents—who grew up in a world of backbreaking toil, outhouses, lousy transportation, and a life expectancy scarcely more than fifty years—nor those of my parents, whose early years encompassed those same joys and World War I besides.

Complaining doesn't appeal to me much even now that I've reached an age when I could do it with some credibility. As a generalist grumbler I wouldn't stand a chance, not while enjoying the comforts of indoor plumbing, air travel, high-speed communication, and a computer that's taken 90 percent of the physical work and half the time out of doing what I do for a living. Even if I took up specialized bitching I'd have a hard time painting my corner of the world, the corner devoted to guns and shooting, in shades of misery. I can work up plenty of high dudgeon over what's happened to the environment and go on some thunderous tirades about how wildlife habitat truly has gone to smash—but I can't bemoan the gun world itself, because the fact is, it's a far from dreary place.

This is especially true of guns priced in the middle range, the market niche that once was home to guns costing $100 to $300, a niche the American arms trade filled with some of the best values in the world—sturdy, handsome guns built to shoot and built to last. If they seldom approached the levels of refinement available from gun trades elsewhere, so be it; they weren't meant to. Their failure to reappear after World War II left a void that never really started to refill until the mid-1960s, when Winchester came up with the grand idea of having guns of American design manufactured in Japan. It isn't quite filled yet, in fact, but it's getting there, thanks mainly to imports from Spain and Italy—guns that occupy the same market turf once held by Fox and Parker, L.C. Smith and Ithaca.

Prices certainly aren't the same, but they're surprisingly comparable. For good or ill, it takes about $12 in mid-1990s money to buy what you could get for a buck in 1940, so the middle range of gun prices today reaches to about $3,500. Quality is comparable, too. In 1940, $250 would buy a DHE Parker, an XE Fox, or a Specialty Grade L.C. Smith with ejectors. Nowadays, equivalent money will buy guns just as well-built—which brings me to the Oxford 90 by Renato Gamba.

As with a number of "new" names that have appeared on the American market in the past few years, Renato Gamba is not really new at all. The guns have been around for a generation or more, and they've even been available here, off and on, since the late '60s—mostly off, though, since like some other foreign makers, Gamba has spent its share of time in the game of Musical Importers. When I field-tested the Oxford 90, in 1991, Gambas were marketed here by Heckler & Koch; now, I believe, the Gamba company is doing its own marketing.

The Oxford 90 is a production-type piece, built in 12-gauge and 20-, with barrels 68 and 70 centimeters, double and single triggers, straight-hand and pistol-grip stocks. According to factory literature, you can also have a semi-beavertail forend, a checkered butt or a rubber pad, and a set of Briley choke tubes suitable for steel shot.

The basic gun to which all these refinements apply is built on an excellent boxlock action fastened by a Purdey bolt, and fitted with decorative sideplates. The plates, in turn, are fitted with a full complement of dummy pins placed exactly where lock-pins would be on true sidelocks. The real Oxford 90 lock-work is a variation on the Anson & Deeley design.

Although I have examined and fired several of these guns in both gauges, quality of materials and workmanship has been remarkably consistent, so I'll simplify this discussion by focusing on the one I used the most.

It's a 7-pound 12-bore with 70-centimeter barrels—in our system, a shade over $27^1/_2$ inches. Chambers are 70 milli-meters, or $2^3/_4$ inches (3-inch chambers are standard for 20-gauges). The barrels are constructed on the monobloc system and fitted with a heavy reinforcing splinter behind the forend loop, which is a particularly good idea for guns that might be used with steel shot. Like many other makers, Gamba bores its longer barrels to modified and full chokes and the shorter ones to improved-cylinder and modified. If you prefer longer bar-rels and open chokes, you can have them honed out, but it won't be an easy job with the Oxford 90, because the bores are chrome-lined.

RENATO GAMBA OXFORD 90
WILLIAM W. HEADRICK

I have mixed feelings about chromed barrels. They're about as corrosion-resistant as bores can be, which is good, but chromium is so bloody hard that altering chokes is difficult, which ain't so good if you want less constriction than the factory gives you. Given my druthers, I'd opt for plain steel and take the trouble to keep them clean.

The Oxford 90 rib is flat with a slight swamp, file-matted across the top, and tapers from a full centimeter at the breech to 5 millimeters at the muzzles. The matte finish is very well done, and the taper offers a nice illusion of additional length. In all the guns I've seen, the barrels are very well struck, with nary a ripple between the muzzles and the monobloc joint. And every set I've handled rings beautifully.

The stocks are attached with a drawbolt and built to standard dimensions: $14^3/_4$ inches pull to center, $14^7/_8$ inches to the heel, and $15^1/_4$ inches to the toe. Standard bend is $1^9/_{16}$ inches at the comb and $2^3/_4$ inches at the heel, with about $^1/_4$-inch cast-off.

The wood is European walnut of good quality, handsomely figured with dark, smoky streaks. The shaping is a bit better than average, although I'm not overly fond of the slightly fish-bellied profile, which is popular in some parts of Europe.

The wood-to-metal fit is good but not flawless; a couple of guns show some random gaps, especially around the top tang. In the same vein, the finish is also good, but just about all the Oxford 90s I've seen could use a few more coats of oil to better fill the pores and bring up a richer patina. The checkering, cut to about 24 lines per inch, is decidedly better than average.

Functionally, I have no complaints at all. The trigger-pulls are a wee bit heavy, but among production guns they usually are. Unlike some production guns, though, Oxford 90 triggers are quite crisp, and although they show a bit of slack, they are altogether free of creep or drag. With sears this nicely fitted, you can live with a little extra weight in the pulls. And, at $4^1/_2$ and 5-plus pounds, these are only about a pound overweight anyway.

The cocking system and ejectors are timed just right. Both locks cock at the same instant, and the ejector sears trip simultaneously just a fraction later. Ejector springs are plenty strong enough to do their job.

Matters cosmetic are largely matters of taste. The Oxford 90 very much appeals to my taste in some respects, rather less so in others. I like the way the frames are sculpted and filed, and the sideplates are better-shaped by far than those on many sideplated boxlocks. Triggers and trigger guard are as slender and graceful as they ought to be.

The engraving, which combines machine-cut scroll and hand-cut line work, is not up to the same quality. To my eye, the gun would look better with only line work and the rosettes on the ends of the hinge pin—especially if the frame, sideplates, trigger guard, and forend metal were blacked or color-hardened, or even if they weren't so brightly polished. Gamba is by no means the only Italian firm that makes guns so shiny; in fact, most of them do, so I can only conclude that I'm among a relative minority who doesn't like it. I'll take good blacking or case colors or the soft silvery-pearl of traditional French gray any time.

But these are minor quibbles, and none so offend my tender sensibilities that I'd refuse to own one of these guns. On the contrary, if you're in the market for a very good gun at a reasonable cost, this one has much to offer. It qualifies as a best-buy value in its price range, and about the only thing the Oxford 90 really needs is to be better known.

Which brings me back to the point I started with—that the good old days are more often a product of perception than of fact. The middle-range guns we have now are different from the ones we used to have, but if you compare old and new side by side, strip away the layers of nostalgia, and take a hard look, you'll have to admit that maybe they can make 'em like they used to.

CHAPTER ELEVEN

GARBI MODEL 101

I've mentioned before that the Spanish gun trade has staked out a niche that is unique in the world. Nowhere but in Spain can you have a high-quality sidelock ejector game gun built to your specifications for between $3,000 and $8,000. You can find the quality elsewhere, but not at a comparable price—and that, as I also have said before, makes the best Spanish guns some of the best bargains in the world.

Pose the question of who the best Spanish makers are, and you'll likely start a debate that'll last at least as long as the Scotch holds out and won't get fully resolved even then. This is as it should be; differences of opinion and taste are what keep our brains from shriveling like raisins. Regardless of the contenders, the name Armas Garbi is certain to come up, and if you haven't had the chance to look over some of these guns, listen well to what their champions have to say.

As companies in the Spanish trade go, Garbi is scarcely more than a youngster, organized in 1959 by five craftsmen who decided to leave the employ of other makers and set up on their own. Along with their skills at the bench, each contributed an initial from his name to form the company name. According to Terry Wieland's excellent book, *Spanish Best*, Garbi, which in the Basque language means "graceful," is an acronym for Jesús Guerena Barrena, Juan Alday, Ramon Churruca, Jesús Barrenetxea, and Domingo Iriondo.

Each man was a specialist at some aspect of gunmaking, and in the beginning they made all the guns themselves. In the 1960s and '70s, however, Garbi expanded its range to include boxlocks, sidelocks, high grades, low grades, the whole works, and expanded the workforce as well. But in 1980, reckoning that the future would not support such diversity, the owners decided to phase out everything except sidelocks made to order. That's how it is today, and Garbi's annual production amounts to about 300 guns, built essentially by hand in the traditional way.

Being well-disposed toward the best Spanish guns, I looked forward to the chance for a full-scale field test with a Garbi.

On a trip to Argentina a couple of years ago with Bill Moore, Garbi's American importer, I spent a day hunting *perdiz* with a very nice little 20-gauge and an afternoon at doves with an equally nice 12-bore. Both gave me an appetite for more. Eventually, Garbi dealer Bob Hunter called to say he'd just taken a used one in on trade and was sending it along.

Technically, it is a Model 101 in 12-gauge with 28-inch barrels, straight-hand stock, splinter forend, two triggers, and general game-gun configuration. The code stamped on the barrel flat says it went through the Spanish Proof House at Eibar in 1992.

This gun was built for someone, to his specifications. If you were to order a Garbi, you could have it made to your specs, and they probably wouldn't be quite the same as these, so I'm not going to bother with stock dimensions and chokes and other such stuff that'll be different from gun to gun. What shouldn't be different is the quality, and I'd rather concentrate on that.

To start at the business end, the barrels are chopper-lump type, and they ring with the sweetest, clearest tone I've heard since the last time I rang a set from a London best. Whoever put them together and soldered on the ribs knew what he was doing. I assume the same man also bored and lapped and struck them, because the bores are consistent within a thousandth-inch and the wall-thickness is consistent within about three thou. (And at .033- to .035-inch, they are thin enough to be lightweight and plenty thick enough to be durable.) All told, this is barrel work worthy of a gun that would cost about three times the $4,400 base price of this one.

The polishing is more in line with the price—which is to say it's quite good but not perfectly mirror-smooth. For that, you really do have to pay more. The blacking is even and apparently deep, because I don't see any particular wear, and this gun had been shot a fair amount before I got hold of it.

It has a Churchill rib, which is an option you don't see very often. A Churchill rib is filed with the sides tapering toward each other, so its cross-section looks like a flat-topped triangle. This one is file-matted on top to create a narrow, dark line that your peripheral vision picks up as you look down the barrels. From a purely practical point of view, I don't consider any type of rib on a side-by-side gun to be better or worse than any other type, but there's something about this one that rather appeals to me.

The forend is a typical splinter with a typical Anson-type

GARBI MODEL 101
MICHAEL MCINTOSH

latch, and it's very well fitted to both the action knuckle and the barrels themselves.

Strangely, though, the forend tip is the only bit of metal on this gun that isn't well filed and finished; the curvature's not right, and a lot of file marks still show. It's an odd thing, because the rest of the metal work is excellent.

That's not to say you can't see the odd file mark here and there, but you have to look damn close, and even then there aren't many. The triggers are especially pleasing—thin and graceful with just the right amount of curve to them. And if this strikes you as being overly nit-picky, just lay two guns side by side, one with slender triggers and the other with the sort of thick, chunky ones you often find on even fairly expensive guns, and tell me which gun looks better overall.

Geoffrey Boothroyd started me thinking about this subject one night years ago, as he and David Trevallion and I were having a working dinner of fish and chips and beer in his wonderfully cluttered office at the top of his house in Glasgow. It forever changed the way I look at guns, because it brought what had long been an unconscious reaction into what's left of my conscious mind. The fact is, putting clunky-looking triggers—or trigger—on an otherwise beautiful gun is no different from dressing a perfectly constructed fashion model in four-buckle galoshes; there's something wrong with the picture, though you might not be able to put your finger on it right away.

This gun is as good in its wood as in its metal, fitted with a handsome piece of *Juglans regia* that Garbi's stockmaker did right proud. For the most part he made it look as if the wood grew around the metal, even that weird, almost unfinished-looking forend tip (I don't mean to dwell on this, but it *is* weird). At any rate, the wood fits the way it should.

Like the man who filed the triggers, the stockmaker was someone who paid attention to detail. He squared off the lock edges perfectly and cut two of the best drop points I've ever seen on a Spanish gun—and in those details you can read a lot about the way a stocker works. Not surprisingly, the grosser work—shaping and smoothing—is excellent. The checkering is good, but Europeans generally aren't as meticulous about it as American stockmakers are, so it has its share of runover nicks and little places where the diamonds aren't fully pointed up.

Although the general run of Spanish engraving isn't quite as good as what you'll see from Italy or England or the United States, there are a few Basque engravers whose work stands up well to any comparison, and the man who did this gun is one of them. Large scroll actually takes more time than small scroll—because it has to be shaded to give it depth—and it's bold enough to readily show the touch of a clumsy or inexperienced hand. You'll find no such thing on this gun, not even under a loupe.

All in all, it looks great. It also shoots great. The stock's too short for me, but with a lace-on pad it feels fine. With the balance point just at the forward edge of the hinge pin, it swings fine, too. The triggers are light and crisp, and the ejectors have never failed to work just as they should. I have thoroughly enjoyed all the shooting I've done with it.

It also figured in a little comedy that had me shaking my head for days afterwards. I was in England during November '95 for some shooting and research, had just boarded the plane at Gatwick, heading home, and was standing around having a last stretch before the long sit-down. Another passenger came up, introduced himself, and said he'd just bought one of my books to read during the flight.

This happens to me now and then, and it always feels a little strange to be recognized; that's for celebrities, not gun writers. I forget, too, that my photo is floating around on the dust jackets of several thousand books (and maybe some post office walls, for all I know).

Anyway, it seems that this chap had been shooting in Ireland—and it turned out that one of the guns in his party was a man I've shot with several times. Small world. But then he said, "By the way, how do you like that Garbi you're reviewing?"

I looked around to see if I hadn't somehow wandered onto the set of a Stephen King movie, and wondered if he was next going to ask whether I still keep my shorts in the top dresser drawer. My befuddlement must have showed, because he laughed and told me, "They said they were going to send it to you when I traded it in. It used to be my gun. . . ."

Sometimes, "small world" doesn't even begin to describe it.

CHAPTER TWELVE

HOLLAND & HOLLAND
SPORTING GUN

The longer I live, the more I'm convinced that what we call "news" is seldom truly new at all but rather a continuing chronicle of events and circumstances as old as mankind. I've also decided that the mass media focus more upon how predictably history repeats itself, day by day, than upon events that own no recent precedent. Were it otherwise, every wire service and network in the world would have told us in 1993 that the British had introduced an entirely new gun.

Had Isabella told Columbus there was war in the Balkans or the Middle East, he would have answered, "So what else is new?" But if you can remember the last time a gun of brand-new design came out of the British trade, you're a lot older than I am. Add in the fact that it's an over/under, and you have an extraordinary event.

Actually, *two* new British over/unders debuted in 1993, which was more extraordinary still. One was David McKay Brown's round-action, and the other was Holland & Holland's Sporting Gun. This review is on the Holland & Holland, but before I get to it, a word about why this was such a remarkable event.

For one thing, the British have had no particular reason to invent new guns, simply because they perfected the sporting shotgun once and for all a hundred years ago, and you can't improve on perfection. That's why the world standard for a best-quality gun, whether it's built in England, Belgium, Spain, France, Italy, or Timbuktu, is a sidelock side-by-side patterned after the London gun as it came to be at the end of the nine-

□ 78 □

teenth century. With literally nothing left to invent, all that remained was to match the level of quality that British craftsmen established at the turn of this century.

Considering what they accomplished with the side-by-side, the British understandably have not nurtured much love for the over/under. Even though the world's first two truly great over/unders were built in England—the Boss in 1909 and the Woodward in 1913—the most important development of the vertical gun has come from the Italians, particularly Daniele Perazzi and Ivo Fabbri. But the tides of world economics have shifted to the point that the English trade's best market is no longer in Britain but rather the United States and elsewhere, and it's a market that takes a definite shine to the over/under.

In part, this is a result of the phenomenal popularity of sporting clays. I don't fully understand why, but I do my best target shooting with an over/under and so do a lot of people I know. You won't see many side-by-sides on a skeet field, trap range, or clays course. Lots of gunners prefer the shooter-friendly qualities of an over/under for game as well—although for my part, and again for reasons I don't fully understand, I shoot birds much better with a side-by.

In response to the demand, a number of British makers—Holland & Holland, Purdey, Boss, Peter Nelson, and McKay Brown among them—offer best-quality over/under guns. Except for McKay Brown's, all are sidelocks and for the most part are variations on older designs. Holland & Holland's new gun is different; like McKay Brown's, it is truly new.

When I first met Holland's Deputy Chairman Roger Mitchell in the fall of 1988, he told me of a project, just then under way—a new over/under, to be created by the company's principal design team of Peter Boxall, Peter Blyth, and factory manager Russell Wilkin, in consultation with Holland gunsmiths, sales staff, and shooting-school instructors.

Their approach was also something new, at least for the English trade—computer-assisted design, with the image of the gun and all its parts created in three dimensions on a computer monitor instead of paper. The Italians—Perazzi, Fabbri, and a few others—pioneered the high-tech approach to sporting guns, and Holland & Holland was the first English maker to use it. More on this as we go.

In the course of my continuing contact with Holland & Holland over the next couple of years, more details emerged. The new gun would be neither sidelock nor boxlock but rather one in which the lockwork is mounted on the trigger plate, a concept that originated more or less simultaneously in Britain and Germany during the 1860s. The Dickson round-action is built on this principle, and so is David McKay Brown's fine over/under. And it's not an entirely new idea to Holland & Holland, either; Henry Holland and Thomas Perkes patented a trigger-plate design for a side-by-side gun in 1879.

Daniele Perazzi and Ennio Mattarelli took the notion a step further in the 1960s with a design that allows the shooter to dismount the locks and install another set in only a moment. As Holland & Holland invented the now-standard approach to hand-detachable sidelocks—in which the head of the main lock pin is formed as a little thumb-lever—it isn't surprising that the company chose to make the new gun's trigger-plate system hand-detachable, too. Unlike the Italian approach, which uses the safety button to unlatch the lock-and-trigger assembly, the Holland latch is part of the trigger guard, located at the rear of the guard bow on the left side. It's clever, completely unobtrusive, and requires only one hand to pull the locks, leaving the other to maintain a firm hold on the gun.

Building a single gun is one thing, but developing a finished design for full-scale manufacture is quite another. Once all the basic elements are worked out on the computer, the data are fed into the computer-controlled milling machines that actually produce the first prototype. Once this is accomplished, traditional gunmaking takes over. A computer can create the beginnings of a best-quality gun, but only human experience can complete the task. This requires time and rigorous testing, both to confirm the virtues and to ferret out the bugs that inevitably show up in a new mechanical system—all the while refining both the aesthetics and the manufacturing process.

Thus two more years elapsed before the piece was ready for public debut. By then, spring 1993, two prototypes and four demonstrators had been built, and together they showed the full range of forms the new gun could take. And by then, a 20-gauge version was in the works as well. I shot all the protos and demos, some of them quite a lot, and while I have some preferences as to the details, I have nothing but praise for the fundamental elements of design.

At first look, the Holland & Holland Sporting Gun is decidedly handsome. This is no mean feat to pull off with an over/under, because its tall, boxy, slab-sided frame is difficult to invest with any great measure of grace. Look more closely and you can see how Holland's did it—lovely sculpting at the top of the standing breech that fairs out to a gracefully shaped bolster, giving the frame maximum strength at minimum weight. The sideplates, purely decorative, lend an impression of length to offset the height, and the effect is a gun that's about as elegant-looking as an over/under can be.

As Holland's intention was to create a fine gun and not reinvent the wheel, certain features are based on existing concepts—which usually proves to be the best way to design a gun and, in large part, is how the English side-by-side came to perfection.

The Sporting Gun's action pivots on trunnions, with the pins mounted on the frame—an idea that's at least as old as the Boss over/under and that has been highly refined by the Italian trade. Some other features also show a distinct Italian influence: the fastening system, with twin bolts midway up the breech face engaging heavy lugs on either side of the lower barrel; the cocking system, a simple, highly efficient arrangement actuated by a camlike tongue in the forend; and of course the drop-out lockwork. All of these are thoroughly time-tested concepts that have come to be standard fare for such great Italian guns as Perazzi and Marocchi. I also see a bit of Boss influence in the replaceable recoil lugs inside the frame.

That these features are derivative doesn't mean they were copied down to the last jot and tittle. On the contrary, Holland's designers came up with some excellent variations. In the Italian system, for example, the cocking slide is a single steel bar; the Holland uses two bars fitted side by side, which probably enhances the mechanical advantage somewhat. The locks are driven by stout U-shaped springs mounted almost vertically, on the order of the Perazzi system, but the lockwork itself appears simpler to me. Though I cannot quarrel with the quality of Perazzi locks, simplicity in gun mechanics always appeals to me.

The selector for the single trigger is completely new, and, in fact, is covered by patent. (This itself is worthy of notice, because English gunmakers have taken out mighty few patents in the past couple of generations.) The selector works off the safety thumb-piece, which will seem familiar because it's one of the standard approaches for boxlock and sidelock guns. But the Holland is the first in which this system has been applied to trigger-plate locks.

Though the Sporting Gun is made to order and therefore is available with all sorts of options, there were originally two models: Sporting and DeLuxe Sporting. You could have either one set up as a game gun or a target gun. The rib could be solid or ventilated, the barrels any length up to 32 inches, with fixed chokes or tubes. The wood was fine-quality European walnut finished in traditional London oil. You could have a slender, game-style forend or a fuller target-type; a pistol grip, straight hand, or—my favorite—the elegant half-hand design generally known as the Prince of Wales grip. Checkered butt, heel plate, or recoil pad—your choice. Whatever the form, the chambers were $2^3/_4$ inches (3 inches upon request) and the barrels approved for steel shot.

The Sporting version was the plainer of the two, decorated with just a bit of scroll engraving—though you could specify that the frame be color-case-hardened. With the maker's name inlaid in gold, it is to my eye extraordinarily handsome.

As the name implies, the DeLuxe was *deluxe*—extra-select wood and large-scroll engraving much like what you'll see on a Holland & Holland Royal sidelock. If you wanted game scenes, carving, gold inlay, or almost anything else, it was yours for a price.

Holland's eventually discontinued the DeLuxe designation, but in name only; all its features are still available as options for the standard Sporting.

Apart from differences in weight, ribs, stock configuration, and all the other options that can have some effect on appearance and handling, all these guns share one essential quality: They work perfectly. The trigger is superb; the pull is crisp and clean, and the weight is properly adjusted to the weight of the gun. The locks cock as they should and trip when they're supposed to. The trigger shifts sears reliably, without hangup

HOLLAND & HOLLAND SPORTING GUN
HOLLAND & HOLLAND

or hitch—provided of course that you release it between shots. I sometimes forget to do this on fast double targets, but I do it with every single-trigger gun, so it's a matter of my failing synapses, not faulty triggers. The ejectors eject every time, consistently. In short, the Sporting Gun does everything it ought to do. I don't know what more you could ask.

I normally spend a fair number of words in these essays evaluating workmanship—how well the barrels are bored and struck, how the stocks are shaped, how everything's fitted and finished. That's in the nature of reviewing. This time, though, it's enough to say that these guns are built by Holland & Holland, and Holland & Holland only turns out best-quality work. Simple as that.

London guns do not tend to be cheap, and at first glance, Holland's Sporting Gun may seem decidedly pricey. As of mid-1996, the standard Sporting begins at about $35,000. But you can spend considerably more on an over/under by Perazzi or Fabbri, and in fact argue that the Sporting is a bargain by London standards. Not having the price of one myself, I won't belabor the point, but I bring it up because anyone familiar with the prices of new best-quality guns these days might well ask how Holland's can sell them so cheaply. The answer lies in the fact that Holland & Holland has the most sophisticated gun factory in all of Britain, where the sort of donkey work once done by hand is executed by computer-driven machinery capable of fine precision. And that minimizes the expensive hand-work required for final fitting.

This doesn't mean the Sporting Gun is "machine made" in the usual sense of mass production and interchangeable parts milled to loose tolerances, but the fact is, virtually every gun built in the world today is made to some extent with power-driven machinery. Now isn't the time for a long digression on the subject, but I would suggest that the real art and craft of gunmaking rests in the last few thousandths of an inch, not in hogging out great chunks of steel with hacksaws and big chisels.

Look at it this way: Michelangelo sculpted *The Pietà* out of solid marble entirely by hand. If he'd had a jackhammer to do the rough work, don't you suppose he would have used it? And so long as it was finished by talented, experienced, loving hands, wouldn't the result be the same? You can say as much for the Holland & Holland Sporting Gun.

By the same token, the Holland & Holland Sporting Gun itself says much. It speaks to me of a fresh enthusiasm in the London trade, of at least one great gunmaker actively seeking to carry fine old traditions into the future, adapting to the present without compromising the standards of excellence from the past.

From some quarters you'll hear all sorts of epitaphs to be chiseled onto the tombstone of the English gun trade. But look in the right places and you'll find guns to prove that the obituaries are decidedly premature. The Holland & Holland Sporting Gun is evidence of this. It is a remarkable achievement.

CHAPTER THIRTEEN

HUGHES CUSTOM FOX

Unlike an alarming number of things that happen to me as I settle ever deeper into middle age, I can remember exactly when and where this project began.

It was January 1991, at the American Custom Gunmakers Guild show in Reno, Nevada. I was sitting in the cocktail lounge with my friend and favorite rifle writer Terry Wieland, gunmaker Steven Dodd Hughes, and a delightful chap named Jim, who is an enthusiastic patron of custom gunmaking. (I also remember Jim's last name, but he prefers to remain anonymous.) Not surprisingly, the conversation was turning mainly on guns, and at some point the question came up: If one wanted to have an existing gun completely customized, what would be the best American piece to start with?

This has been posed to me before. In fact, I've toyed with the notion myself—even to the point of writing up a detailed set of specs. I would have gone ahead with the project long ago, save for the fact that my bank account hasn't yet been sufficiently flush. So it's an easy question to answer: If the gun were to be mine, it would be a Fox.

As I discuss the A.H. Fox gun in a couple of other chapters here, I won't belabor the details again, except to say that to my taste it's the handsomest boxlock ever built. And for various mechanical reasons I consider it the best of the American classics. The fact that Foxes weren't always the best-finished guns is just one more reason why a Fox would be my choice as the basis for a custom job. Even the lowest-grade Foxes show an intrinsic beauty in line and form. To me, no Fox is so ugly a duckling that I cannot readily see the swan beneath; so it's easy to

imagine what a lovely thing one could be if some master craftsman brought out its full potential.

We kicked all this around the table for quite some time
there in Reno, building hypothetical guns from the raw material of imagination. That most guns created this way remain
unbuilt doesn't much matter; just dreaming the dreams is pleasure enough.

This time was different, though. Steve Hughes phoned me
a week or so later to go through everything again. And yet once
more a few weeks after that. The talk grew steadily more specific as to exactly what sort of Fox might be best for reworking
and what could be done with the piece to create a lightweight
game gun of essentially English character. I was writing a book
on Ansley Fox at the time, so Fox guns were much on my mind
anyway, and by the time Steve told me he'd decided to actually
do what we'd been talking about, I was as excited over the
prospect as he was.

For nearly three years after, I followed the progress with
keen interest, happy to assist in any way I could. Except for
providing some initial consultation in finding the right gun and
serving as a sounding-board for Steve's own ideas, I didn't really contribute that much, but talking about it and seeing the
gun take shape in the photos he sent was all great fun. I wish
I could have watched first-hand, but I live in Missouri and
Steve was in Oregon at the time, so we were a bit more than
commuting distance apart.

The first Hughes Fox was completed in 1993, and Steve
sent it to me for a close look and some shooting. For the first
week or so, it was scarcely out of my hands. I shot targets with
it, studied it from across the room, went over it end to end with
a jeweler's loupe. I missed it when I sent it back home.

Simply put, it is a mightily impressive piece of work. And
in a larger sense, the project raises some issues that are topics
of current interest in the gun world and that seem likely to
prompt even more discussion in the future.

In keeping a close eye on what's happening in the shot-gunning community, I've noticed a trend developing over the past few years: ever-increasing activity in the business of performing extensive work on existing guns, particularly American guns. The nature of this work tends to fall into one or another of just a few categories. There's restoration, which is the matter of returning a well-used, or even misused gun to the same mechanical and cosmetic condition it was in when it left the factory.

Then there's upgrading. This is a matter of transforming a gun to a grade higher than it was originally. The degree can be modest—say, turning a Field Grade L.C. Smith into a Specialty Grade—or it can be as extreme as making a Parker VHE into an A-1 Special or an AE Grade Fox into an FE Grade. In any event, the objective is to duplicate the higher grade as precisely as possible.

Then there's the true custom job—which, to my thinking, is quite different from either restoration or upgrading, even though it takes in certain elements of both. Instead of recreating the appearance of a factory gun of any particular

HUGHES CUSTOM FOX
STEVEN DODD HUGHES

grade, the custom gunmaker seeks to create something wholly new, something unique, something unmistakably different from what he started with.

The Fox that Steven Hughes remade is an excellent example of this. If you haven't already, study the photo for a few minutes and notice certain things.

Hughes started with a 12-gauge Sterlingworth Field Model with 28-inch No. 3-weight barrels. When it left the Philadelphia factory about 1925, the gun was a typical Sterlingworth in every respect: a sturdy, well-made shotgun but plain-Jane all the way—no engraving, some machining marks still visible on the outside and lots of them remaining inside, completely unremarkable wood, and so on. In other words, it was a typical American field-grade piece, and the lack of cosmetic attention is why it could be sold at a retail price of $36.50.

Now, however, this Sterlingworth not only has some features that Fox applied only to its highest-grade guns, but also others that never appeared on any factory Fox. Notice that Hughes refiled the frame completely, rounding off the ends of the traditionally pointed frame panels and reducing size and weight in nearly every dimension. He filed the rear edges in the graceful, fancy-back scallops that you'll see on some very high-grade factory guns. He also rebated the frame top and bottom and rounded the tops of the fences to follow the contour of the barrels—as Fox did with its XE, DE, and FE grade guns from about 1914 on.

Look closely and you'll see a narrow bead running along the rear of the fences, from the barrel flats right around to the top of the standing breech. Factory Foxes were filed with a short section of beading at the bottom of the fences, but none were beaded this extensively. Such work is a common English motif that few American makers went to the trouble of copying. Parker and L.C. Smith were the notable exceptions, but only on their highest-grade guns—and if you wonder why, the fact that Hughes formed his beads the traditional way, by removing surrounding metal with chisel and file, should be answer enough. It's painstaking, time-consuming work, but the effort shows.

And so does the rest of Hughes's metalwork—from the re-struck barrels, new forend tip and anchor, reshaped forend shoe, top lever, safety button and brand-new trigger guard to the scalloped steel heel and toe clips. I turned every part in every direction under strong light, and except for some very slight waves on the surface of the barrels, I couldn't find a dis-cernible dip, waver, or irregularity anywhere.

Hughes tells me he hand-polished all the internal parts as well. I really wanted to have a look inside, but I trust you'll for-give me (as I knew Steven would) if I didn't put a screwdriver to those perfectly slotted, pristine pins.

As every top-notch craftsman will, Hughes had some jobs done by specialists. Dennis Potter deepened the chambers from their original $2^5/8$ inches to just over $2^3/4$ inches, honed out the chokes to .007-inch on the right and .029-inch on the left, and polished the bores. They're mirror-bright and were polished so carefully that they still measure no more than .003-inch over the nominal 12-gauge standard of .729-inch. Com-bining this with Hughes's judicious barrel-striking (and the fact that most American guns were overbuilt to begin with), nowhere are the barrel walls less than .030-inch thick. If this were an English gun, it would pass proof without a whimper.

Doug Turnbull did the color case-hardening, using the pack process to get a result that's very close to the original Fox col-ors. Color case work is a genuine art, practiced by few and mastered by even fewer. Having seen a lot of guns he's hard-ened, I can tell you that Doug Turnbull is as good as they get.

The engraving is by Eric Gold, a young Arizona craftsman whose work I saw for the first time on the Hughes Fox. I don't know what his background is or who taught him, but he's one to watch in the future. His flowered screw heads and pins are perfectly symmetrical, his bar-and-ball bordering is clean as can be, and his lettering and inlays are flawless. Judging from what I saw under my loupe, he cuts his English scroll with a hand-graver; at any rate, I couldn't see any of the tiny step-marks that are the typical signature of a hammer-and-chisel job. His circular cuts are extremely smooth, his shading superb.

The stockwork belongs entirely to Hughes. The wood is a killer piece of California-grown English walnut, splendidly fitted and shaped. Not even the loupe showed a significant gap at the head (and a fancy-back frame can be a real bear to fit perfectly). From there to the butt, every surface is a curve, the belly properly concave to lend a lean, elegant look. And Steve left just enough wood to accommodate a bit of freshening up before it lies at the same plane as the metal. By "just enough" I mean you can feel a slight step, but you can't see it.

I knew from photographs that Hughes hollowed out the stock to refine the balance and then plugged the hole with a slab cut from the butt—but I couldn't find the seam where he fitted the plug, not even in direct sunlight wearing my strongest reading glasses.

If you forced me to quibble, I might say the necks of the drop-points are just a wee bit too thick and that I can see a few slight imperfections in the checkering—but take that as a quibble and nothing more.

Hughes built the gun for himself, and the stock dimensions are his, not mine, so I missed a few targets before I figured out just where the shot was going. After that, though, it proved a deadly little thing from every angle. At nearly 7 pounds, it's light enough to be pleasant, heavy enough to swing smoothly, and the weight is distributed just as it should be for dynamic handling.

Besides polishing all the lock parts to make them operate more smoothly, I believe Hughes reduced the size of the tumblers as well—a reduction in weight that also tends to make the lock time faster. I have no way of actually measuring lock time, but in shooting the gun I got a sense that it's a bit quicker than the typical factory Fox. It feels right, at any rate. And so do the trigger pulls; they're crisp as glass and trip at about 4 pounds of pressure.

As I said earlier, American guns in particular are getting more and more attention as the basis for custom work, and there's good reason for it. All the great American guns were factory items, produced in quantity and meant to deliver reliable performance at modest prices. Obviously, they were highly successful at doing so. Very few, however, were finished with the sort of meticulous hand work that characterizes the finest guns of Britain and Europe. This is one reason why comparing English and American guns is neither fair nor productive for any valuable insight—but it also is a good reason to consider them for custom work.

We built the best factory-made guns in the world, especially the plain, workaday pieces we generally know as field grades. In almost every case they were mechanically identical to the higher grades. They were durable, reliable, reasonably handsome, and the fact that they were not filed and finished down to the last degree of perfection takes nothing away from their intrinsic virtues.

Turn the economic issue the other way around and consider this: Even if the factories didn't perfect these guns because they couldn't afford to, what's to say that someone shouldn't have one perfected if he *can* afford to? And what's the difference between shelling out several thousand dollars for a beautifully built English boxlock and spending a similar amount to have an American gun brought up to the same level of refinement? Given materials and mechanics of comparable intrinsic quality, the money will go for exactly the same thing in either gun—the experience, skill, and time of the craftsmen who do the work. And craftsmanship is what fine gunmaking is all about.

Which brings me back to where this began—to my longstanding belief that even the plainest American gun can be a thing of remarkable beauty waiting to happen; and, more specifically, that a Fox is the one to start with. Steven Dodd Hughes's first custom Fox tells me I was right. It also tells me that the results can be even better than I imagined.

CHAPTER FOURTEEN

KRIEGHOFF K-80
GAME GUN

For more than a generation now, Krieghoff has been known almost exclusively for top-quality target guns, although target
guns are not what Ludwig Krieghoff and his partner Herr Sempert had in mind in 1886. The city of Suhl, in the old German
state of Thuringia, was one of eastern Europe's traditional
armsmaking centers, and there Sempert & Krieghoff, as the
firm was originally called, built sporting guns and rifles for
nearly sixty years.

Sempert & Krieghoff disappeared in the shambles of
post–World War II Germany, but the Krieghoffs didn't. With
Thuringia annexed to the Soviet-controlled East Germany,
Ludwig Krieghoff's son and grandson moved the family far to
the south, to Ulm, where the Iller River flows into the Danube.
There, Heinrich and Heinz Ulrich Krieghoff leased some fac-
tory space, reassembled their gunmaking machinery, and on
July 1, 1950, established H. Krieghoff GmbH.

At about the same time, Heinrich Krieghoff bought the design and manufacturing rights to one of America's greatest
guns. Remington had stopped making its Model 32 over/under
in 1942, when the American arms industry converted virtually
its entire resource to wartime weapons production. Afterward,
with repeaters showing every sign of dominating the sporting-
arms market for a long time to come, Remington concluded
that it could no longer sell enough Model 32s to justify the cost
of manufacture.

Heinrich Krieghoff must also have known that mass-
produced over/unders were no economic match for auto-

loaders and pump guns, but the target-shooting market, then slowly reviving in Europe, was another matter. Serious target shooters have always valued reliability and consistency far more than low price, and even though they represented a minuscule share of the gun market at the time, it was a share worth tending to.

Krieghoff made some small revisions in the Remington 32 design, renamed it the Krieghoff Model 32, and during the 1950s turned out a few guns every year. Meanwhile, the roughly six thousand guns that Remington had built were hot items on the American market, sought after by skeet and trap shooters who liked the wonderful way the old guns handled and the way, shot after shot after shot, they turned clay targets into satisfying balls of dust.

The first Krieghoff 32s reached the United States about 1961, and both an American agency and a dealer network were in place by 1967. By then, it was the gun of choice for a goodly number of those who shot targets in serious competition and for big-money purses. Over the following years it evolved in various specialized forms at about the same rate that target-shooting interest continued to grow—trap guns in both over/under and single-barrel style, skeet guns in every gauge. Krieghoff wasn't the first maker to devise multi-gauge, inter-changeable barrel sets for skeet shooters, but it was the first to do so with a genuine measure of success.

The mix-and-match approach can create some interesting results. Within certain limits, the ability to attach different bar-rels and stocks to a single frame offers a versatility that took a while to fully explore. The Krieghoff I field-tested in 1990 is a good case in point.

Technically, I suppose it's best described as a hybrid target/game gun, since the heart of it was the further-revised Model 32 action that Krieghoff introduced about 1980 under the designation K-80. In this instance, however, the style is more game gun than target piece—the lightweight alloy K-80 frame fitted with 28-gauge barrels, a straight-hand stock of game-gun dimensions, and a slimmed-down, schnabel-tipped forend.

The lightweight frame was a key element. Krieghoff essentially builds only one frame, of 12-gauge proportion, and if this one had been steel, the gun would have been a monster. At $7^{1}/_{4}$ pounds, it was no featherweight even at that, but in hand you might've guessed as much as a pound less. With the forend in place, the barrels—28-inch tubes monoblocked into a 12-gauge-sized breech—were slightly heavier than the frame and stock, and that tipped the balance slightly forward. Which of course gives your leading hand something to work with and promotes a smoother, more controllable swing than the short, wispy tubes too-often put on smallbore guns.

Traditionalists and those who insist upon fine aesthetics can find plenty of bones to pick. No one ever accused the Model 32, whether by Remington or Krieghoff, of being a raving beauty in the first place, and hanging a pair of 28-gauge barrels on a 12-gauge frame doesn't help. If you want a gun that delights your eye, that wasn't it.

On the other hand, if you want one that shoots like a demon, that was it.

Come right down to it, all the decoration and style that could possibly be applied to a gun isn't worth a damn if the thing has poorly bored barrels, a bad trigger, and clumsy dynamics. But in those areas, Krieghoff truly shines.

A bit ripply on the outside, the Krieghoff didn't have the best-struck barrels I've ever seen, but you'll search a long time to find a pair more meticulously bored and lapped. To comply with some vagaries of the German proof laws, the chambers were bored to 3 inches and the forcing cones were quite long.

At the time, I was afraid the chambers might prompt a cartridge company to revive the old, unlamented long 28-gauge case, but mercifully, none did. Personally, I wouldn't lament the passing of Winchester's 1-ounce 28-bore either, which had just come on the market when I was testing the Krieghoff. It was the only gun I've shot, before or since, that could handle that load both comfortably and efficiently. The long chambers and cones and what I suspect was a bit of overboring combined to turn those vicious-kicking, shot-stringing little bastards into something almost like an effective load. I know some shooters who swear by them, but all I've ever been inclined to do is swear *at* them—except in the Krieghoff.

The trigger was magnificent—clean, light, and suffering neither creep nor over-travel. Regardless of the firing sequence, under/over or over/under, the lower-barrel sear broke at just a bit under 3 pounds and the other at about a half-pound more. It was, in a word, perfect.

The trigger also was one of the first to be made adjustable for position, to accommodate the size of your hand and the length of your trigger finger. By loosening two Allen-head set-screws, you can slide the trigger forward or back about a quarter-inch. With it set in the middle position, the stock measured $14^{1}/_{4}$ inches to center and heel, and $14^{1}/_{2}$ inches to the toe. The butt was checkered. Bend was $1^{1}/_{4}$ inches at the comb and $1^{3}/_{4}$ inches at the heel, high enough to be deadly on rising targets and also to accommodate some alteration if you wanted to lower it a bit.

The stock also was detachable and, unlike most quick-change stocks, formed an exceptionally close wood-to-metal fit in every dimension.

Typical of K-80 target guns, the safety was non-automatic and fitted with Krieghoff's nifty little lock-out button—a handy feature if you're a target shooter and in no way inconvenient if you aren't.

Everything about it, from the ejectors to the overall quality of fit and finish, was consistent with Krieghoff standards. The wood was oil-finished and nicely checkered; the frame was treated to graceful, hand-cut, large-scroll engraving.

Unfortunately, I had no opportunity to try it on game, but I did shoot a lot of sporting clays with it, using standard $^{3}/_{4}$-ounce Winchester AA skeet loads for the closer shots and the 1-ounce shells with No. $7^{1}/_{2}$ for the longer ones. And I must say it earned me some good scores—a few, in fact, every bit as good as I could've shot with a 12-gauge. The credit rightfully belonged to a first-class pair of barrels and a superb trigger, all in one gun that handled beautifully.

As I said before, no Model 32 is likely to win any beauty contests, but it's well to remember that beauty often is as beauty does. When it came to doing what a gun is supposed to do, that was one that did.

KRIEGHOFF K-80 GAME GUN
WILLIAM W. HEADRICK

CHAPTER FIFTEEN

LANBER

––––––––––––

Reviewing guns is not dull work, but it's rarely adventuresome. I get to shoot a lot, of course, but reviewing is mostly a matter of looking and thinking—studying everything about a gun from the gross anatomy of shape and line to the minute details of fit and finish; thinking about how it feels and how it works, about its pedigree and its place in the firmament of guns in general. That's how I believe reviewing ought to be done.

But this one was different. This time I went about a quarter of the way around the world, stumbled almost by accident upon a gun I'd previously given little attention, watched it being built, found myself shooting one in the most challenging formal sport ever devised for the shotgun, and in the process discovered what may well be one of the world's best guns for the money.

It started simply enough. In the spring of 1994, Jack Jansma and I had plans for a visit to some gunmakers in Spain—mainly Arrieta, for whom Jack is an American importer. But upon returning from the European sporting trade show in Germany, Jack called to say he'd met the president of Lanber, who had invited us to visit his gun factory and to be his guests for an afternoon of pigeon shooting.

Now I have to confess: I was aware of Lanber guns to about the extent of a passing glance. I knew them as inexpensive, machine-made over/unders that seemed little different from similar pieces turned out by a whole slew of European makers. Not unattractive guns, but not the sort whose charisma grabs you by the neck from fifty yards off. I figured I'd eventually get around to having a closer look but felt no great rush to do it. Clearly, however, the time had come.

Just being on the northern coast of Spain along the Bay of Biscay east of Bilbao is enough to get you cranked up. It's incredibly beautiful country, where the eastern end of the Cantabrian Mountains segues into the Pyrenees. You'd think you were in Austria or on the western slope in Colorado. It's Basque country, gunmaking country. Virtually the entire Spanish gun trade exists within the few kilometers of the narrow Ego River valley, from Eibar to Elgoibar to Zaldibar. Lovely place.

I could wax equally ecstatic about our home base, the romantically beautiful city of San Sebastian, but this is a gun review and not a travelog. Suffice it to say that there we rejuvenated ourselves from the long flight with a stiff drink, a hot shower, a few glasses of *vino tinto,* and a splendid piece-meal dinner at the *tapas* bars in the old section of the city, a hotelward stroll under the ancient tamarind trees in Cervantes Park beside the harbor, another stiff drink, and about ten hours of sleep. Next morning we set off for the Lanber factory in Zaldibar.

In meeting Lanber's president, Señor Felix Aldabaldetreku, my friend Mr. Jansma struck something very much like gold. I've met some good people in the gun and shooting world, but none more gracious. Lacking an ear for the Basque language, I won't even attempt a phonetic rendering of Señor Aldabalde-treku's surname. Everyone knows him as Felix anyway. He's been head of the company since the beginning.

In a trade where pedigrees often reach back a hundred years, Lanber is a newcomer, founded in 1963. The name is derived from a Basque word that translates as "new work." At first, Lanber built only side-by-side guns, then added over/ unders and eventually dropped the side-by-sides in favor of an autoloader. With sixty-six employees and an annual production of twelve thousand guns, Lanber is now the largest shotgun manufacturer in Spain. Half are sold in Spain and the rest go all over the world, from Finland to South Africa to New Zealand. Only about a thousand come to the United States each year.

This shrewd reluctance to consign too many eggs to any particular marketing basket helps explain why you don't see racks of Lanbers in every gun shop and discount house. The American gunner who wants one will have to go to some effort, but it's worth the trouble.

Lanber guns are machine-made and built almost entirely in-house. Of the roughly three hundred separate operations required to turn chunks of steel and wood into a gun, only the stock finishing is done outside the factory, sent to a specialty house in Eibar. Everything else, from boring barrels and machining frames to final fit and test-firing, is performed in the factory, mostly by highly sophisticated, computer-controlled machinery. Even the checkering is done by machine, and I don't mean with a little hand-held electric buzz-saw cutter. All the machine requires is that someone clamp in as many as four freshly turned buttstocks or forends and push the right button. With that, the tool head comes down and starts buzzing back and forth, making precisely spaced cuts of a pre-determined length while the cradle slowly rotates the wood. The result is a panel of checkering that's astonishingly well done.

Designwise, the gun is a simple boxlock with a monobloc breech, a trunnion hinge, and a thin, full-width underbolt fastener. All the major springs are coil-type—including the ejectors, which are housed entirely in the monobloc. The single trigger works on a simple inertia shift. All in all, there isn't much to go wrong.

Now, building a shotgun by machine is relatively easy, given the fact that computer-controlled machinery can mill highly complex parts with such precision that the tolerances actually are too close for gun work. A gun lock fitted as closely as the technology is capable of would jam on a drop of oil or a speck of dust. So building a gun that fires isn't the trick; any decent home-shop tinkerer can make one that'll go *bang*, but a shotgun probably is the most intimate functional object ever devised, and the trick is building one that shoots, that responds in dynamics, fit, trigger pull, balance, and all the other ergonomic qualities required of a gun.

In my experience, this is where the typical factory piece comes up short. It may look like a gun, sound like a gun, and, to a point, act like a gun, but somewhere in there is the line that separates a mere tool from an object that somehow is capable of functioning as a separate yet still integrated body part. It's a quality that can scarcely be captured in words, but one that speaks clearly in feeling alone. I haven't come across many machine-built guns that truly have it, but Lanber is certainly one of them.

I learned this the following Sunday afternoon on a mountaintop above Eibar, where the Shrine of the Virgin of Arrate stands next to a small hotel from whose terraced lawn on a clear day you can see all the way to the ocean, twenty kilometers off. The view alone is worth the drive up the narrow, winding mountain road, but there are other attractions as well. For example, the hotel, like several others in the area, is also a pigeon-shooting club.

Now, I've never written much about the sport of box-bird pigeons, for several reasons. One is that I don't shoot flyers very often. What few pigeon clubs we have in the United States are mostly private, members- or invitation-only affairs. What holds me back is not a lack of invitations but rather a lack of funds; it's expensive enough that I'd be bankrupt in no time if I shot as much as I'd like.

The main reason, though, is that the sport not surprisingly raises ire and activism among the animal-rights loonies. Protecting pigeons makes as much sense as a Save the Rats campaign, and yet those most vehemently opposed—who wouldn't know a pigeon-shoot from a crapshoot—don't seem to mind if municipalities execute the birds in a slow death by poison. Go figure. So you're not likely to see any pigeon shooting on ESPN, although it used to be an Olympic event.

But I will tell you this: Apart from *columbaire*, in which the birds are launched by professional throwers with pitching arms like the one Nolan Ryan used to have, box pigeons are the most difficult game you can play with a gun—and by far the most addictive. People who've never done it think I'm making a joke when I say that, for my part, you might as well boil down the whole experience to a few cc's, draw it up in a syringe and inject it straight into a vein.

Layouts vary somewhat, but essentially the game is played in a ring about thirty meters in diameter surrounded by a two- to three-foot fence. Arranged in the center are five to nine box-like traps, each holding a single pigeon. The shooting stand is typically a concrete strip graduated in yards or meters, and handicapping is by distance. In the United States, you may be placed anywhere from twenty-six to thirty-six yards back from the traps; in Europe the maximum distance may be even greater, and the rings often are larger.

Regardless, the rules are the same everywhere: You take your position, mount your gun, ask the trapper if he's ready, and call for the bird. Thereupon, one trap—you never know which it'll be—springs open, and the pigeon is free to do what-ever it wants. It may sit there or fly off at any height, speed,

LANBER MODEL 99E PLUS
COMLANBER · S. A.

or angle, in any direction. You are allowed two shots with which to drop the bird inside the ring. If it gets over the fence—alive, wounded, or stone dead—it's lost. The flight can be blazing fast and highly erratic. And with pigeons being extraordinarily tough, you'll see more than a few absorb two solid hits and still have enough juice to flutter out before they're retrieved.

For obvious reasons, a proper pigeon gun is a highly refined, highly specialized piece, with a premium on handling, pattern density, and trigger pull. If you want to be a serious pigeon shot, you need a serious gun. (I have always done my very best box-bird shooting with Ivo Fabbri sidelock over/ unders, borrowed, of course. I take this as just one more bit of evidence to prove that I don't make nearly enough money to accommodate my tastes.)

Anyway, the plan was that we'd shoot a few birds during the practice session before the weekly tournament started. From the three new-in-the-box Lanbers that Felix had picked at random from factory inventory, I chose a 28-inch barreled clays model, mainly because I liked the feel of the forend a bit better. Otherwise, all three felt the same. A few minutes tinkering with choke tubes got the business end set up the way I like for box birds—improved-cylinder for the first shot, full in the top barrel.

I hadn't a clue how the trigger would feel, but the first bird brought an extremely pleasant surprise: possibly the best factory-adjusted trigger I've ever found on a gun in this price range—and better than those I've found on some guns that cost a whole lot more.

Not having fired a gun at anything in almost two months, I missed the first bird and the second and finally managed to find the groove on the third. It wasn't the gun's fault. In fact, I was mightily impressed by the way it handled and performed—which was a good thing because just then Felix walked up, gave me a handful of plastic chips (which tell the judges the entry fee's been paid), grinned, and said something to the effect that, "You're in this tournament, my friend, shooting for the greater glory of Lanber Armas."

Oh, shit. Just what I needed—a sterling opportunity to trot my 30-percent average out among some really good shots and win a monumental dose of humiliation. Jansma was grinning like a Cheshire cat—until Felix gave him some chips, too, and said he was the official Arrieta gunner. The grin faded but, unlike the Cheshire cat, Jack remained.

The practice birds had already told me it was going to be tough shooting. The wind was blowing up the mountainside at about twenty knots from right to left, and the birds were small, dark-colored, and hard to see—especially as very few of them got more than five or six feet off the ground. To make it worse, Spanish pigeons are small-bodied with ungodly big wings that can scoop a lot of air. Most simply caught the tailwind and went streaking low over the grass, straight for the fence. I'd seen a lot of them fall dead out of bounds.

Mercifully, it was only a six-bird race at twenty-eight meters—to be shot in sets of two, as there are two rings at Arrate. It went as such things usually do when there are seventy-odd entrants: Shoot a bird in the first ring, go immediately to the second for another, and then wait for about an hour and a half until it's time to shoot again.

The Arrate club is fairly high-tech in that the traps are sprung by voice-activated electronics. When it's your turn, you drop one of your chips into the control box to turn on the current. The trapper stands just behind you, holding a microphone on a long handle. When you're set, you say, "¡Listo!" (Ready!). He says, "¡Listo!" in reply, flips the switch and holds the microphone close to you in a way that won't interfere with your shooting. The next sound you make—cough, sneeze, belch, "Pull," whatever—releases a pigeon. It is not a good idea to clear your throat, or your lower intestine, before you're ready to shoot.

I don't much enjoy competition anymore, but box birds do make me concentrate, and on the first set I was about as focused as I get. Praise be, it worked. I smacked each bird solidly with the first barrel and carefully ground-swatted them with the second. (This is perfectly legal in pigeon shooting, and in a serious match you're riding for a fall if you don't do it.)

By the time the first rotation was finished, I was in a twenty-three–way tie for first place and liking the Lanber gun a whole lot.

The first bird of the second set started out as a hard driver, and I shot just a fraction too quick and behind it, then the damn thing turned into a spinner and cut a turn that should have broken its neck just as I let off the next shot. I don't know where that one went. In the second ring I got a straight-away grass-clipper from the center trap that died before it flew ten feet.

Then I was in an eleven-way tie for second and liking the Lanber more by the minute.

Time was, I would have spent the next hour sitting in some quiet place practicing the imaging technique I used when I was serious about competitive shooting: focusing my mind's eye on seeing myself making perfect shots from every angle. Instead I stood around talking with my friends, taking photographs, watching the shooters, frittering away any competitive edge and letting my poor old knees and lower back get good and achy.

So in the last set I handled my gun as I usually do—like a man being attacked by hornets—and both birds flew off to be fruitful and replicate so that years from now their progeny can show some other silly bastard his real place in the scheme of things.

I wasn't overly happy about it, but the event turned out better than I expected, and I found a truly admirable new gun in the bargain.

A few days after I got home, a letter from a reader showed up in the mail. "I'm on a pretty tight budget," he wrote, "but if you can recommend a good over/under for less than $1,000..."

Ah, friend, do I know just the gun for you.

CHAPTER SIXTEEN

MAROCCHI CONQUISTA

Even on a small scale, serendipity is a lovely thing.

In the mid-1980s, having rediscovered the pleasures of skeet after almost twenty years away from the game, I was shooting about a thousand targets a month, and among my most frequent companions in this was a chap whose penchant for gun-trading made him something of a legend at our club. To say that Don never showed up with the same gun twice is an exaggeration—but not by much.

To me, the only thing more fun than shooting is shooting with different guns, so between my own, those that came along as review and field-test pieces, and whatever Don hauled out of the back of his van, I was having in those days what you might conservatively describe as a hell of a good time.

One Wednesday afternoon, a day the club traditionally is the province of retired guys and those who, like me, don't have "real" jobs, I was on my way to load the high-house trap when Don strolled in carrying a dark-blue, molded-plastic case. As we passed, I asked what was in it, and he said, "A Marocchi." Because he has a soft voice, and because I have trouble hearing thunder with my left ear, I thought he said, "A Miroku." But what I picked up a while later from the clubhouse rack was not one of those well-built Japanese guns that have come along under a variety of names and guises.

What I picked up was a strikingly handsome over/under whose tall rib and buttstock design said this gun was built for international skeet, a low-gun game whose extra-fast targets put a premium on balance and dynamics. One swing and mount made clear that this gun possessed those virtues in abundance. The word *Marocchi* was engraved on one side of the beautifully sculpted, polished, and blacked frame, *Contrast* on the other.

Except for fine lines around the contours and small sunbursts at the ends of the hinge pins, it bore no decoration at all—and it was one of those guns that don't need any. Everything about it, from the wood to the fit and finish, spoke clearly with a single word: quality. Unmistakable, first-rate, top-notch, whack-you-right-between-the-eyes quality.

Now, I've told you all this in the past tense, but everything I've said about the gun is still true. It's lying on the desk next to me right now, in fact, looking as impressive as it did the first time I saw it. When that afternoon was over, Don left with a VH Parker and my old Superposed skeet gun (which I got back later in another deal), and the Marocchi came home with me.

That was almost ten years ago. I don't know exactly how many cartridges I've put through it, but I do know the number has six digits. It's shot ducks and pigeons here and in Argentina, skeet in several states, and sporting clays targets all over the country. I try not to mistreat my guns, but they go where I go, in all weather, and I shoot them unmercifully. That's what guns are for. Through it all, my Marocchi Contrast has shown exactly one mechanical glitch, which was a broken ejector stem, soon repaired. Considering the use it's had, I can live with that.

Finding myself with a splendid gun by a maker I'd never heard of naturally made me curious to learn something about Armi Marocchi and its other products. The process took a good while, largely because the guns were scarcely known at all in this country. Eventually, though, I learned that Armi Marocchi has been in business since 1922 in Brescia, the traditional center of Italian gunmaking. Like many other small companies in the Trompia Valley, it's a family business, currently in the capable hands of third-generation gunmaker Mauro Marocchi.

In the course of these seventy-odd years, Armi Marocchi

has manufactured everything from side-by-side game guns and over/under target guns to rimfire rifles, combination guns, even air guns—and from inexpensive boxlocks to best-quality sidelocks built to order.

Sile Distributors, of New York City, has imported the less expensive Marocchis for years, but the top-quality guns were almost completely unknown in this country until Competition Arms, of Lafayette, Louisiana, began importing them in 1979. Competition Arms's main interest was the line of world-class target and pigeon guns built on the Contrast action. Unfortunately, they made little headway in a market dominated by Perazzi, Beretta, Krieghoff, and a few others. Lester Trilla Imports, of Chicago, became the Marocchi agent in the early '80s, and once again the market simply failed to respond. By the late '80s, virtually the only Contrast-action guns coming into the country were pigeon guns made on special order.

In 1990, Precision Sales International, a solidly based company with a good marketing program, took on the task of importing high-end Marocchis. Happily, this amounted to the proverbial third-time charm, and it came about just at a point when Armi Marocchi had some new projects on board.

First came the Avanza, a lightweight over/under that offers exceptional value at a price of less than $1,000. When I saw one of the prototypes, I had a feeling it would find a niche, and subsequent history seems to have borne that out. Now, the Avanza is available in 12-gauge and 20, in both game-gun and clays configurations.

By 1990, I was convinced that the Contrast was one of the finest over/under actions ever invented, and in all my conversations with Precision Sales chief Alan Johnson, I kept asking about it: When will the Contrast line be readily available? Will Marocchi build it as a smallbore? Will they make it available with game-style stocks? On and on, until I'm sure I sounded like a broken record. Alan, ever the patient gentleman, kept telling me that Marocchi believed the Contrast could be better yet, that there was something new and highly interesting in the works—assurances that didn't really sink in until the UPS man delivered a brand-new Marocchi Conquista.

The Conquista is not the Contrast reincarnated. It is the Contrast evolved. And that makes it yet another of the finest over/under actions ever invented.

To see what makes the Contrast/Conquista great, it helps to consider the differences between over/unders and side-by-sides. The heart of virtually every modern break-open side-by-side action is the barrel lump. A semicircular hook in the front end matches up with a cross-pin in the frame to form the action joint. The rear end of the lump may also be a key point in the fastening system, machined to accept either a single or double horizontal bolt. A side-by-side may also be fastened by a rib extension and top hook, by a cross-bolt, or in some other way not associated with the lump—but the lump is a central component. The horizontal arrangement of the barrels allows the lump to be relatively large, relatively deep, and therefore provide optimum strength and stability to the action while still allowing the profile to remain trim and shallow. This, in turn, affects a gun's weight and balance.

Turning the barrels to the vertical, however, instantly creates some design problems. You can still use a barrel lump, but the deeper it is, the taller an already-tall profile becomes. This adds additional weight. Make the lump shallow and you take away some strength from the joint, because the shallower the lump, the smaller in diameter the hinge pin has to be.

This is not to say that a barrel lump cannot be successfully used in an over/under. The Browning Superposed, for many years the standard by which over/under guns were judged in this country, has a lump. It even has an underbolt fastener that's placed on the same plane as the hook—and nobody's ever seriously accused the Superposed of being a weak action.

Other makers, notably the Germans, have combined a barrel-lump hinge with various kinds of top fasteners, usually to great mechanical success. But never to much aesthetic success; barrel lumps and top fasteners make for very tall frames with awkward-looking bulges at the top, all of which are ugly as butt hair and seldom very lively in handling.

To see a much better approach, look at some of the best Italian over/unders. Perazzi, Beretta, Marocchi, and others use joint and fastener concepts that date back to the world's first truly great over/under—the venerable Boss, patented in 1909. In these guns, there is no full-width action pin but rather trunnions mounted on either side of the lower barrel. (In technical cannonry, trunnions are pins or gudgeons integral with the barrel; if there's another word that denotes the opposite arrangement—pins on the frame and recesses on the barrel—I don't know it. Let's just call them trunnions, too, wherever they happen to be.)

The trunnion system promotes the shallowest possible over/under frame. This makes for an optimal weight-to-strength ratio, because extra steel can be placed to enhance durability, not just to create enough room to accommodate a lump. Moreover, positioning the hinge virtually at the center of the under-barrel's bore substantially lessens stress on the action, and placing the fasteners so they emerge horizontally about midway up the breech face offers additional mechanical advantages without all the clutter of extensions and cross-bolts.

Thus it was with the Marocchi Contrast. Add in wonderfully simple lockwork and ejectors, all powered by coil springs, a splendid single trigger, finish it up in a neat, handsome package matched with a pair of barrels beautifully bored and polished, and you have a great gun.

The Conquista is all this and more. I said earlier that it represents the Contrast taken an evolutionary step further. The lockwork and cocking system are virtually unchanged. The ejectors are slightly different, in that the sears are in the forend iron. Good as the Contrast ejectors are, the Conquista's are a better, more durable design.

Its action, too, is somewhat improved. In the Contrast, the trunnions are milled integrally with the monobloc breech. They work fine, but they'll need expert metalwork if the joint ever needs to be refitted. In the Conquista, the trunnions are fastened to the frame and are removable, which will make re-jointing infinitely easier.

My Contrast has a non-selective, mechanical shift trigger and the sweetest pull of any gun I own. The Conquista's trigger is selective, shifts sears on recoil, and is equally sweet. The selector is linked to the safety button and operates in the old Browning-type H pattern. Personally, I think selective triggers are unnecessary for practical purposes, adding only another layer of something mechanical to go wrong, but the shooting world by and large doesn't see it that way, so Marocchi made the right choice.

They also came up with a gem of a trigger. It shifts sears exactly as it should, and the pulls are crisp. Like almost every factory trigger in the world these days, it's a bit heavier than it needs to be (thanks to our absurd product-liability laws), but

MAROCCHI'S CONTRAST AND CONQUISTA MODELS
WILLIAM W. HEADRICK

unlike most, it does not require full-scale surgery to make it lighter. This one is gunsmith-adjustable—which means a 'smith who knows what he's doing can lighten the pull with a tool instead of a hone. If you choose to have it done, find a 'smith who knows triggers. Don't try it yourself unless you know them, too; triggers are easy to bugger to the point of being dangerous.

Mauro Marocchi tells me the Conquista was designed from the ground up as a clay-target gun, and like some other such pieces, it has several features that target shooters will like. For one thing, the trigger position is adjustable. Pushing a little spring-loaded button on the left side lets you slide the trigger blade forward or back to where it best suits the size of your hand and the length of your finger. The total range covers about a half-inch, which should accommodate all but the most extreme hand sizes.

I believe Daniele Perazzi was the first gunmaker to devise a means of changing buttstocks quickly and easily. You simply push a long-shafted Allen-type wrench through a hole in the center of the butt, engage the drawbolt, take off one stock, and put on another. Shooters who want to use the same gun in different target events have long found this useful and economical. Marocchi adopted the same system with the Contrast and carried it over to the Conquista. Even if you never have more than one stock, it's handy for getting at the lockwork for cleaning and periodic lubrication.

Every one of the better Marocchis I've seen has extremely high-quality wood, not necessarily highly figured but always good quality. The Grade II Conquista I tested does have well-figured wood, well shaped and finished. The buttstock is typically chunky. The forend is trim, which I like, and finished off with a schnabel tip, which I don't like—but that's because my own peculiar way of holding a gun isn't very comfortable with a schnabel.

The Conquista's barrels are excellent, both in terms of workmanship and performance. Boring and striking are very precise. Wall thickness is consistent, tapering just as it should without any humps, bumps, or ripples. Both bores measure precisely .725-inch. A full set of flush-fit choke tubes comes with each gun.

According to the stampings, the chambers are 70 millimeters ($2^3/_4$ inches), but my chamber gauges show them to actually be $2^7/_8$ inches, which should help reduce kick a bit. Conquista barrels are factory-approved for steel shot, so you can use it at target clubs where non-toxic shot is required and also take it wildfowling if you want.

Standard barrels are 28 inches, 30 inches, and 32 inches, and you'll be pleasantly surprised to find that a Conquista with 32-inch tubes is just as lively and responsive as one with shorter barrels, because each Conquista is individually hand-balanced. You'd expect this in a gun made to order; that it's done with production-line guns is truly admirable. In any case, you can feel the results.

At $8^1/_4$ pounds, it isn't a featherweight—but on the other hand, a featherweight 12-bore is not my notion of a serious target gun. My Contrast is almost as heavy, and sometimes, either in tournaments or on days when my desire to keep shooting overrules good sense, I wouldn't be unhappy if it weighed a pound more.

The fastening system is one difference between the old Contrast and the new Conquista that I'm not yet convinced is an improvement. In the Conquista, Marocchi abandoned the mid-breech bolt in favor of an underbolt. This probably was done for reasons of manufacturing economy, which is a valid concern for any gunmaker. I can't call it a weakness, because other best-quality over/unders get along quite nicely with underbolts, and I can't quarrel with it on aesthetic grounds, because the Conquista bolt is extremely thin and doesn't add anything to the height of the frame.

In fact, the bite, which is the notch the bolt engages, is placed on a plane slightly below the hinge; theoretically, this should make its mechanical advantage greater than if it lay in

the same plane, and the system may therefore be just as efficient as a mid-breech bolt. It depends to a great extent upon
how cleverly the bolt is hardened, and now that the Conquista has a few years under its belt, time seems to speak
well for the change.

So, I can say without reservation that if you're looking for
a top-notch gun with a fine pedigree, you ought to have a look
at this one. As the test gun made the rounds of clays courses,
it began to lose its new-gun stiffness and the action took
on that silky feel that high-quality guns achieve with use. I
looked less and less forward to the day when it had to go back
to the importer.

Besides, it just looked good standing in the safe next to my
dear old Contrast. Together, they looked like serendipity incar-
nate. They looked like quality.

CHAPTER SEVENTEEN

MERKEL 147E

—————————

My students used to be especially fond of debating the notion of which is more important, form or content. My short answer was always "yes." I had a longer answer, of course, because that's how teachers earn their pittance, but it all boiled down to a view that form and content are equally important—and are in fact as indisseverable as yin and yang.

To me, this is true of almost everything, from literature to music, automobiles to clothing, guitars to guns. I can best appreciate content, character, and craftsmanship when it's presented in pleasing form.

Consequently, German guns have always been something of conundrum for me. It's hard to fault the best craftsmanship that has come out of Germany and Austria (their approaches to gunmaking are essentially identical), but the form rarely appeals to me. Plenty of yang, too little yin. It's solely a matter of taste, of course; I just don't happen to care for the look of square frames with odd bulges, fish-bellied stocks, cheekpieces, or heavy, baroque carving of either wood or metal.

There are a few exceptions. Simson and J.P. Sauer and Austrian-built Charles Daly side-by-sides typically show an aesthetic form that truly complements their excellent craftsmanship. And so does the Merkel Model 147E I tested in the summer and fall of 1995.

Apart from Krieghoff, which enjoys a vast, well-earned reputation among target shooters, Merkel probably is better known in the United States than any other German maker. Gebrüder Merkel—Merkel Brothers—first came on the scene in the 1920s in the ancient gunmaking city of Suhl, and by the time World War II disrupted everything, their sporting guns were highly regarded in America—highly enough, if fact, that when the Soviets imposed postwar trade restrictions against exporting firearms from East Germany, the prices for Merkels that had already found their way here went sky-high.

The restrictions eased a bit as political tensions thawed briefly in the late '70s, but importation of new Merkel guns remained largely haphazard and amounted to little more than a trickle until the early '90s, when Soviet trade barriers went down the tubes along with the Union itself. Now GSI, of Trussville, Alabama, imports Merkels in good numbers.

The test gun is a boxlock ejector patterned on the old Anson & Deeley action. According to the catalog, the 147E is available in all the gauges, including 16, with pistol- or straight-hand stock and two triggers or a selective single.

This one is a 28-bore fitted with a straight stock, two triggers, and 68-centimeter barrels—which translates to 26³/₄ inches and is the only length available in either 20- or 28-gauge. The 12s and 16s come with 28-inch tubes, and if anyone at Merkel is interested in my opinion, I think the smallbores should, too. They'd handle better, and besides, these barrels

MERKEL 147E
MICHAEL McINTOSH

are so nicely made that having an inch or two more of them would represent just that much more gun for the money.

They're hinged on a typical dovetail lump, and the action is fastened with a Purdey-type double bolt, a Greener cross-bolt as a third grip, and side clips on the fences. It is, in a word, overkill, but multiple fasteners are virtually a signature of German gunmaking. There's nothing wrong with wanting a secure, positive lockup, but having more bolts than the county jail means a trade-off in additional weight and can levy an aesthetic price as well.

It means in this case a 28-bore that weighs $6^{1}/_{4}$ pounds. That isn't necessarily a bad thing; I'd rather have the gun a bit too heavy than a bit too light, but doing away with the Greener bolt, which is mechanically redundant, would reduce the heft to about 6 pounds even and would allow the frame to be shallower at the standing breech. This is the one beef I have with the way the gun looks; it would please my eye a good deal more if the frame didn't have to bulge out on top to accommodate the extra fastener.

The tubes are well-struck, showing just a few slight ripples, and the bluing is deep and uniform. The bores are very well polished and highly consistent—.551-inch on the right and dead on the nominal 28-gauge standard of .550-inch on the left.

The chokes are indicated at improved cylinder and modified, but they measure out at .009-inch and .020-inch constrictions. The smaller the bore, the less constriction is required to tighten the shot swarm, so dimensions that would be improved cylinder and modified in a 12-gauge amount to modified and full in a 28—and that's how the Merkel behaved on my patterning plate. At twenty-five yards, which is about where most quail, grouse, and woodcock are shot, the main swarm from the right barrel was only about eighteen inches in diameter, from the left one about fourteen inches, all with Winchester AA skeet loads. This naturally reduced the scope of the middle ground between a clean miss and a bird shot to dollrags, so if this gun were mine it would go off for some aftermarket reaming.

The wood is handsome indeed—dark, straight-grained walnut with some subtle, streaky figure to it, and both forend and butt appear to come from the same blank. The forend is technically a splinter but is fairly thick and as wide as the barrels; it doesn't look bad and feels great. It's held on by a Deeley finger-lever fastener. The stock is very well shaped: It's slender and crisp-edged where it ought to be and shows almost none of the fish-belly profile that can make even the daintiest gun look clunky. My only quarrel with the dull oil finish is that a bit more of it would fill the pores of the wood better. Fit, both wood-to-metal and metal-to-metal, is nearly flawless.

The length of pull, which I assume to be Merkel standard, is $14^1/_2$ inches; for pitch, it measures $14^{11}/_{16}$ inches to the heel and $14^{15}/_{16}$ inches to the toe. The drops are $1^1/_2$ inches at the comb and $2^1/_2$ inches at the heel, and it's cast off about $^1/_4$-inch. Even though the stock is a good $^3/_4$-inch too short for me, it feels surprisingly good.

Actually, the whole guns feels good, and that, too, came as a surprise. With the short barrels and a point of balance only two inches from the breech face (which puts it exactly on the hinge pin), I didn't imagine I'd shoot it very well. Slightly more than half the total weight is in the barrels and forend, but I take such a relatively long hold with my left hand that I expected to find it twitchy as a whip.

And a little twitchy it is, but not nearly as much as I expected, and I only needed about four shots to get used to the dynamics. It's a quick little gun, and like most quick guns it responds better and better the less you try to rush it. At $4^1/_2$ pounds each, the trigger pulls are theoretically heavier than they should be. A heavy trigger in a light gun usually makes a poisonous combination, but the Merkel triggers are so crisp that you don't really notice the weight of the pulls.

Mechanically, the gun never failed to function perfectly. The action joint and fasteners were stiff, which is to be expected from a brand-new gun, but they began to smooth up after about three hundred rounds. The safety—automatic, by

MERKEL 147E □ 119

the way—was also a bit stiff and stayed that way for as long as I had the gun.

A 28-gauge, like a .410, is hard on ejectors. The cartridge cases—very slender in relation to their length—set up a lot of friction in the chambers and often don't want to kick all the way out. The Merkel's ejectors, designed after the Southgate pattern, are strong enough and the chambers are polished well enough that only three or four cases refused to make a complete exit. An impressive performance.

The same three words pretty well sum up my experience with this gun. I ended up liking it more than I thought I would —a lot more, in fact—and that served as a good lesson: Preconceptions may be endemic to human nature, but they're best approached with eyes and mind well open. Otherwise, we're apt to miss out on some truly good things.

CHAPTER EIGHTEEN

PACHMAYR / PERAZZI MX20
SPECIAL EDITION GAME GUN

In 1963, Daniele Perazzi was a little-known gunmaker quietly plying his trade in Brescia, Val Trompia, the centuries-old center of Italian armsmaking. A year later, every competition shooter in the world knew his name.

It happened through an acquaintanceship with Ennio Mattarelli, a splendid shot and gifted designer who wanted a gun for the 1964 Olympics in Tokyo. Mattarelli had a headful of ideas about how an International-style trap gun should be made, and he found in Daniele Perazzi just the man to render them in steel and wood. Mattarelli won the gold medal, the two men subsequently formed a partnership, and by the mid-'60s, Armi Perazzi was turning out some of the finest target and live-pigeon guns in the world.

The majority of Perazzi's early converts were European shooters. That the guns took a bit longer to catch the American fancy had less to do with their intrinsic merit than with the general mindset of American target shooters. As Don Zutz rightly points out in *The Double Shotgun*, the 1960s saw a substantial change in the way American clay shooters approached the games. For several generations, only the most serious-minded of them were willing to spend much money for high-quality guns tailored specifically for targets. Few, in fact, owned target guns at all, and if they did it usually was a Winchester Model 12, a Remington Model 31, or an autoloader. Winchester offered the Model 21 in trap and skeet versions; Browning did the same with its Superposed. A few really serious types shot Krieghoffs at trap and skeet. All of them were by contemporary standards hellishly expensive, and the man who owned one might as well have had "Hotshot Target Shooter" embroidered on the back of his vest.

But the American economy prospered in the 1960s, and more and more casual shooters decided they could compete with the champions if they had guns like those the champions used. Don Zutz puts it well: "People who just a couple of years earlier would have shuddered at the thought of spending $300 on a double, suddenly began spending $3,000." Browning enjoyed the first fruits of the new attitude, as did Winchester's Model 101, but the one that finally blew all the others away was Perazzi.

One of the first things Ennio Mattarelli and Daniele Perazzi did after setting up shop was to start thinking about a trap gun for the 1968 Olympics in Mexico City. They already had the '64 Tokyo gun, which was on the market as the Perazzi Mirage—first-rate barrels, a frame with more steel than a VW engine block, flawless locks and ejectors, and a superb trigger that was part of an ingenious arrangement by which a shooter could drop out the trigger/lockwork assembly and slip in a new one in a matter of seconds.

Thinking of Mexico City's high altitude and relatively thin atmosphere, Mattarelli designed what at the time was an astonishingly tall rib in order to get the shooter's line of sight as far as possible from the shimmer of heat waves coming off the barrels. Its real advantage, as Mattarelli well knew, was that it lowered the barrels in relation to the shooter's shoulder, permitting an extremely high-combed stock that could be mounted low on the shoulder and therefore deliver noticeably softer recoil. The MX-8, as the gun came to be called, kicks just as much as any other in terms of foot-pounds of energy, but since the barrels are in line with the shoulder, the recoil tends to come straight back and doesn't whip the barrels around as much as other over/unders. That means you're less likely to get socked on the cheekbone and also means less muzzle-jump to overcome for the second shot.

There would have been something poetic about it if Ennio

Mattarelli had taken a second gold medal at Mexico City, but he didn't. What he did was show the target-shooting world the gun of the future. Now, some thirty years later, almost everybody who builds serious target guns offers high ribs. Then, only Al Ljutic and Perazzi made them. The gun Mattarelli used in '68 had a screw-in choke in the bottom barrel; these days, there are screw chokes in almost everything that shoots.

Medals notwithstanding, the MX-8 brought Perazzi to the forefront of target shooting worldwide. In 1970, Ithaca Gun Company began marketing the guns in America, and as trap-shooters like Dan Bonillas and Ray Stafford began using them to set new all-time records, demand in the American market bloomed like dandelions.

In the early '70s, Perazzis were available in three models: Competition I, a basic target gun built in both trap and skeet versions; the Mirage, which Ithaca and Perazzi positioned in the world market as a live-pigeon gun; and the MX-8, offered as the ultimate high-tech competition piece. Ennio Mattarelli worked up yet another Olympic gun for the 1976 games in Montreal, this one called the MT-6. It didn't take the gold (Don Haldeman won the trapshooting medal with a Krieghoff), but the MT-6 took Perazzi innovation a step further by having screw-chokes fitted in both barrels. If memory serves, it was the first factory over/under built that way.

The Ithaca-Perazzi relationship lasted until 1978. After that, Winchester marketed the guns for a couple of years, until Perazzi U.S.A. was established at Rome, New York, about 1981. By then, a steadily worsening economy was cutting into the gun market, and the '80s brought some lean and difficult years. Flagging sales prompted Perazzi to bring out the MX-3 as an economy model. A price tag of better than $2,000 made economy a relative term, but the MX-3 gained a respectable popularity, and that's what it was meant to do.

Early in 1988, Perazzi U.S.A moved to Monrovia, California—the same town that's home to Pachmayr Ltd. And therein, as they say, lies a tale.

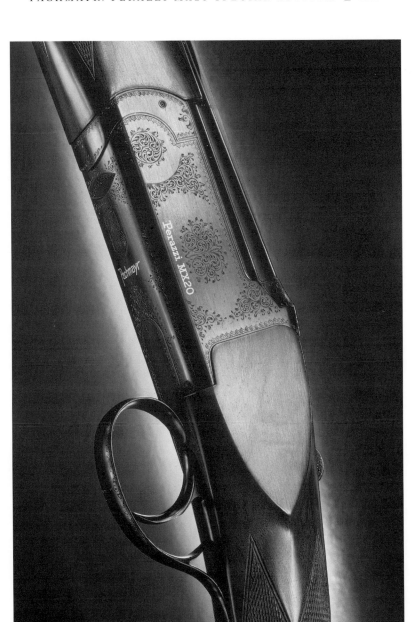

PACHMAYR/PERAZZI MX20
WILLIAM W. HEADRICK

Though Perazzi has always built side-by-side game guns, the majority of its efforts went to the over/under target guns as the cornerstones of the firm's reputation. A lightweight 12-gauge over/under game gun appeared in the early '70s and went out of production after only two years. In the mid-1980s, the MX-3 became available in a 20-gauge version, but it was built on a 12-gauge frame and was of far more interest to skeet shooters than to hunters. The typical 12-bore Perazzi frame creates a much heavier gun than most hunters want to lug through the woods.

Then came the MX20—a 20-bore gun built on a 20-bore frame—and to help bring Perazzi quality into the hunter's world, Pachmayr Ltd. contracted a special series of them set up as game guns. Judging by the one that Rich Giordano, of Pachmayr, sent to me for testing, this is a gun to warm the heart of any bird shooter fond of stack-barrel doubles.

At 7 pounds exactly, it's no willowy switch of a gun—but no 20-gauge that will accept a 3-inch cartridge ought to be. It's extremely comfortable to shoot with $7/8$-ounce loads, which is as heavy a 20-gauge round as I care to fire; if I need more shot than that, I'll fire it in a 16 or a 12.

Perazzis have a certain feel about them, brought about by a thick, stout frame combined with barrels struck fairly thin, so that the weight is concentrated in the center, between the shooter's hands. Consequently, even the biggest Perazzi trap gun is surprisingly nimble. The special edition MX20 has that feel; you can get it moving quickly, without any of the manic whippiness that some 20s have, and you can keep it moving. That, to my mind, is how a game gun ought to feel.

The Pachmayr guns all have $25^{11}/_{16}$-inch barrels with screw chokes that bring them to an even 26 inches. The whole affair would look better to my eyes if the choke tubes fit entirely inside the muzzles, but that's not how Perazzi makes them. The tubes themselves are $1^{13}/_{16}$-inches long overall and are extremely well machined. You can screw them all the way in with your fingers alone and seat them firmly with one twist of the wrench. The ones in the test gun stayed put through all the shooting I did. Each gun comes with five tubes: skeet, improved-cylinder, modified, improved-modified, and full.

Because the barrel walls are thin, the muzzles are slightly expanded to accommodate the tubes, but not enough that you notice it until you peer down the side of the barrels. At the other end, they're fixed to a monobloc breech milled in the typical Perazzi style—square-bottomed with recesses on each side that match up with heavy lugs inside the frame. The side ribs aren't slotted as they are on most target guns these days; barrel heat may dissipate a bit more slowly, but you won't have to go through the tedium of swabbing chaff or rainwater from between the barrels. The flat vent rib is $1/4$-inch wide, matted on top, and fitted with a small metal front bead. Pachmayr will install a center bead at no charge if you want one.

Stocks are European walnut. The forend is trim, finished off with a graceful schnabel, and it fastens to the barrels by a Deeley-type latch.

One of Perazzi's best innovations is the quick-change stocks. The drawbolt is fitted with an Allen-type head, and all you have to do to swap stocks is push the stock-wrench (which comes with the gun) through a small hole in the buttpad, unscrew the bolt, and install a different stock the same way. Trap and pigeon shooters are particularly fond of the system, because it lets them use one gun and still have the advantage of stocks tailored to each different event. It's a handy feature even for someone who has only one stock, because you can easily dismount it to clean or dry the lockwork.

Wood-to-metal fit is very tight and accurate, but as with nearly all Perazzis, it stands out proud all around, as much as $1/16$-inch in places. This is the price you pay for having all stocks fit all guns.

The test gun's wood is quite handsome in both stock and forend, though, as is typical, there's no attempt to match the grain between them. The walnut is dense enough to hold extremely fine checkering, which is well executed but not perfectly so. Instead of a pad or heelplate, the Pachmayr guns are given checkered butts, quite skillfully done.

On the practical side, where it really counts, the stockwork truly shines. The grip, which is something between full- and half-pistol, is comfortably shaped. Length of pull is $14^1/_2$ inches to center, $14^5/_8$ inches to the heel, and 15 inches to the toe—which amounts to a good, standard pitch. With drops of $^{15}/_{16}$ inch at the comb and $2^3/_{16}$ inches at the heel, the stock is rather straight by American standards, but as there's no pitch to the rib, it's deadly on rising targets without requiring too much daylight on crossers.

The game gun doesn't have Perazzi's famous detachable trigger, but it does have a trigger that performs to Perazzi standards. It's selective, which is unusual among Perazzis, and is designed on the inertia-shift principle. The selector works off the safety button. There's a bit of slack in this trigger that you wouldn't find in a Perazzi target gun, but you'll never notice it shooting at game. All told, it performs beautifully, with no hesitation; there's just a clean, crisp release that happens when you want it.

With the selector set to fire the under barrel first, the first sear lets go at $3^1/_4$ pounds' pressure, the second at a shade over 4 pounds. When the selector is set the other way, the upper-barrel sear breaks at the same 4 pounds, the lower at $3^1/_2$. To see if the lighter second sear might be liable to jar-off, I shot a round of skeet doubles in the over-under firing mode; there were no double discharges.

The Pachmayr guns are decorated differently from standard MX20s, treated to some nicely done scroll engraving on the frame, top lever, top tang, safety button, trigger guard, forend iron, and forend latch. *Perazzi MX20* is inlaid in gold on the left side of the frame, *Pachmayr* on the bottom, and S, O, and U on the top tang. The Pachmayr emblem is engraved, unobtrusively, on the bottom of the frame.

The whole package—gun, stock wrench, choke wrench, and five choke tubes—came in a molded-plastic trunk case.

Prices ranged from $3,995 to $4,600 new, depending on the figure in the wood.

I don't know how many guns the special edition comprised, but as I conducted the field-test in the summer of 1988, I seriously doubt there are any left in new condition. Used ones don't show up on the market very often, but the quality is such that tracking one down would be well worth the trouble.

CHAPTER NINETEEN

RIZZINI B. PREMIER SPORTING

First a word about the maker. Rizzini is not exactly the Italian equivalent of Smith or Jones, but there are, let's say, more than a few in the phone book. There are several on the rolls of the Brescian gunmakers' association and several whose marks are registered with the Italian National Proof House— Zoli & Rizzini, Salvino Rizzini, Armi Techniche di Emilio Rizzini, Tecni-Mec di Isidoro Rizzini, Fratelli Rizzini, and Battista Rizzini.

Of those currently active in the gun trade, Fratelli Rizzini (Rizzini Brothers, in English) is a small shop in Gardone where Amelio and Guido Rizzini and their sons turn out about two dozen side-by-side guns per year, each one handmade to the highest standards of the craft. Tecni-Mec di Isidoro Rizzini is a medium-scale factory in Marcheno that builds machine-made sporting and target guns. Battista Rizzini, or Rizzini B. as it's commonly known, is a high-volume factory, also in Marcheno, that makes everything from guns to auto parts and from textile machinery to small electrical appliances.

This piece is about a gun by Rizzini B., and I have to confess I wasn't overcome with enthusiasm when William Larkin Moore, an American importer, called to say he was sending a "Rizzini." I knew it wouldn't be one of Fratelli Rizzini's magnificent pieces and figured it would be some middling-quality gun bearing the Rizzini name, such as those I've run across occasionally over the past ten years or so.

I figured wrong. The price of the Rizzini B. Premier Sporting is middling; the quality isn't.

According to the latest catalog, the Rizzini B. line includes

three models of over/under guns, all meant for target shooting
and all boxlocks (one, the S2000 Trap, has decorative sideplates). The Premier comes in three forms—Sporting, Skeet,
and Trap—each available in 12- and 20-gauge.

The test gun, a 20-bore Sporting, is highly appealing to look
at. It's sculpted in the mold of Perazzi and Marocchi, which to
my eyes are a couple of the handsomest boxlock over/unders
ever built. Scaled to proper 20-gauge proportions, the frame is
small but substantial and gracefully milled. It's also well polished and deeply blued, with the maker's name in gold on one
side, *Marcheno* on the other, and *Premier Sporting* on the bottom, all done in small, unobtrusive lettering. The whole effect
is every bit as handsome as good color case-hardening and, to
me, far more so than metal that's polished bright.

The barrels are 75 centimeters long, which translates to

RIZZINI B. PREMIER SPORTING GUN
MICHAEL McINTOSH

$29^5/8$ inches. The catalog shows 71 centimeters (28 inches) as optional. They're assembled on a monobloc breech, chambered at 70 millimeters ($2^3/4$ inches) and fitted with ventilated side ribs and a low, ventilated top rib 10 millimeters wide. The tubes are smoothly struck but not highly polished.

My gauge says the bores are slightly oversized. The nominal 20-gauge standard is .615-inch; these measure .624-inch in the bottom and .625-inch on top. Wall thickness varies somewhat around the circumference, but there are no thin spots.

The Premier Sporting comes with five flush-fit choke tubes, which the bore gauge shows are constricted .000-, .011-, .019-, .027-, and .037-inch—in other words, cylinder, improved-cylinder, modified, improved-modified, and full. The threads are fairly wide and should help keep the tubes from getting sticky. The tubes are easy to put in and take out, and they stay put.

My only beef with the barrels is with the front bead. Actually, it's not a bead at all but rather a squared-off $^{11}/16$-inch bar of fluorescent red plastic, something on the order of the old Ithaca Ray-Bar sight. It looked like hell on the Ithacas and is no better on the Rizzini. If this were my gun, that sucker would be history in nothing flat. Sounds picky, I know, and I suppose it is, but this is otherwise such an elegant-looking gun that putting red plastic on it is like hanging fuzzy dice in a Porsche. Besides, a shotgun bead is only a reference to be picked up by the shooter's peripheral vision, not some neon abortion that calls attention to itself. Get distracted looking at anything but the target and you might as well save the shell because you're about to miss behind.

The wood is lovely: Honey-brown European walnut figured with dark streaks, nicely oil-finished. The forend is beautiful— fairly long, slim, comfortably rounded and made with a finger-groove at the top. The stock is what has come to be the standard among Italian target guns, which is to say it has a big full-pistol grip with palm-swell and altogether enough wood to stock two .410s, a .22 rifle, and a dozen Colt Dragoons. It's quick-detachable via a hole in the buttpad, a system developed years ago by Perazzi and since adopted by a number of Italian makers.

The stock is too big and thick to have any particular aesthetic grace, but as is usually the case with guns of this sort, it feels terrific. The standard dimensions are good—14⅝-inch pull, drops of 1⅛ inches at comb and 1⅞ inches at heel, and about ¼-inch cast-off. There are some advantages to having such a big stock on a target gun, but the Premier Sporting would also make a dandy game gun, especially with the stock slimmed down and reshaped with a Prince of Wales grip. Lord knows there's plenty of wood to work with, for that or just to have the dimensions custom-tailored.

You can also order extra stocks in whatever configuration you want, including field style, for about $250 apiece. Thanks to highly accurate milling and the quick-detach design, they don't need to be hand-fitted.

At 7 pounds, 3 ounces, the Premier Sporting is not exactly a featherweight, but then a target gun shouldn't be, and the dynamics are such that it feels lighter than it really is. Combining the long barrels and a balance point set just forward of the hinge, it's a wonderfully smooth-swinging piece. I find that it points every bit as precisely as it should for clays, and I love it as a skeet gun.

The mechanics are pretty much current Italian standard as well—trunnion hinge and wide underbolt fastener. The mainsprings are coil-type, and the sears engage at the tops of the tumblers. The ejectors are a variation on the Gamba design, with sears and springs fitted to the monobloc rather than to the forend iron. They're well-timed and strong enough to pitch a pair of empty hulls about ten feet.

The Premier Sporting's trigger is selective (the selector's part of the safety thumbpiece) and shifts on recoil. It also is an absolute jewel. There's not a smidgen of creep, drag, or hesitation. In either firing sequence—under-over or over-under—the first sear breaks at exactly 3 pounds and the second at a half-pound more. It is one of the best triggers I've tested in quite some time.

The gun alone would be a bargain at its $2,495 retail price, but the Premier Sporting comes in a molded, hard-plastic case with a full set of choke tubes, a choke wrench, a stock wrench, and even a spray-can of gun oil.

Finding the unexpected gems is one of the pleasanter aspects of reviewing guns. It's admittedly not an unpleasant occupation in the first place, but some guns turn my crank with more torque than others. This is one such. In fact, by the time I'd finished testing it I was already rummaging through my small battery of personal guns, trying to decide if there were any I'd be willing to sell or swap as a means of adding a Rizzini Premier Sporting to the bunch.

CHAPTER TWENTY

RUGER RED LABEL

So much exquisite artistry has accrued to the gun that it's tempting to overlook the commercial nature of gunmaking. A fine gun may be a work of art, but it isn't built solely for art's sake. It's built to sell—and to sell, moreover, at a profit sufficient to support both the gunmaker and the continued existence of his trade.

Since the beginning, gunmakers everywhere have sought to apply technology to their trade, to convert wherever possible laborious and expensive handwork to efficient, economical machining. The exact proportion of machining to handwork has always depended upon the level of quality in fit and finish that the maker set out to achieve, but virtually every modern gun since the days of Joe Manton has been, to some extent, machine-made.

In terms of value—what a buyer gets for the money he spends—a well-built machine-made firearm has no peer, and nowhere has machine technology been more successfully applied to gunmaking than in the United States. All of our greatest makers have been disciples of machine manufacture—Colt, Winchester, Remington, Parker, Lefever, Fox, Smith, Browning, all of them. Nowhere have value and quality reached a better balance.

Sadly, the American trade isn't what it used to be. Global and domestic economics have seen to that. The great tradition of American gunmaking—the ability to offer a remarkably high-quality product at a price that makes every penny count—is wearing thin. But for Bill Ruger, it would be thinner still.

In common with the great American gunmakers of the past, Bill Ruger has a particular gift. Like Samuel Colt, Dan Lefever, and Ansley Fox, he combines a brilliant grasp of mechanics with a fine artistic eye. Like Charles Parker and William Baker and others, he has a keen sense of manufacturing technique. Had he been born fifty years earlier, we would think of him now as we think of the others—with admiration and with some regret that he's no longer around to build guns the way they used to be built.

The admiration is well deserved and the regret unnecessary. More than any other contemporary gunmaker, Bill Ruger has helped keep the old tradition alive. He's been at it nearly fifty years and is at it still.

His various autoloading pistols and carbines and double-action revolvers offer unquestionable value, but the most important guns, the cornerstones of Ruger's success, are those that demonstrate his uncanny ability to adapt great designs of the past to manufacturing techniques of the future: the single-action revolvers derived from the old Colts and Remingtons; the elegant single-shot rifle adapted from the Scottish Farquharson action; the classic, Mauser-inspired bolt-action rifle; and the shotgun that has for some time now been the only production over/under built in America.

Ruger introduced the Red Label over/under in 1977 as a 20-gauge skeet and game gun. It was typical of Bill Ruger's best guns—plainly finished but intrinsically handsome in its clean, graceful lines; thoughtful and simple mechanically; extremely well built; and at a retail price of $480, an exceptional value.

Bill Ruger's great contribution to manufacturing technique is his pioneering use of investment casting. Instead of milling frames and receivers from bars and blocks of steel, Ruger early on adapted to gun manufacture much the same technique that artists use to cast bronze sculpture. It amounts essentially to casting molten metal into a nearly final shape as the initial manufacturing step. Since the molds can accurately accommodate highly complex shapes that require only mini-

mal machine work, investment casting is tremendously efficient, economical both of time and material. Moreover, as the
molten steel is injected into the molds under pressure, the re-
sulting parts are of extremely high quality, uniformly dense,
and free of internal flaws. It's a brilliantly innovative way to
make gun parts, and a generation of Ruger guns is ample evidence that it works.

Enough time and clear thinking went into the original design that the Red Label has remained essentially unchanged.
The first guns were made only with 26-inch barrels; 28-inch
tubes were introduced in 1978. A 12-gauge version appeared in
1982. At first, the 12-bores were built, like the 20s, with blued
frames; about 1985, Ruger began making them with stainless-
steel frames and forend irons. Blued frames were revived as
options in the early 1990s, and a scaled-down, 28-bore version
was added in 1995.

Such variations aside, all Ruger Red Label guns are mechanically the same: Anson & Deeley–type lockwork driven by
stout coil springs, rebounding tumblers and firing pins, and a
fastening bolt that engages two lugs on the face of the lower
barrel. A lug on the bottom of the lower barrel extends through
the frame to form a third fastener.

Thanks to the rebounding locks, cocking force is not applied until the action is partway open, which makes the Red
Label an easy-opening gun. Better yet, it's an extremely safe
one. The tumblers cannot reach the firing pins unless the lock-
ing bolt is fully forward, and even then they're held fast by
Ruger's unique hammer interrupter. This device, which operates on the same principle as the intercepting sear developed
in England about a hundred years ago, locks both the tumblers
and the trigger. The only way to fire a Ruger is to close the action, click the safety off, and pull the trigger. The locks won't
work any other way.

The barrels are fitted to a monobloc breech, and the whole
assembly pivots on trunnions integral with the frame. With no
barrel lump for either the hinge or the fastener, the Red Label

is about as trim of profile as an over/under can be; the 12-gauge frame measures only about $2^3/8$ inches to the top of the standing breech, the 20 naturally is smaller, and the new 28-bore even smaller yet.

The Ruger single trigger is designed to shift mechanically from one sear to the other, so you're not left at the mercy of a dud cartridge or an empty chamber. An inertia block prevents doubling. The barrel selector works off the safety thumb-piece, which pivots from side to side to set the firing order and slides forward to disengage. It's in some ways a more reliable system than the old Browning H-pattern selector because it rides in only a single slot in the top tang and therefore can't hang up in the middle. But, having the button cocked to one side or the other takes some getting used to.

The ejectors and springs are fitted to the monobloc and the ejector sears fastened to the forend iron. As in Marocchi, Rott-weil, and some other guns, the system is cocked by studs on the ejector stems that engage slots inside the frame; it's good, simple, and reliable.

I've shot both game and targets with various 20-gauges over the years, but the test gun for this project was my first experience with a 12—a stainless-steel-frame gun with 28-inch barrels and screw chokes. After several hundred skeet and sporting clays targets, a few dozen more shots at the patterning plate, and a careful look at the thing from end to end, I can only marvel at what Bill Ruger has wrought.

Every time I pick up a Ruger of any sort, I'm struck by the obvious quality of it—not necessarily of the finish, although the finish doesn't really leave much to quarrel with, but more by the precision with which the various parts are shaped and with which they all fit together; by the quality of the wood (better-than-average American walnut has always been a Ruger signature of sorts) and the skillful way it's shaped; simply by the lean, graceful lines. I've seen some lovely custom-engraved specimens, but decoration doesn't add as much to a Ruger as it does to some other guns. Even starkly plain, they're handsome enough. And I'm always struck by the fact that this excellent quality is available at prices unmatched by virtually any other gunmaker in the world.

The test gun certainly struck me this way, which requires a certain perspective in outlining the bones I have to pick with it. It's easy to criticize a Ruger as if it were a gun that cost twice as much—because it's easily as much gun as you could expect for twice the money.

On the happy side, the gun works perfectly. It's never misfired, balked, hung up, or faltered. It fires when I pull the trigger and delivers a charge of shot right where I look. The stock is a tad short but it fits me well enough, and all the parts fit one another with scarcely a gap. Metal-to-metal fit is excellent, wood-to-metal fit almost as good. Where it counts, in stock heading especially, wood and steel come together quite well indeed. The finish of both wood and metal is good, although the checkering is coarse and not particularly well done.

It works equally well at the business end. Both barrels shoot to the same point of hold, and the choke tubes essentially deliver the pattern percentages they're supposed to, although all of them tend to be on the tight side. The tubes are flush-fitting and therefore do not mar the gun's appearance.

The ejectors kick out the empties neatly, both at the same time, the action opens readily, and it's easy to reload—more than I can say for some guns that cost many times as much.

Even though I have some axes to grind, none is serious enough to keep me from buying a Red Label. The test gun is ungodly heavy, $8^{1}/_{2}$ pounds. Four pounds of that is in the barrels, which are plenty stout enough for steel shot (and factory-approved for steel), but the weight of them, combined with a large stainless-steel forend iron, makes the gun decidedly nose-heavy. The point of balance is about 6 inches ahead of the trigger.

The overall weight and balance disqualify the 12-gauge Red Label as an upland gun, in my view. It's just too heavy to carry around all day and too slow getting into action to be a really good quail, grouse, or woodcock gun. As a waterfowler, on the other hand, it should be a dandy.

I'm not wholly enthusiastic about the trigger, either. Mechanically, it works fine, shifts as it should, has never doubled, and has only a fraction of slack in it. But it's a heavy beast to pull. No matter how the selector is set, the first sear lets go at better than $4^{1}/_{2}$ pounds, which isn't bad considering the weight of the gun. But the second goes clear off my scale: way over 5 pounds. The actual let-off is crisp enough, but takes more muscle than it should to get there.

But would I refuse to buy a Ruger on these grounds? Not at all. If I wanted it as an upland gun, I'd buy a 20 or 28; they handle beautifully. For a fowler, I'd be happy with the smooth swing and recoil-damping weight of the 12.

I would not, however, be content to live with the trigger-pull. Even though Ruger is adamant about not authorizing any alterations to its guns (understandably, considering the absurd judgments in product-liability suits), any Red Label of mine would immediately go off to a first-class gunsmith to have the sears adjusted.

In a more expensive gun, I would expect the maker to provide a better-tuned trigger, but I could spend some after-market money on a new Ruger with no qualms at all. With a Ruger, you're money ahead from the beginning.

At one time, you could say as much for a lot of American guns, but those days are all but gone. Our great tradition of excellence in factory-built, machine-made shotguns is fading, and it probably won't come around again. So it's well that we have Bill Ruger, because he takes us back to where we started.

CHAPTER TWENTY-ONE

RUGER SPORTING CLAYS

The Ruger over/under occupies a warm spot in a lot of gunners' hearts. And it's an affection easy to understand, both in terms of the gun itself and in terms of what it represents in American armsmaking. You'll find a discussion of Bill Ruger's place in the history of our gun trade in the preceding chapter, so I won't rehash it here, except to point out that the Red Label came along at a time when the rest of the industry was throwing up its hands in despair of ever again being able to produce a high-quality double gun in the United States.

When the Red Label appeared in 1977, it was one of only two over/unders still built in this country, and when Remington took its excellent but ultimately ill-fated Model 3200 out of production in 1984, Ruger had the stage all to itself. At an initial price of $480—more than a third less than the least-expensive Model 3200 of the time—the Red Label represented an exceptional value. It still does, although like everything else, it costs more than it did twenty years ago.

Manufacturing technology, which includes the use of investment castings, has allowed Ruger to keep production costs comparatively low and quality high, but that's only half the story. The other—and in some ways more important—half is that the Red Label is a brilliant piece of engineering. The lockwork is simple yet sophisticated, highly efficient, and fitted with an interrupter-type secondary safety system that truly works. The action pivots on trunnions, so the frame is shallow. The ejectors are simple and reliable, as is the trigger.

Not even the pickiest critic could level a serious indictment against the Red Label on grounds of durability and strength. As witness to their ruggedness, you don't have to look far to find any number of Rugers that have digested shells by the boxcar-load and are still at it. As for strength, California gunsmith Butch Searcy has converted quite a few 20-gauge Rugers to rifles as large as .375 H&H, without having to make any substantial change in the action or fastening system. A shotgun able to accommodate that would seem to me strong enough.

Theoretically, a gun of good design built from quality materials should be adaptable to any purpose, but how well it truly serves depends upon what the maker does by way of adaptation. Virtually every outfit in the world that makes over/unders these days offers at least one model tailored to sporting clays. But how much actual tailoring they do varies greatly. Some seem to do no more than stick a certain model name on an otherwise standard gun and let it go at that. Others go whole-hog with special ribs and screw chokes,

RUGER SPORTING CLAYS
MICHAEL McINTOSH

adjustable triggers and stocks, you name it. Even in the middle ground, which most makers choose to occupy, you'll find differing approaches.

The reason is that no one format is necessarily "best" for sporting clays—which is what lends the greatest interest to both the game and the guns. Sporting targets offer vast variety, and that means the guns should be as well suited for a close overhead incomer as for a crossing target at thirty yards. This kind of adaptability has little to do with chokes (though you'll have a hard time convincing the average shooter of that), even less to do with ribs, and much to do with smooth, lively dynamics and a good fit. It also helps if the maker takes some pains to achieve good patterning performance, since even the largest sporting targets aren't very big, and the smallest are scarcely larger than golf balls.

In short, it seems to me that some of the characteristics becoming more or less standard among clays guns are of little practical value, while others are important indeed. And for a gun of its price range, the Red Label Sporting strikes me as being set up in an eminently sensible way.

I mention price because it's an important point. You can drop a serious bundle of cash on a clays gun that has all the bells and whistles, or considerably less on one that has only a few, such as the Ruger. The trick is to find a gun that offers the economy of the *right* features, and the Red Label's relatively few adaptations are exactly that—refinements that have more to do with practical performance than with cosmetics or features only marginally useful. Therein lies its value.

In most respects, the Sporting version is identical to every other Red Label—the same handsomely shaped stainless-steel frame, the same lockwork and fastening system and trigger and ejectors and stock dimensions, with the length of pull at $14^{1}/_{8}$ inches and bend of $1^{1}/_{2}$ inches at comb and $2^{1}/_{2}$ inches at heel. All typical Ruger fare.

The refinements are in the barrels and balance, and in these the Red Label Sporting shines. Like many another clays gun, it has 30-inch barrels, but unlike any other in its price range—unlike most, in fact, of several price notches higher— the barrels are overbored and treated to some other attention that pays a genuine return in performance.

Although it's about as old as gunmaking itself, the practice of overboring barrels has been discarded and rediscovered many times, at least three times in this century alone. It's well in vogue at the moment, but unlike some other cyclical trends in gunning, overboring truly does make a difference. No one fully understands the phenomenon, but enlarging a bore by a few thousandths typically improves the distribution of pellets within the bore's patterns. Combined with a carefully regulated choke, overboring also can produce unusually tight, dense patterns, but evenness is the most important aspect, especially in a target gun. A barrel that prints patterns with no target-sized gaps will break more clays, on the whole, than one that doesn't.

According to factory literature, Ruger bores its clays-gun barrels at .741- to .745-inch, which is considerably larger than the nominal 12-gauge standard of .729-inch. My bore gauge shows actual dimensions of .747-inch in the test gun's under barrel and .744-inch in the top—which helps explain why it shoots the way it does. With No. $7^1/2$ shot in both $1^1/8$-ounce factory cartridges and my 1-ounce handloads, these barrels pattern beautifully at every distance from 20 yards to 40. I really don't see much room for improvement.

Ruger also claims to bore the clays guns with "long" forcing cones, which, like overboring, can help reduce kick and improve patterns. At about half an inch, the test gun's cones are longer than some, shorter than others. As standard practice, Ruger bores all Red Labels with 3-inch chambers, and these can create an effect similar to long forcing cones when you fire $2^3/4$-inch cartridges. In any event, the test gun is as comfortable to shoot as it is efficient.

Sheer mass has a recoil-damping effect as well, and at $8^1/4$ pounds this is no lightweight. All 12-gauge Rugers are hefty—

too much so to qualify as ideal upland guns in my opinion— and they're not very well balanced. The Sporting gun wouldn't make much of an upland piece, either, but it's not meant to be. It certainly is not too heavy for a target gun, though, and the balance is exceptional.

The test gun's barrels alone weigh $3^3/4$ pounds, $4^1/2$ pounds with forend attached, which puts the balance point right at the forend iron. For one who likes to shoot with his leading hand well extended, as I do, this divides the overall weight nicely between the hands and creates a much more dynamic feel than you might imagine in a gun this heavy. It's lively without feeling whippy, and smooth without seeming ponderous.

As you might expect, the Sporting comes with screw-in chokes. At $2^7/16$ inches, they're longer than standard Ruger tubes and therefore cannot be used in other Red Label 12-bores. The Sporting tubes are stainless steel, are easy to screw in and out, stay put without overtightening, and in general deliver the pattern percentages they're supposed to. Two skeet tubes, one improved-cylinder and a modified, come with each gun; full and extra-full tubes are available at additional cost.

Unlike other Red Labels, the Sporting gun does not have side ribs, which makes it a bit easier for the barrels to shed heat. Nor does it have the wide rib that has become *de rigueur* for a lot of clays guns. Instead, Ruger opts for a nicely matted, floating, parallel rib $5/16$-inch wide. Twelve-millimeter ribs are fashionable, but I'm not convinced they offer any real advantage. They do no harm, of course, except to increase the price, and in that regard, I think Ruger is wise to forego the expense.

The barrels are not factory ported, either, which may or may not suit your fancy. There's no question that porting does help tame muzzle-jump, and a lot of clay shooters insist on it. I find the Red Label behaves perfectly well as it is. My shooting partners also appreciate not having muzzle-blast and powder flakes blowing back at them, which is porting's chief lapse in social grace.

My only quarrel with this gun is the same beef I have with

every Red Label—the trigger has too much slack and the pulls are too hard. A light, crisp trigger is especially important for a target gun, and I wish Ruger would make more effort to get it that way at the factory. It requires expert hand work, but a properly tuned trigger would be well worth a few dollars added to the price.

Because the fact is, at less than $1,400 retail, it's a remarkably inexpensive gun to begin with, especially considering what you get for your money. If you're a serious competitive shooter, you'll probably opt for something more highly refined and spend big bucks to get it. But for those who shoot clays just for fun and want a good gun at a minimal price, the Red Label Sporting is just the ticket.

J & L RUTTEN

I don't suppose it would come as any surprise if I said it's a pleasure to test and review top-quality, meticulously built guns that carry five-digit price tags. What's not to like, right?

There's also a genuine pleasure in finding a good meat-and-potatoes gun that's well-made, reliable, not bad to look at, and available for relatively little money. One that you can feel confident will serve you well if you go hunting or target shooting when the weather's a bit dicey, when the going is likely to be rough, or when you head for some far-flung foreign country. Or one that represents a good first gun for a young person or for a recent convert to this lovely sport of ours. The Lanber over/under is one of those, and so is the J & L Rutten over/under.

It is the product of two Belgian gentlemen, brothers named Rutten, which they pronounce "Roo-ten." They work in Herstal, which along with nearby Liège forms the ancient center of gunmaking for a trade that once supplied much of the world, civilized and otherwise, with firearms ranging in quality from gaspipe-grade to best. It's probably best known to American shooters as the trade that built many of John Browning's most famous guns, including the Auto-5 and the Superposed. As gunmakers, the Ruttens are, let's say, not without pedigree.

As I write this, in December '95, the guns are available in two models and one gauge, 12. Both are boxlocks, though the Model 285, the one I have, is fitted with decorative sideplates that give it a handsome look. I haven't seen the less expensive Model 100, but I assume the two are mechanically identical. The importer tells me that smallbores are in the works.

The test gun has 28-inch barrels, bored, as Continental guns tend to be, a wee bit on the tight side—.727-inch in the under barrel and .728-inch on top. The bores are uniform down to a half-thou. I don't know exactly how thick the walls are because, like a lot of guns with screw-in chokes, the barrels won't slide over the indexing stud of my gauge. But they are not the ultra-thick, overbuilt tubes you find on some current machine-made pieces. They're thick enough to be perfectly safe (after all, they passed Belgian proof, which imposes some of the most rigorous standards anywhere) and yet thin enough to feel like a set of gunbarrels rather than a length of railroad iron. They're built on the monobloc principle and fitted with a flat, 7-millimeter vent rib and solid side ribs. Chambers are 70 millimeters. Exterior surfaces are extremely well struck, polished, and deeply blacked.

Each gun comes with a set of five choke tubes, nominally ranging from cylinder to full. Dimensionally, they go from a couple of thousandths constriction to very tight, and that's pretty much what showed up on my patterning plate. I shot a bit of everything—from my light handloads to Estate pigeon loads—and the gun distributed all the swarms about equally well.

The whole gun weighs 7 pounds, 10 ounces, with just enough weight in the barrels to put the balance point slightly forward of the hinge. Which means it's heavy enough to be enjoyable through a couple of hundred targets in an afternoon, light enough to carry comfortably around the field for a few hours, and balanced to promote a very smooth, dynamic swing.

The action pivots on a trunnion-type hinge and is fastened by a Greener cross-bolt. The hinge promotes a relatively shallow frame, but the fastener offsets this, so it's about the same size as a 12-bore Superposed—not the sleekest over/under around, but not the clunkiest, either.

The locks and ejectors are driven by coil springs, which I like. There's certainly nothing wrong with a well-made and properly tempered V-spring; the ones in my John Wilkes have been performing perfectly since 1916, and last winter I shot pheasants with a Purdey hammer gun powered by springs made in 1879. But coil springs have one advantage in that they usually keep on working even when they're broken.

The Rutten ejectors are entirely self-contained in the monobloc, like those you'll find on several of the best Italian guns these days. But they're also under spring tension even when fully extended, and that's a mixed blessing. Spring assistance for simple extraction means you shouldn't have any stuck shells and also helps pop the action open, but compressing springs every time you close the gun, fired or not, puts a strain on the hinge that other systems don't. I haven't used the Rutten long enough, and won't be able to, to learn whether the ejectors will make the joint sloppy before its time, but that'll be one sign of how well the bearing surfaces are hardened.

Triggerwise, this is a field gun, or one for informal target shooting. By that I mean the pulls are slightly creepy, somewhat rough, and heavier than the 5-pound maximum my scale can measure. But not much heavier, I suspect. I'd raise hell about them if this were marketed as a highly refined target gun, but it's fine for game shooting and targets for fun.

The single trigger is built on the inertia-block principle and is selective. The selector is a little button fitted to the safety thumb piece, the same way Beretta does it. It's also designed in the Browning image, firing the bottom barrel first when the selector is set to the right, which I think is the wrong side for a right-handed shooter. But although I can make it switch barrels as I push the safety off, I can't make it hang up in the middle and not fire at all—a mark definitely in the Rutten's favor, so far as I'm concerned.

The wood is exceptional for a gun of this price, very handsomely figured European walnut, and the stock and forend either came from the same blank or from two so nearly alike that it doesn't matter. It's nicely but not perfectly shaped, and satin-finished with what looks like a urethane compound.

The checkering could be better, especially on the pistol grip. The recoil pad is fairly thin ($^3/_4$-inch), not very attractive, and not very well fitted, but it's soft enough to effectively help dampen kick.

The standard dimensions are excellent—length of pull 14$^7/_8$ inches, bends of 1$^1/_2$ and 2$^1/_8$ inches at comb and heel, respectively, and about $^1/_4$-inch cast off. This stock should be a good fit for just about any shooter of average build.

The medium-scroll decoration is minimal and uniformly crisp. Some of it appears to be rolled-in, and some appears hand-cut, possibly with a pneumatic or electric graving tool.

Wood-to-metal fit deserves high marks, while the metal-to-metal fit shows some gaps around the sideplates, trigger plate, and screw heads.

Overall, the Model 285 Rutten strikes me as a good value for its $1,495 price tag. In fact, it's a slam-dunk for anyone who wants a versatile, reliable over/under that doesn't have to be coddled or fretted over. I'd want to shoot it more than I have before I drew a final conclusion, but I have a notion this would be an excellent travel gun. It has all the right virtues to be the sort of meat-and-potatoes piece I described at the start, with enough additional charms to place it several cuts above the merely functional.

It is not, shall we say, a gourmet meal of chateaubriand, but it's a dandy filet at a T-bone price.

CHAPTER TWENTY-THREE

IGNACIO UGARTECHEA

Whether it's a matter of arithmetic or geometry I can't decide, but more diverse interests accrued to this story than usually apply to a gun review. For one thing, it showed that a fine old gunmaker managed to dodge a potentially lethal bullet, and for another it proved Shakespeare's adage that the uses of adversity can be sweet. It also was the only time I had the chance to test a pair of guns for my *Shooting Sportsman* column, and thus explore the historical and technical implications of twins.

So, all things considered, I guess the final tally proved to be more geometric because, like a good gun itself, it amounted to more than just the sum of its parts.

The maker in question is Ignacio Ugartechea, founded in Eibar in 1922, making it the second-oldest surviving company (after Aguirre y Aranzabal) in the Spanish trade. Terry Wieland's excellent book, *Spanish Best*, contains a good outline of the company's history. For a while in the early 1990s, however, the key question was whether that history had come to an end.

Although he set out to build only high-quality guns and Express rifles, the founding Ugartechea soon recognized the potential of mass production, and by the 1960s the company was one of the largest makers in Spain, annually turning out as many as nine thousand side-by-sides and over/unders in a wide range of quality. The second Ignacio, son and successor to the founder, trimmed things back a bit by dropping the over/unders and the real cheapies, but in the late 1980s annual production still amounted to about six thousand pieces.

Most of the Ugartechea shotguns that showed up in this

country at that time were boxlocks sold under the Parker-Hale marque and, in smaller numbers, as Bill Hanus Birdguns. They were inexpensive but remarkably well made, and seemed to me a tremendous value.

Then some labor dispute brought it all to a halt in 1994. Production ceased, the factory closed down, and for a while it seemed a foregone conclusion that Ignacio Ugartechea, S.A., had bitten the dust—one more casualty in a gun trade that's been shrinking steadily for more than twenty years.

But like AyA in the aftermath of the Diarm debacle, the owners of Ugartechea chose to drop the mass-production side and reorganize as a small operation specializing in high-quality guns made to order. Both the tradition and the expertise were already in place. Fine custom-built guns had always accounted for a portion of Ugartechea's output—never more than about three hundred per year, according to Wieland, but still substantial by anyone's standards. The quality was there, too. One of my friends had a pair of 1960s-vintage Ugartechea sidelocks that he often used for dove shooting in South America. They were beautifully built and took the pounding of high-volume shooting without even a whimper.

Ugartechea's resurrection came as good news, but it raised other questions: Could the company take enough orders to make it work, and would the proper level of quality continue to come through? It's still too soon to answer the first one, but if the brand-new pair I tested in mid-1995 are any indication, there's no call to worry about the second.

The notion of using more than one gun at a time originated in England and Europe, and it dates to flintlock days, when sporting gentlemen realized they could do a lot more shooting if they had a second gun and a ghillie to do the loading. The two guns were often similar but not even necessarily by the same maker, and except in rare instances they certainly were not identical.

The idea of two or more identical guns came on during the late Victorian Era, in the heyday of Albert Edward, Prince of

Wales, when game shooting was a British social institution. With virtually the entire upper classes of society out every weekend of the season blazing away at driven pheasants, additional firepower held obvious attractions. What few three- and four-barreled guns the British trade produced were built during this period. The most sensible course, however, wasn't adding extra barrels but rather extra guns—especially as cost was scarcely a consideration. English makers charged relatively low prices for their wares to begin with, and the customers were anything but short on money.

So by the turn of the century any gentleman who was anyone owned at least one pair of fine game guns and retained a loader among his staff of servants. A few went a step further, using sets of three guns. With his three hammer Purdeys and two loaders, Lord Ripon, universally acknowledged as the finest game shot in England, could have six pheasants dead in the air at once—and on one occasion at Sandringham, he killed twenty-eight birds in sixty seconds.

Though the truly golden age of English gunning is long past, multiple guns are as useful as ever. In fact, more high-volume shooting is available now, and in more places, than ever before. Doves and ducks in Central and South America, a multitude of species in Africa, driven pheasants in England and Europe, partridge in Spain, grouse in Scotland—these are all venues for which a pair or set of guns would be entirely appropriate.

And before I get to the pair of Ugartecheas, allow me a digression on terminology. As George Bernard Shaw remarked, the Americans and the British are two peoples separated by a common language, and it's nowhere more apparent than in gun words. To the English, a *pair* is what we often call a *matched pair*—two identical guns built at the same time, with consecutive serial numbers. In England, *matched pair* denotes two identical guns built at different times; in other words, you own one gun to begin with and have another made to match. We call this a *composed* or *composite pair*. Three or more identical guns are called a set—although the English occasionally describe a set of three as a *garniture* or *leash*. For the purposes of this piece, let's just use *pair* to mean identical guns built at the same time.

Which is exactly how the Ugartecheas were made, and it provided an unusual opportunity to see just what sort of work the maker is capable of. Pairs of guns (and sets, too, of course) are built simultaneously, not one after another. Moreover, the work is done step by step. The barrelmaker starts with four tubes and, switching from one to the other at each step, makes two sets at the same time. The actioner, ejector man, stockmaker, finisher, and all the rest do the same. The stocker, for instance, heads up one blank, then the other; fits one trigger plate, then the other; inlets one set of locks, then the other; and so on.

It's demanding, painstaking work because pairs should be

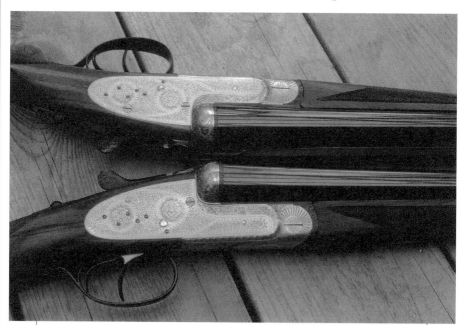

IGNACIO UGARTECHEA MODEL 119
MICHAEL McINTOSH

more than merely lookalikes; they should be identical in every detail of dimension, weight, balance, trigger pull, you name it. The chokes might be different, if the customer wants them to be. So can the decoration—and in fact often is, especially when it involves game scenes. But if the engraving is all scroll and flowers or simply scroll, that too should be a perfect match.

Not surprisingly, matching wood is a perennial bugaboo. The stocker makes the stocks, but nature makes the wood, and I doubt that two perfectly matched blanks ever existed. Some are awfully close, though, and they are exquisitely rare and expensive. In general, matching blanks are priced according to the rule of two-for-three—which means you pay as much for two matched blanks as you would for three of the same quality that don't match.

The same premium typically applies to the price of the guns themselves: A pair will cost 10 to 15 percent more than you'd pay for two non-identical guns. The English trade calls this "pairing money," and it's appropriate because making two guns exactly alike is considerably more difficult than simply building two guns. As one English maker told me, "If you make a mistake on one, you have to make the same mistake on the other." The craftsmen themselves sometimes call it "PITA money," which stands for "Pain in the Arse."

The guns I tested were what Ugartechea calls Model 119— round-body sidelock ejectors. Because they were made to order for someone, the gross specs are largely irrelevant, but for the record they are 12-bore guns with 77-centimeter (27⅞-inch) chopper-lump barrels and matte-filed Churchill ribs, straight-hand stocks, splinter forends, and double triggers.

What's more important in this case is how well they're made and how well they're matched. To my thinking, they earn an A- and an A, which is to say the workmanship is extremely good but not perfect, while the matching could hardly be better. Considering that they cost less than $10,000, including a 12-percent pairing fee, that's pretty impressive. If you're spending $80,000 to $100,000 for a new pair of London or Italian bests, you're entitled to pick all the nits you want, but at this price the maker deserves a bit of slack.

Not that much is needed. The metalwork is mostly excellent, disappointing only in that both sets of barrels show more faint ripples than they should, and wall thickness consequently varies a bit more than it should. This is acceptable, certainly, but the barrels would have benefited from some additional striking.

Inside, though, the tubes are almost perfect. The left bore of the No. 1 gun shows a variation of .001-inch between the two points where you typically measure them. The other three bores are exactly the same everywhere. The screws that hold the locks in place have some gape around the heads. There are no cocking indicators on the tumbler axles, which I consider an omission rather than a flaw. Otherwise, metal-to-metal fit is exemplary.

The wood is of very good quality, figured with subtle streaks and on the whole nicely matched. Shaping is excellent and wood-to-metal fit virtually flawless; the only gaps—and they're minute—are around the forend escutcheons and tips. The checkering, at about 26 lines per inch, is quite good, too, showing only a few waves.

My only functional complaint is that the rear trigger of the No. 1 gun is a wee bit creepy. The pulls on both are slightly heavier than I'd want, but not much, and I have no quarrel with the way the sears feel.

The ejectors are properly timed and never failed. And they're fitted with a powerful set of springs: They'll consistently pitch empty hulls better than ten feet and throw snap caps, which are heavier, almost as far. I don't think the owner will have to fool with any stuck cases in the midst of a drive or on a hot dove pass.

Nor will he be troubled by any functional or dynamic differences between the two guns. Stock dimensions are exactly the same. Each gun weighs 7 pounds, 4 ounces on my scale.

Each set of barrels, with forend attached, weighs an ounce under 3 pounds, and the points of balance fall at precisely the same place.

For a practical test, I had a friend stand behind me, where a loader would, and we passed the guns back and forth while I swung each one as if shooting driven birds. I've handled pairs of guns that I was eventually able to tell apart by the way they felt, which surprised me. But not these. I asked to be handed the No. 1 gun first but paid no attention to how many times we switched; and ten minutes later I didn't know which one I had. I guessed and was wrong. You really can't ask for better than that.

All in all, these strike me as yet another example of one of the most important things to happen in the gun world over the past decade—which is that American shooters have finally discovered the high quality and relatively low prices available from the Spanish trade. International economics being what they are, I rather doubt we'll see any new Spanish makers come on the scene, although it could happen. For the moment, the survival of those that already exist is good enough.

CHAPTER TWENTY-FOUR

WEATHERBY ATHENA

If ever an award is given for the Quietest Long-Term Presence in the American shotgun market, Weatherby is certain to be the winner. Or if the prize is for the Longest-Term Quiet Presence, Weatherby would win that one, too, since its first shotguns came on the market thirty years ago.

The situation didn't come about by design, but the fact is, the shooting world so thoroughly perceives the company as a rifle and ammunition maker that it scarcely gives Weatherby's shotguns a second thought. Which is unfortunate, because they deserve better. Actually, they deserve a lot better.

Weatherby's shotguns have never been built in this country. The earliest, an over/under called the Regency, was made in Italy by Antonio Zoli from 1967 until 1982. The Olympian, another over/under, was in production from 1977 to 1981, manufactured in Japan by Nikko Kodensha. Since 1982, all Weatherby shotguns, including the short-lived pumps and autoloaders, have been built by the New SKB Company of Japan.

The manufacturing connection has led to some confusion and misperception, especially in instances when the Weatherby is dismissed as nothing more than a flossed-up SKB. The implication is that the flossing-up does not justify the additional cost—even though SKB guns have earned a fair measure of respect in the thirty-odd years since Ithaca imported the first ones to appear in this country.

Weatherbys *are* SKBs, on the one hand, and on the other, they aren't. The actions are basically the same, featuring a trunnion hinge and a modified Greener cross-bolt fastener. Weatherby and SKB use the same ejector system, the same

Deeley-type forend fastener, and share a few other details—all of which are points in favor of either gun. The trunnion hinge is ideal for an over/under. The Greener bolt, which operates transversely in the top of the standing breech and engages stout lugs on either side of the top barrel, isn't the prettiest affair ever designed. But there's no question of either its mechanical merit or its durability.

The ejector system is excellent. The springs are mounted in the monobloc breech rather than in the forend; the cams are studs on the ejector stems and fit into slots milled into the frame. It would be hard to come up with a simpler arrangement, and where ejectors are concerned, simplicity is a paramount virtue.

If the similarities speak well for both guns, the ways in which Weatherbys differ from SKBs are equally worth considering—and let's be clear that from here on I'm talking solely about Weatherby.

Some differences involve fit and finish. Weatherby specifies that all the metal parts of its guns be hand-fitted, and the

WEATHERBY ATHENA
MICHAEL McINTOSH

tolerances generally are quite close. Weatherby also specifies high-grade wood, which among the guns I've seen ranges from striking to spectacular to a few I could only describe as kaleidoscopic.

There are functional differences as well, and the cleverest of these is a safety linkage that so far as I know is unique to Weatherby. The safety itself is a straightforward non-automatic design; it does not, in other words, shift to the on-safe position when you operate the top lever. But it also is fitted with a little spring-loaded plunger that blocks the trigger until the action is fully closed, regardless of how the safety is set. With the safety off, the sear will not trip even if you pull the trigger and hold it while you close the action. To engage the sear, you must release the trigger, which in turn releases the block.

During the field test, I spent half an hour trying to override, bypass, or otherwise fool the mechanism—unsuccessfully. Like every other safety system, it's no substitute for sensible gun handling, but it isn't meant to be. For its purpose, it works perfectly.

Besides offering an additional edge in preventing the guns from going off when they shouldn't, Weatherby also devotes attention to what happens when they should. Forcing cones are bored extra-long and all the 12-gauge barrels are slightly overbored to .735-inch. Both the overboring and the long cones do good things for patterning efficiency, and the cones help reduce the sensation of kick as well. Like nearly every other gun in the world these days, Weatherbys come with screw-in chokes, but unlike many, the tubes are stainless steel and are certified for use with steel shot, even the full choke.

Customarily I write these reviews after spending some time with one or two specimens. In this instance, I had the opportunity to shoot sporting clays for two days with eleven different Weatherbys—game guns, skeet guns, clays guns, the whole works—in 12-, 20-, 28-gauge, and even in a .410-bore. About twenty other people were doing the same, so those guns digested roughly six thousand cartridges among them.

Now, an average 500-odd rounds per gun is hardly a demolition test, but the shooting was fairly intensive at times. Besides, with that many guns, you could expect a few hang-ups of one kind or another—a wanky trigger or a sticky ejector or something. In fact, though, there wasn't one malfunction of any kind. Every gun opened and closed every time without a hitch and went bang when it was supposed to and didn't when it wasn't; every ejector popped every empty case every time. The results were, in short, impressive.

I can give Weatherby equally high marks in performance. Every gun, from the biggest 12-gauge clays model to the little .410, felt good, well balanced. Stocks are nicely shaped, triggers and grips properly aligned, forends comfortable to hold, ribs unobtrusive. For the price range, the triggers are exceptional—light and crisp, free of creep, drag, hitch, or glitch. The pulls could be a bit lighter for the lightest-weight pieces, but it wouldn't need to be much.

My objections are almost entirely cosmetic. The checkering is coarser than it ought to be. I don't care for high-gloss stock finish or flared pistol grips or white-line spacers, all of which became Weatherby hallmarks in the 1950s. Appearances aside, though, the flared grip feels just fine, and the radius is exactly right for allowing good trigger control without cramping your wrist. And for those who prefer a more traditional look, both the Athena and sister model Orion are available with field-style stocks—rounded half-hand grip and slender forend, all oil-finished.

On the other hand, I find some aspects of Weatherby appearance highly appealing, notably the Athena's decorative sideplates. It seems to me that designing sideplates for an over/under is a more demanding job than for a side-by-side, mainly because of the over/under's relatively tall frame. Plates that are too narrow make even a small frame look bulky and out of proportion, spoiling the lines of an otherwise well-shaped gun. The Athena's plates complement the frame beautifully, and the whole effect is quite handsome.

I didn't shoot any game with the Weatherbys, but there's no reason why they wouldn't be as good for birds as for clays. And they are dandy for targets, all of them, not just those designed for the target games. The 20- and 28-bores are especially nice to handle. The 28 is made on the 20-gauge frame, but as Weatherby frames are fairly small, the slender barrels don't look at all out of place.

Some things, it seems, just take a while to catch on, and I have a notion that Weatherby shotguns fit that category. Perhaps their next thirty years won't be so quiet as the first.

PART TWO

THAT'S OLD

BUT STILL AVAILABLE

CHAPTER TWENTY-FIVE

THE SUPERPOSED:
JOHN BROWNING'S MASTERPIECE

If you want to start a good argument in a roomful of shooters, ask them to name John Browning's greatest gun. The more heterogeneous the group, the livelier the debate will be. The riflemen most likely will nominate the Model 94 Winchester, now more than a hundred years in production, or maybe even the grand old Hi-Wall single-shot. Pistoleros are sure to bring up the Model 1911 Government .45 and the Colt Woodsman .22.

The shotgunners could have a field day just among themselves. Some pumpsters will cite the Winchester Model 97, others the Model 17 Remington (which in a later incarnation became the Ithaca Model 37). You'll hear an even larger contingent arguing in favor of the classic squareback A-5 autoloader.

Take a step back to get a broader view, and one thing is certain: No other name in gunmaking could provoke a similar debate on anywhere near the same scale. As a firearms designer, John Moses Browning was the greatest of the modern age, perhaps of any age. Cut it any way you like: the total number of successful designs, the variety of them, the number of specific guns still in production seventy years after the man's death—you name it. Pick apart virtually any repeating arm, sporting or military, built anywhere in the world today, and chances are you'll find some basic mechanical principle that was first applied by John Browning.

In view of that kind of accomplishment, it's no wonder you can hear so many different answers to the question of which

Browning gun is the greatest of all. But if it were up to me, my tastes being the way they are, I'd have to say that John Browning's masterpiece is the last gun he designed—the one he called the Superposed.

Besides a genius for mechanics, Browning had an uncanny ability to recognize unfilled niches in the firearms world; in 1922, when he started tinkering with what would become the Superposed, it was a world vastly different from the one we know today. Now almost every maker in the world builds over/under guns; in the 1920s, only a handful did.

Back then, the best of them came from the English trade— from Boss, Woodward, Beesley, Lang, Westley Richards, Lancaster, and a few others—all splendid guns and splendidly expensive. American over/unders didn't exist at all and wouldn't for another ten years. The great Remington Model 32 didn't come on the market until 1932, the Marlin Model 90 until 1937, and the Savage models 420 and 430 until 1938.

As it turned out, the Superposed didn't make its debut till the 1930s either. It was delayed by John Browning's fatal heart attack the day after Thanksgiving, 1926, at the Fabrique Nationale factory in Belgium, where he and his son Val had gone to work out the last engineering details while FN tooled up for production. Finally, though, the new gun came to the American market in 1931, and was featured in the first catalog issued by the newly formed Browning Arms Company.

In those early days, the Superposed was a 12-bore fitted with ejectors, two triggers, and a solid rib. It came in four grades—Standard, Pigeon, Diana, and Midas. A vent rib and "Twin-Single" triggers were options.

The trigger was the one element John Browning had not yet fully worked out before he died. He had intended the Superposed to be a single-trigger gun all along, but in the fall of 1926 he was still experimenting with an inertia-block system for shifting the sears. Val Browning, a first-rate engineer in his own right, took up the problem in turn, but by 1930 he hadn't found just the right mechanism either. He had, however, come up with an interim system that the catalog called the Browning Twin-Single.

This amounted to two triggers, each capable of tripping both locks. The front one fired the under barrel first, then the over; the rear trigger simply reversed the order. This was not a new concept even in the late 1920s, as English, German, Czech, Spanish, and Italian gunmakers had built similar gizmos. Browning's was among the better ones, though highly complex and sometimes very difficult to put right if it got out of whack.

It was mainly a stopgap measure, anyway, and Val Browning kept working on the inertia-shift idea. By 1938 he had a system that suited him; it became standard for the Superposed the following year, and it's been part of the gun ever since.

Inertia-shift triggers own one inherent characteristic that's not always endearing: They depend upon recoil to disengage the block from the first sear. If you drop the hammer on an empty chamber, a dud cartridge, or a snap-cap, you can keep pulling that trigger for the rest of your life and it just won't shift. Unlike some other inertia systems, you can shift a Superposed trigger by clicking the safety slide back and then forward again; otherwise, the universal cure is to give the gun a sharp rap on the butt. There have been a few times in the game fields when I've wished I could do the same thing to the inventor.

That aside, however, Val Browning's trigger is one of the best ever made. I've never shot a Superposed that wasn't crisp and quick and light on the let-off. I'm sure some have developed mechanical ills, but I haven't seen one.

Addition of the single trigger brought the Superposed to its final form, mechanically at least. From there, all that remained was the evolution of various configurations and grades. The Lightning model had been introduced in 1935. The 20-gauge version came on the market in 1949, magnum chambering the following year. At the same time, the grading went from names to numbers—and changed back to names in 1960. Ventilated ribs became standard in 1955; 28-gauge and .410-bore guns were introduced in 1960.

Through it all, the Superposed earned a splendid reputation for reliability, quality, and value. Though never truly cheap, it was for a long time not overly expensive, either. As the 1931 catalog put it, "Browning Superposed is the first overunder gun offered at a price which is not prohibitive." True enough. That year the Standard Grade sold for $107.50. Best-quality English over/unders cost $1,500 or more at the time—and none of them was fifteen times the better gun.

Production costs inevitably crept upward. In 1965 the lowest-priced Superposed sold for $360; by 1970 it was $420. At the same time, the market was growing ever more competitive, with good, modestly priced over/unders from Italy claiming a larger and larger share. Winchester was doing quite well with its Japanese-built Model 101. Following Winchester's cue, Browning Arms shifted more and more of its manufacture to Japan, beginning in 1971 with the BT-99 single trap and BSS side-by-side. The Citori was introduced in 1973, the same year FN brought out a less-expensive Browning called the Liège.

The Liège was not a true Superposed action, and most of the measures taken to reduce production costs also reduced the quality as well. It so underwhelmed the market that Browning discontinued production in 1975.

At once encouraged by the excellent Citori's growing success and discouraged by steadily flagging sales of the Superposed, Browning stopped regular Superposed production in 1976 and announced the following year that it would be available only on special order. It still is. And the Citori continues to be the mainstay of the shotgun line.

One of the gun writers whose work I used to devour with great relish in the 1960s (I'm not being coy about his name; I just can't remember which one he was) once remarked that he had a sure-fire formula to fall back on any time he was stuck for a story: Take some time-honored, meat-and-potatoes gun or cartridge and flog the hell out of it in print. Argue, for instance, that the Model 12 Winchester is really a piece of junk or that the venerable .30-30 is possibly the most inefficient round ever developed, that sort of thing. I suppose there is some mileage

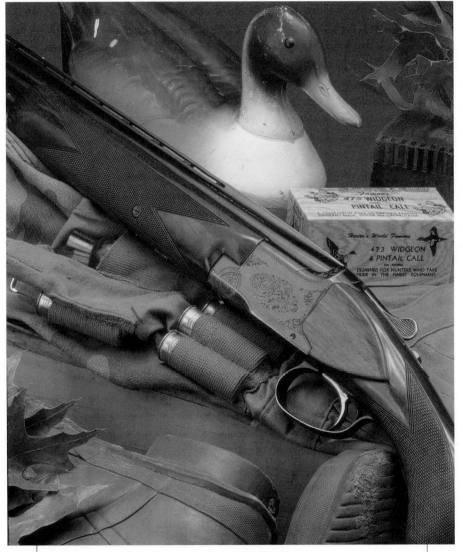

BROWNING SUPERPOSED
WILLIAM W. HEADRICK

to be made in goring sacred oxen, but I've never been inclined to try it myself—at least not without tongue in cheek—and I'm not going to start now. The good old Superposed is not the handsomest over/under ever made, nor the best-designed, but it's one of the greatest nonetheless.

None of John Browning's guns are particularly simple, and if you want to see why production costs of the Superposed got to be so burdensome, just look inside one, at the roughly half-zillion little parts that require an ungodly amount of milling and fitting. If the workmanship or materials were of even frac-tionally lesser quality, the guns would suffer a lot more me-chanical breakdowns than they do. But as the Browning ads used to say years ago, they are rugged as the Rockies, smooth as silk.

I'm not overly impressed by the inventor's choice of a barrel-lump action and underbolt fastener. Trunnions and mid-breech or top fasteners are better and make for a shallower frame besides. Yet a Superposed will absorb a world of use and no small measure of abuse before it needs a new bolt or re-jointing.

The forend system makes no sense at all. As I'm sure you're aware, you don't actually remove the forend from a Superposed to take it apart; you unhook the latch, pull it down, and slide the forend forward about three-quarters of an inch. You can find the same concept, applied to the side-by-side, de-scribed in a British patent issued to Charles Osborne Ellis and Edward William Wilkinson in 1877—but you'll look a long time to find a gun actually built that way. It's unnecessarily compli-cated and unnecessarily expensive to make, but like almost everything else about the Superposed, it was so well made that it always works.

One thing that doesn't always work is the trigger selector. It's handy enough; all you have to do is move the safety button to one side or the other—to the right for the under-over se-quence, to the left to fire the top barrel first. This H-pattern arrangement has since been copied by more gunmakers than you can count. And to my thinking, almost every one of them has made the same mistake Browning did.

Now, a Superposed safety is smooth enough to begin with, and it gets even silkier with use. The problem is that, being right-handed, I tend to push on a right-to-left diagonal rather than straight ahead, and with the selector set in the standard under-over sequence, the button can easily get hung up in the center of the H. Which means the safety's still on when I pull the trigger. If the mechanism were reversed—with the under-over position on the left instead of the right—this wouldn't happen.

It's a problem with every gun that has a Browning-type selector, not just those made by Browning. I probably think of it as mainly a bug in the Superposed because I've owned more of them than any other over/under. But a bug it is. There was a certain 20-gauge Superposed years ago—one of the sweetest-handling guns I ever had—that was notorious for safety jams, and I swore at it for nearly an entire quail season before giving up and having a gunsmith block the selector altogether. I've had a bad attitude toward the mechanism ever since.

If you own an older Superposed or are thinking of buying one, you should be aware of the famous "salt wood" problem. This was very real, and it trashed some otherwise good guns. In the mid-1960s, Browning Arms got hornswoggled into buying a whole bunch of stock blanks that were full of salt. Probably some bozo tried to hasten the drying process by packing the wood in it. Sodium chloride certainly is a desiccant, but it also has a nasty habit of dissolving steel, and a lot of these blanks got made into gun and rifle stock before anyone— Browning Arms least of all—realized they were poison. The company rightly offered to replace these at no charge, but considerable damage was already done and a lot of guns were literally eaten up inside. Most of these probably have been identified and corrected, or else junked, by now, but some are no doubt still out there.

So if you have a Superposed that was built from about 1966

to about 1975, check it for internal rust. The easiest way is simply to pull the butt-plate screws. If they're clean, the wood probably is okay; if they're rusty, find a good gunsmith in short order.

Other than that, there are no "bad years" for the Superposed. The quality of materials, workmanship, fit, and finish has been uniformly high for sixty-five years now. That's not a bad record, by any standard.

CHAPTER TWENTY-SIX

A.H. FOX

I consider the A.H. Fox to be the best gun ever built in the United States. I don't say this to start an argument with those who fancy Parker or L.C. Smith or any other, but simply because I believe it.

At one time or another I've owned specimens of all the American classics (several of some), shot many hundred birds and thousands of clay targets with them, and experienced most of the mechanical problems that some are known for. By the same token, I've appreciated their virtues, so it's been an enlightening experience, and it's brought me to the firm conviction that Fox is the best of a good lot.

Mechanically, the Fox is impressive in almost every regard. One of the great virtues of the boxlock gun is that its mechanics can be very simple. Not all boxlocks are, by any means, but they can be, and I don't know of any simpler than a Fox. The cocking system and lockwork, covered by a patent issued to Ansley Fox on October 17, 1905, comprise only three working parts in each lock (one of which is the mainspring) and a single cocking piece between them. The cocking piece, a spring-loaded slide mounted on the barrel lump, engages the tumblers directly, so there are no intermediary levers.

All told, the Fox system is even simpler than the original Anson & Deeley boxlock. Its closest forebear—in principle, anyway—is W.W. Greener's Facile Princeps action, patented in 1880.

About the only thing the Fox leaves to be desired are rebounding locks, inasmuch as the strikers are integral with the tumblers. If the strikers were separate parts, it wouldn't matter

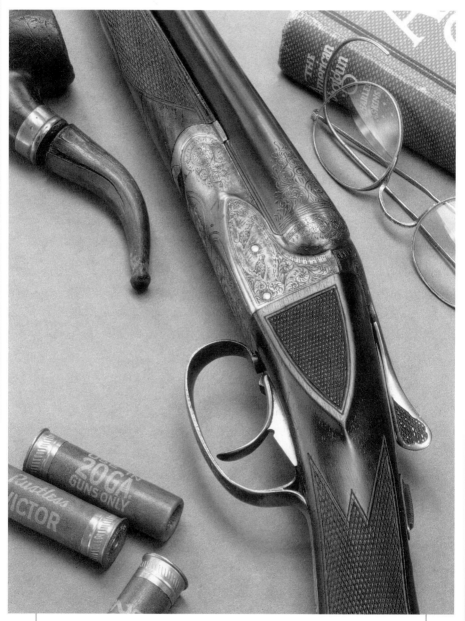

A.H. Fox CE Grade
WILLIAM W. HEADRICK

because they could retract under spring tension after hitting the cartridge primers. But with the integral strikers and non-rebounding locks, the pins remain protruding through the breech face until the cocking lever begins rotating the tumblers. A worn, damaged, or mistimed cocking system can therefore allow the strikers to drag against the primer or case head and make the gun difficult to open.

But though the potential exists, this sort of thing rarely afflicts Fox guns, thanks mainly to very stout lock parts made of high-quality, well-hardened steel. And the non-rebounding locks have one advantage in that the tumblers seal the striker holes against gas blowback from a pierced primer or ruptured case head.

Fox's fastening system is not greatly different from those of other American guns, notably L.C. Smith. In fact, an earlier version, used in the guns built by Philadelphia Arms Company, is so similar to the Smith's that I've often wondered why the U.S. Patent Office accepted it. The classic Fox fastener, patented January 16, 1906, is a bit simpler, but both involve a rib extension engaged by a cylindrical hook mounted inside the standing breech.

Along with Purdey's double-bite underbolt, the top fastener is one of the world's greatest systems for bolting a break-open action. Among the various stresses that come to bear upon a side-by-side gun at the moment of firing are forces that flip the muzzles downward and therefore seek to pull the barrels away from the top of the standing breech. A properly fitted Purdey-type underbolt clearly is enough to hold everything together through several lifetimes of shooting. But a positive top fastener (and by "positive" I mean a barrel extension that's actually engaged by a bolt) is an extremely strong, highly efficient system and does much to enhance the durability of the guns that use it.

Good as it is, the Fox fastener is neither immune to wear nor to malfunction. The most common malfunction—though it is relatively rare in Foxes—is for the action to pop open all by itself when the gun is fired; this usually is the result of an improper radius on the hook or of insufficient contact between the hook and the rib extension.

Fox used two different ejector designs, one for a brief while, the other for more than thirty years. The first system was the work of George A. Horne, a gunsmith who worked at Syracuse Arms Company from 1888 until he hired on with Ansley Fox at Philadelphia Arms Company about 1904. He stayed on with the A.H. Fox Gun Company when it took over Philadelphia Arms in November 1906. In all, Horne designed four different ejector systems, three of which were for Syracuse Arms. The fourth, for which he and Ansley Fox jointly filed a patent application in July 1907, became the original Fox system.

It wasn't an altogether bad design, but it had its weaknesses. The sears are rather delicate, which probably forced Fox to do quite a few repair jobs under the terms of its typically broad guarantee. The system's greatest shortcoming, though, is that the ejector springs act as an assist to the extractors. If you open the gun without firing it, the extractors are mechanically cammed out for only about the first $1/8$-inch; then the springs take over and push them farther. At the time Fox used this system, L.C. Smith's ejectors worked much the same way.

Spring-driven extractors may sound good in theory, but in practice they're a pain in the butt. Both the Fox and Smith systems used coil springs, but they weren't always strong enough to force a swelled cartridge out of a chamber, especially a dirty chamber, and swelled cartridges were common as cockroaches in the old days of thick paper cases. The worst problem, though, is that the shooter compresses the ejector springs each time he closes the gun, whether he's fired it or not; this puts considerable strain on the hinge and makes the gun hard to close.

The U.S. Patent Office took a sweet long time to accept the design—possibly because it was so similar to the Smith's—and didn't issue the patent until May 1909. By then, Fox knew full well that the company needed something better.

By 1910, Horne was no longer at Fox, and plant manager

Frederick T. Russell started working on a new ejector system. At the end of the year, even before the patent application was filed, Fox announced its new "Model 1911 ejectors" to the trade. As it turned out, the announcement was not premature. The Patent Office quickly accepted Russell's design without amendment and issued the patent May 2, 1911.

The Russell system owes something to the Boss design, in that it's powered by coil springs fitted around the ejector stems and is controlled by a fairly straightforward sear, but the whole thing is quite creative and mechanically solid. You don't see many Fox ejectors go on the bum.

Fox always used high-quality materials. The earliest guns have Krupp steel barrels. The tubes were expensive, and by the early 1910s the political situation in Europe served to threaten the supply. Enter Chromox, trade name for a chromium-nickel steel made in Belgium. I have a notion it's precisely the same steel Fox had been using for Sterlingworth Grade guns since 1910, under the trade name Sterlingworth Fluid Compressed Steel. In any case, Chromox is splendid stuff, and about 1912 Fox began using it for barrels and frame forgings alike, first in smallbore guns and then, as the inventory of Krupp tubes ran out, for 12-gauges as well. (This transition lasted until after World War I, so you will see plenty of early smallbores with Krupp barrels, and some guns built in the 1920s have them as well.)

Because internal parts are few and because the fastening system doesn't use an underbolt, the Fox frame is the smallest of any American boxlock. To my eye, it also is the handsomest boxlock frame in the world—which is strictly a matter of personal taste and therefore not part of my argument that Fox is the best American gun. Nonetheless, I love the look of its sleek, simple elegance, especially in grades XE and higher, which were treated to somewhat more detailed sculpting than the lower grades.

Until the Super-Fox came along in 1922, Fox used only two different frame sizes, one for 12-bore guns and the other for

16s and 20s. The small frame strikes me as being a wee bit closer to 16-gauge scale than 20, but this, too, is a personal impression, and some of my Fox-collector friends disagree with me. At any rate, it's an exquisitely lovely thing, a precisely scaled-down version of the original 12-gauge.

Frame size contributes quite a lot to overall gun weight, and Foxes by and large are the lightest American guns. Twelve-bores of less than 7 pounds aren't at all unusual, and some 20s barely exceed 5 pounds—which makes them lighter than the typical Parker .410.

With the development of the Super-Fox, two more frames came into being, one for 12-gauge and one for 20. The Super, also known as the HE Grade, is the only American gun designed from scratch as a long-range wildfowler. How it came to be is a story too long to tell here, replete with a cast of characters that include the famous gunsmith Burt Becker, Charles Askins, John Olin, Nash Buckingham, and others. Suffice it to say that in terms of quality and performance, the Super-Fox was super, indeed. It also is among the rarer Fox models, for total production amounted only to about three hundred in 12-gauge and only sixty 20-bores.

On the whole, Fox used better-quality wood, grade for grade, than any of the other makers, and the quality of stock work seems to be the best in the American trade, although the shaping and finish aren't quite as good for guns built after about 1934. Fox was owned by Savage Arms then—had been since November 1929—and the lapses in craftsmanship, which are apparent but not radical, were the result of Depression-era economics. All of the American gunmakers had to pinch pennies just to stay in business, and they did so by reducing the amount of hand work that went into the guns.

Fox decoration is more problematic. Neither the quality of the engraving nor its aesthetic appeal seem to me as consistent among Fox guns as among Parkers and, especially, Lefevers. Some early Foxes are among the best-engraved American guns I've seen, and I haven't found many, from any period, that I could describe as poorly engraved. But overall, the quality is uneven.

There are two distinct eras in Fox engraving. From 1905 till about 1913, guns of B Grade and above were decorated with some form of scroll, while the A Grade was treated with subtle, nicely cut line work. William H. Gough, an Englishman trained in the Birmingham trade, became head of Fox's engraving department about 1910 and soon set about designing new styles of decoration. The early 1910s were difficult years for Fox, and Gough's mission was to come up with engraving patterns of appropriate coverage that required less actual working time—and therefore lower production costs. He succeeded extremely well, although how appealing you find the results is a matter of taste.

The new styles began to appear about 1913, and by the end of 1914 the transition was complete. Except for C Grade, whose pattern remained virtually unchanged, second-era Fox decoration is boldly leafy and floral. In some grades—the XE, for instance—the effect is particularly handsome; in others it is less so to me, but it's all in the beholder's eye.

About the same time the new look was in place, Fox began offering Joseph Kautzky's single trigger as an option. Kautzky was an Austrian-born gunsmith who emigrated to America in 1893, settled first in Perry, Iowa, and then moved fifty-odd miles north to Fort Dodge, where he lived for the remainder of his life. He patented at least two single-trigger designs, the first in 1906. The second, awarded patent protection in April 1911, he sold to the Fox Gun Company in 1914, and he spent several months in Philadelphia that year teaching Fox gunsmiths how to make it.

None of the old-time American single triggers quite measure up to those available today. All were relatively complicated and rather delicate. Probably having learned an expensive lesson from its early ejectors, for years Fox steadfastly refused to install a single trigger in its guns until the Kautzky version came along. As it turned out, both the early hesitation and subsequent faith were justified. Although it requires careful filing to properly shape its roller-and-cam shift mechanism, the Fox-Kautzky trigger is as reliable as any and more so than most.

Actually, you can say as much about virtually any aspect of the Fox gun. None of the old-time gunsmithing books have much to say about Fox, simply because they seldom break down—which is remarkable, considering the pounding many of them have taken. Until the 1930s, short-cased cartridges were standard fare in the United States—$2^9/_{16}$ inches for 12- and 16-gauges and $2^1/_2$ inches for 20—and those were the standard chamberings for Philadelphia-built Foxes.

Longer chambers, $2^3/_4$ and 3 inches, were available upon request in both 12- and 20-gauges from the beginning, and $2^3/_4$ inches was standard for Super-Foxes, with 3-inch chambers on request. But by far the majority of Fox guns made before 1930—and a great many made after that—left the factory with short chambers. So, it's a good idea to measure the chambers of old Fox guns and either consult with a good gunsmith about having them deepened if they're short, or switch to $2^1/_2$-inch cartridges.

Nowadays, slightly short chambers don't cause much of a problem. Modern cartridge cases are thin-walled, and plastic wads create little friction. In the old days, however (by which I mean any time to about 1960), thick-walled paper cases and rough fiber wads could cause a significant pressure blip in a chamber even a fraction too short—of itself, not enough to blow out a barrel, but certainly enough to put considerable strain on fastening systems, hinge joints, frames, and stocks. The cumulative effects of this are one reason why a lot of older American guns have loose joints and split stocks, but you won't find many Foxes suffering such ills. By the time the Fox came along, Parker already had the nickname "Old Reliable" sewed up (and to a great extent Parker deserved it), but the moniker would have applied just as well to Fox.

Which of course is exactly what Ansley Fox had in mind

from the start. He wanted to build the best American gun ever, and to a great extent, he succeeded. He described it as "The Finest Gun in the World," which it wasn't. But it was America's finest, and in the gun world, that's territory enough.

CHAPTER TWENTY-SEVEN

ORVIS-ZOLI SUPERFIELD

Imported guns marked with house-brand names and sold by large retailers represent the oldest form of shotgun marketing in America. For the first hundred years or more, American gunmakers were mainly riflemakers, and what guns were sold here generally came from somewhere else—England, at first, then Belgium, Germany, a few from France, and a handful from other countries. Such American-made pieces as Parker and Lefever were the exceptions to prove the rule.

From about 1880 until World War I came a veritable flood of contract guns—most from Belgium, some made here, none particularly good—for sale by hardware merchants and mail-order houses. What few didn't fall apart years ago are virtually worthless today.

But these two-dollar specials weren't the only game around. Charles Daly was the house brand of Schoverling, Daly & Gales from the turn of the century until about 1930, and the best of the Daly guns, built in Prussia by H.A. Linder, rightly fetch big dollars today. In the 1930s, '40s, and '50s the Abercrombie & Fitch Knockabout was a plain, yeoman boxlock—but made by the fine old Belgian firm of Auguste Francotte. It was a bargain then and still is, at several times the original price.

The playing field is smaller nowadays, and the sources are different, but the situation otherwise hasn't really changed. The ultra-cheapies are mercifully all but gone, but some of the larger retailers and mail-order companies still offer house-brand guns of good quality at reasonable prices.

As the oldest American mail-order retailer of anything (not just sporting goods), Orvis has maintained a fine reputation for quality products, and no small part of the reason is that Orvis goods are, in general, intelligently designed. Unlike companies that sell yuppie toys designed by marketing committees, Orvis contracts products for real sportsmen who engage in real sport. Case in point: the Orvis house-brand gun called SuperField.

As I said, sources have changed. Italy and Spain now supply most of America's contract guns, while the Belgian contribution has dwindled to a trickle. Orvis, in fact, has sold guns from all three countries—excellent Arrieta side-by-sides, over/unders by Beretta, and a Belgian-built Browning, all more or less made to customer specs. The SuperField is Italian, built by Antonio Zoli, and at just over $2,000 it was the lowest-priced piece in the Orvis line. Orvis discontinued it in 1996.

Not surprisingly for the price, the SuperField came only in standard specifications—but not necessarily the same standards we've come to expect in machine-made factory guns. This isn't surprising, either, given Orvis's ability to design things for practical use. Some of the compliments the gun deserves are a direct result; others have to do with the current state of Italian gunmaking.

I've argued elsewhere in these essays that the Italian gun trade is now doing with the over/under exactly what the Lon-

ORVIS-ZOLI SUPERFIELD
THE ORVIS COMPANY · INC

don trade did with the side-by-side a hundred years ago—namely, perfecting the form. The Italians are accomplishing this the same way the British did, by adopting certain mechanical designs that time has proven to be both efficient and reliable—designs that work just as well in inexpensive guns as in hand-made pieces bearing mega-dollar price tags.

Look inside almost any current side-by-side, top-notch or otherwise, and you're apt to find a Scott spindle, Purdey bolt, Holland & Holland or Anson & Deeley-type action, Southgate ejectors, and so on. Look inside the Orvis SuperField (which you can readily do because the buttstock is quick-detachable, using the wrench that comes with each gun), and you'll see shades of Perazzi, Marocchi, Renato Gamba, Beretta, and others.

The mechanics are wonderfully simple—overhead sears and coil mainsprings. The cocking slides lie in the bottom of the frame and work off a tonguelike cam in the forend. The single trigger, which is selective, shifts sears through the inertia of recoil. The barrels are mounted to a monobloc breech that also contains the ejector mechanism. The action is a notch-and-trunnion affair fastened by a broad single underlug.

All this is largely standard fare in the Italian trade and represents a goodly share of the reasons why Italian guns are the best boxlock over/unders you can buy.

The three Orvis versions are equally straightforward. The SuperField Uplander is a 20-bore with 26-inch barrels and a straight-hand stock. The Sporting gun is a 30-inch 12-gauge with a wide clays-style rib and a pistol grip. The All-Rounder, the model I tested, is also a 12-bore, set up with 28-inch barrels, a 7-millimeter matted game rib, and a pistol grip.

Actually, these barrels are 71 centimeters, so they measure $27^7/_8$ inches. The chambers, similarly, are 76 millimeters and therefore just a skosh deeper than the nominal 3 inches. With the forend attached, they weigh 3 pounds, 13 ounces, which accounts for just over half of the gun's $7^1/_2$-pound total weight; this puts the balance point 2 inches forward of the standing breech, right on the hinge, and gives the gun a good, lively feel.

The bores are consistent, chrome-lined and a wee bit undersized—.726-inch in the bottom tube and .725-inch on top. (Why anyone thinks he needs 3-inch cartridges is beyond me, but be forewarned: In a gun this light and thus bored, Roman candles are going to give you a wicked whack.) Wall thickness is fully sufficient but not nearly as consistent, due mainly to uneven external surfaces. The under barrel of the test gun was especially ripply. This would be unacceptable in a more expensive gun, though no more than minor cosmetics in practical terms. Still, I should think Zoli's machinery is capable of better.

You shouldn't really expect hand-polishing in this price range, and all the metalwork shows a faint patina of grit marks. More cosmetics. The blacking, on the other hand is quite good.

The SuperField comes with screw-in chokes, nominally skeet, improved-cylinder, and modified. The tubes fit flush with the muzzles, are accurately threaded, and, if you seat them properly, stay put. The wrench is fitted with a highly useful thread cleaner for the bores.

By actual measurement, the three tubes mike out at .726-, .717-, and .704-inch. Compared with the bores, this amounts to cylinder, loose improved-cylinder, and tight modified, respectively. They all pattern appropriately.

But good as they are, I have a bone to pick. These tubes are marked with notches for identification, but the owner's manual doesn't say what they mean, so you have to measure the bloody things to learn what's what. Moreover, the system apparently is exactly the opposite of what most Italian makers use—the more notches in the tube, the more open the choke— and it's inconsistent to boot: The cylinder tube has no notches at all, whereas the improved-cylinder tube has four and the modified three. Gimme a break—at least a chart in the handbook, if not etching C, IC, and M on the tubes themselves.

Woodwork is where the SuperField really shines. The walnut itself is exceptional; I've seen guns costing three or four times more that didn't have wood this good. It's well fitted and shaped besides. The forend is comfortably slender, finished off with a slight schnabel. The pistol grip fits my hand perfectly, and though the buttstock is substantial, it still is far slimmer than the gigantic hunks of wood you find on a lot of current over/unders. The leather-covered buttpad is both handsome and functional.

Orvis deserves a big compliment on its standard dimensions. The $14^3/4$-inch length is still a bit short for me, but whoever set up the specs clearly knows the average shooter is taller nowadays than five-foot-six to five-foot-eight, which is the range at which 14-inch stocks truly fit. Drop is $1^1/2$ inches at the comb and a shade over 2 inches at the heel; there's about $^1/4$-inch cast-off at the heel and $^5/8$-inch at the toe. It is altogether an extremely well-designed stock that should suit a great many shooters very well.

Both checkering and engraving are machine-cut. Engraving is minimal but tasteful. The checkering is machine-perfect, but because it isn't given any touch-up by hand, don't be surprised if you see a raggedy spot or two where a pulpy streak in the wood fuzzes up; the test gun's forend has one. At 20 lines per inch, the checkering's fairly coarse stuff, but certainly affords a good grasp. Unfortunately, the borders are grooves deep enough to divert rainwater from a base-camp tent, which makes the panels look more pasted-on than cut-in.

The ejectors are patterned on a system originally designed, if memory serves, by Renato Gamba. It's the same system you'll find in the old Marocchi Contrast, and it's a good one.

The trigger selector is a little button mounted on the safety thumb-piece, and the under barrel fires first when the button is set to the left—a sensible arrangement because it means a right-handed shooter can't accidentally hang it up between the sears while disengaging the safety.

The pulls are crisp and free of creep, but they're too hard for a gun of this weight. Both sears go clear off the scale on my pull-gauge, which means they break at better than 5 pounds. The crispness helps mitigate this somewhat, but pulls at least a pound lighter would be an improvement.

The spring that holds the inertia block against the sears apparently is a bit stiffer than most. It failed to shift a couple of times with extra-light $1^{1}/_{8}$-ounce loads. In those cases, it's possible that I didn't have the gun seated firmly enough against my shoulder—a recoil-activated trigger needs a certain amount of resistance in order to work—but it failed to shift several times with $^{7}/_{8}$-ounce loads, which leads me to suspect a stiff spring. It worked fine with everything else I used—the whole gamut from standard light target loads to live-pigeon loads.

All in all, this is a quality piece worth the price, especially as it fulfills quite well the function implied by its name, All-Rounder. It's light enough to carry comfortably in the field, yet heavy enough to shoot comfortably through a hundred-target round course of sporting clays or skeet without making you flinchy from recoil. Best of all, it has the balance and pointability to handle smoothly regardless of whether the target is wearing feathers or a coat of orange paint. At a time when specialized guns are becoming the order of the day, it's nice to find one with that kind of versatility.

CHAPTER TWENTY-EIGHT

Parker

In any discussion of the great American guns, Parker is almost certain to be the first name that comes up. Parker is to American guns what Purdey is to guns in general—the one name everybody knows.

In part it's because the Parker was the first American gun factory-produced in significant numbers, dating back to 1867, and because Parker guns remained in production longer than any other American gun. Although few, if any, were actually built after about 1942, the last Parker shipped—a GH Grade .410 bearing serial number 242387—left the Remington warehouse in 1947. And as yet another factor in its fame, for most of its eighty-year life in active production, the Parker was advertised and promoted as extensively, and intensively, as any gun ever has been. The Parker reputation did not come to exist by accident.

Its production history is both complex and interesting, and you can find the story, told in varying degrees of detail, elsewhere. For our purposes here, history is largely irrelevant. Here, the questions are more practical: Is the Parker truly the be-all and end-all of American guns, as the mystique would have it? Is it "America's Finest Shotgun," as the subtitle of Peter Johnson's 1961 book declares? And just how good—in terms of materials, fit, finish, and function—is the typical Parker gun?

The short answers to these are: No, no, and pretty damn good.

If there's a useful comparison to be made, it's that the Parker has most of the same virtues, and shares most of the same shortcomings, as the Browning Superposed. Both are decidedly more mechanically complex than they need to be. This is especially true of old-style hammerless Parkers, built between 1889 and 1917. The post-1917 guns are considerably simpler, but still relatively complicated. Like the Superposed, however, Parkers were so well-built, so closely machined and fitted —and their various parts so well hardened and tempered—that for the most part they just go on working despite the Rube Goldberg nature of their mechanics.

In practical terms, Parker quality is essentially the same regardless of grade—including the plain, economy-model Trojan Grade introduced in 1915. The Trojan frame was milled with almost none of the graceful contours of the other grades, and after about the first ten years of production it wasn't made with the distinctive (and basically useless) doll's-head rib extension. But as a gun that sold for $27.50 in 1915 and for about $75 when it was discontinued in 1939, it was a lot of value for the money. And still is, especially in view of the often-nonsensical prices at which higher-grade Parkers are offered for sale.

Quality materials are the first step in building a quality gun. Parkers were made of good stuff, some of the best available at the time, although the correlation between materials and the various grades of gun weren't always quite what the company implied. Barrels, for example. Before World War I, Parker offered Krupp steel barrels on request, and until the mid-1920s barreled the highest grades—AAHE and A-1 Special— with English Whitworth tubes. Otherwise, the barrels of all grades were made of the same steel, even though the company stamped the ribs with a variety of lofty-sounding names implying that the higher the grade, the better the barrel steel. In fact, the only real differences among barrels marked Trojan Steel, Vulcan Steel, Parker, Titanic, Acme, or Peerless are the names themselves.

Chambers can be a problem, however, because a lot of older Parkers were bored to the 2⅝-inch depth standard in the early part of the century. Quite a few have been deepened since, but by no means all, so take care to have the chambers measured. If they're short, you can either use $2\frac{1}{2}$-inch cartridges, which are readily available, or consult a gunsmith about having them rebored.

Parker's walnut is generally quite good, though I'm of the opinion that Fox used somewhat better wood, grade for grade, and employed the best stockmakers in the American trade. But this isn't to take anything away from the Parker stockers, who were no slouches at their work. A lot of Parkers are stocked to impossible dimensions, however; stocks tend to be short and made with the extreme drops that were standard in the old days of American gunmaking. These old doglegs are so difficult to handle well that if you buy a Parker to shoot, you're likely to need the services of a good stockmaker, either for bending and lengthening, or for new wood altogether.

PARKER VH GRADE
WILLIAM W. HEADRICK

Regardless of what grade you might choose to buy, you can be assured of getting one of the best-finished guns built in the United States. Even the Trojans and VH Grades were put together, polished, and finished with a degree of attention that no other American factory quite matched, and the high grades are simply superb. Along with Lefever Arms, Parker used the best engravers available at the time, and it shows.

Dynamics are similarly good. I've owned quite a few Parkers over the past twenty-five years, including some big old things that should have been ponderous as a bridge timber. There wasn't a one that didn't handle with surprising grace.

This isn't to say the typical Parker is a wispy switch. On the contrary, most of them are heavier than a proper game gun should be, even the smallbores. Though it's true that Parker used more different sizes of frame than any American maker—from No. 7, which is the size of a Volkswagen engine, down to No. 000—the actual differences among them are in some ways more apparent than real. From No. 2, the standard 12-gauge frame after 1917, to No. 0, the standard 20-gauge frame, you'll find some reduction in width, very little in length and depth. The Nos. 00 and 000 frames are simply No. 0 frames with varying amounts of steel milled out of the action bar to reduce the weight.

Because the frames are all essentially of equal depth, smallbore Parkers look progressively more disproportionate when you compare barrel diameter with frame size. Some shooters and collectors go into raptures over 28- and .410-bore Parkers; to me they're so thick-framed as to be downright ugly, and no amount of finish or engraving can hide it. The eye of the beholder . . .

Whatever mechanical problems might crop up are most likely to be in the ejectors or the single trigger. The ejector system dates to 1901, the single trigger to 1922, and neither design is particularly good; they're complicated, delicate, and can be an utter nightmare to put right when the parts get worn or, especially, if they've been tinkered with by some ham-fisted clod who didn't know what he was doing.

If you're thinking of buying any older gun as a shooter, you'd do well to have it vetted by a competent gunsmith who, for his part, should be looking for any evidence of incompetent work performed on it in the past. You probably wouldn't be surprised at how many old guns have been dinked around by shade-tree amateurs, but you might be astonished at the crudity and utter stupidity of what's been done to some of them. It's not pretty.

But old Parkers in sound condition can be a delight. They were built to shoot, and apart from the problem of stock dimensions, a lot of them still have several lifetimes of good service left to offer.

Even though I think A.H. Fox is a better gun, both mechanically and aesthetically, there's not much question that Parker is one of America's greatest—and when it comes to durable, reliable factory-built guns, nobody ever made them any better than we did.

CHAPTER TWENTY-NINE

PARKER-HALE 645E

The shooting world has always had a place for the inexpensive,
well-made gun. It has, in fact, been the foundation of the arms
industry worldwide. For every maker that has achieved the
best-gun level, you'll find a dozen that have produced thousands of plain, sturdy guns that have stood yeoman service.
The same makers often have turned out both.

This has been particularly true here in America, where
machine-made factory guns have reached levels of quality
higher than similar guns made anywhere else. The best American doubles, now cherished as artifacts, built their reputations
on reliable performance and sensible economics, not on lavish
decoration. FE Grade Foxes and A-1 Special Parkers may
now fetch handsome prices, but they do so in part because
they're rare and in larger part because the Sterlingworths and
Trojans proved themselves in the marshes and fields. You can
say as much for Smith or Ithaca or Remington or any of the
others—the high grades were the icing, but the field grades
were the cake.

From the late 1940s until the '60s, when Winchester tapped
Japan as a source, virtually all of the doubles on the American
market, whether jewels or junk, came from Europe. The big
sporting-goods houses like Stoeger and Abercrombie & Fitch
sold their share of London bests, but they sold a lot more mid-
priced guns, often as house-brand items.

None defines its particular niche better than the Knockabout, built by Francotte in Belgium and sold here by Abercrombie & Fitch. It was a trim boxlock, well finished but not
highly decorated, inexpensive but not dirt-cheap. It sold for

$425 in 1961, when prices for new Purdeys started at $2,800.

In its way, the Knockabout came to represent a whole class of guns that offered excellent service and good value, guns that did what you asked of them and did it well. And the investment was modest enough that you didn't mind taking them out on a rainy day or flogging through the brush or exposing them to water, mud and oafish-footed dogs in a boat or duck blind. Given reasonable care, they'd continue to perform through more than a lifetime of hard use.

There still is a place for the knockabout gun. At a time when the shooting world is rediscovering the delights of fine guns and when more and more shooters are willing to lay out heavy cash to own them, the knockabout's niche may be more important than ever. The sheer weight of the investment it takes to own a Piotti or a Fabbri or a London best or a high-grade American classic demands that you give the piece all the protection you can. They're all made to be used, but they simply cost too much to justify risking serious damage. So either you stay home on drizzly days and stay away from barbwire fences, heavy cover, and rocky ground, or else you own a knockabout to use when the going is likely to be rough.

If the world economy were still what it was in 1961, today's equivalent of the Abercrombie & Fitch Knockabout would cost something in the neighborhood of $7,500. Fortunately, things financial haven't become quite that screwy even yet. Almost everything costs more than it used to, but most of the inflation in the gun trade has been at the top end. So, even if prices for fine guns have escalated sharply, there still is plenty of value available at reasonable cost.

Currently it seems that $1,000 generally is the dividing line between high quality and high risk among new double guns, but if you know where to look, you can buy a lot of gun for less than that, and Parker-Hale is an excellent case in point.

Through most of its hundred-year history, Parker-Hale has been a rifle works. A. G. Parker, an Englishman fond of competitive rifle-shooting, started the business in Birmingham in

1880, manufacturing sights and other target-shooting accessories. He soon brought in his nephew, A.T.C. Hale, as a partner, and the firm earned a vast reputation worldwide for its support of competitive marksmanship and for its products, which today include lovely sporting rifles built on original Model 98 Mauser actions.

Parker-Hale has never built shotguns, but in the early 1970s it saw in the British gun market the same thing that's occurred elsewhere, including America—a growing interest among people who couldn't afford the ever-increasing cost of a best English gun and a continuing interest in good, low-priced utility guns among those who could. Parker-Hale contracted with Ignacio Ugartechea of Spain to supply a line of double

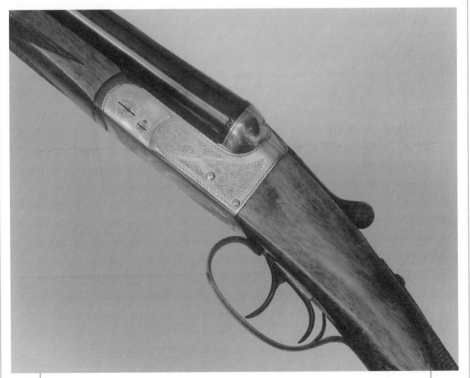

PARKER-HALE 645E
MICHAEL McINTOSH

guns to be sold in England under the Parker-Hale name. British shooters bought hundreds of them. Parker-Hale's American importer, Precision Sports of Cortland, New York, began selling the guns here in 1986.

The line included four models—two boxlocks and two side-locks, all available in 12-, 16-, 20-, and 28-gauge, and .410-bore. The sidelocks were special-order items. The boxlocks came ei-ther with extractors (Model 640) or ejectors (Model 645) and were available in either American or English configuration, identified by an "A" or "E" added to the model number. The American style has a non-selective single trigger, beavertail forend, pistol-grip stock, buttplate, and flat rib. The English version has two triggers, splinter forend, straight-hand stock with checkered butt, and a hollow rib. In the fall of 1988, when I tested a Parker-Hale, prices for the boxlocks began at $529.95.

As a variation in both the boxlock ejector and sidelock guns, Parker-Hale offered a model set up in the image of Robert Churchill's famous XXV gun, and that's what I chose— a slender 28-gauge of English character, with 25-inch barrels and Churchill rib. Parker-Hale called it the Model 645E-XXV.

Robert Churchill was one of England's great shooting in-structors and owned a streak of genius for marketing. In the 1920s and '30s, when 28- and 30-inch barrels were standard fare among game guns worldwide, Churchill insisted that 25 inches was plenty. Although the whole thing was largely an attempt to create something new that his company, E.J. Churchill, could use to advantage in a flagging gun market, he was right—ballistically, at least. In earlier days, barrels needed to be long in order to allow black powder to work up maximum thrust; nitro powders, on the other hand, reach their peak sooner, in a shorter length of bore, and 25 inches is more than enough.

Churchill also argued that a gun could have short barrels and still be balanced to swing relatively smoothly, and he was right about that, too.

He also designed a special rib for his stubby-barreled guns, one that creates an optical illusion. The Churchill rib tapers from breech to muzzle and is shaped like a flat-topped pyramid; both the taper and the narrow plane at the top are intended to give the illusion that the barrels are longer than they actually are.

The illusion actually does work, but the concept belies the basic premise of short barrels: If short barrels are so good, what's the need in making them look longer? And besides, any shooter who's looking at the rib instead of the target is about to miss way behind. The whole thing ravishes logic, but there it is, and Churchill turned it into a remarkable success.

Though it's been a very long time since I've had any fondness for short barrels, especially on smallbores, it also had been a few years since I'd done any shooting with a Churchill-type gun, so with the opportunity there, I figured what the hell.

And in the end, I was glad I took it. The test gun didn't have the odd, stubby look that short barrels usually create—in part because of the slender barrels and in part because it's well-proportioned overall. Ugartechea builds them on three different frames, one for 12s and 16s, one for 20s, and a third for 28s and .410s. I've always thought the 16s should have been made on the 20-gauge frame rather than the 12, but a real 28-gauge frame was a special delight, particularly in that price class.

The stocks, too, are nicely scaled. The 28's splinter forend could be a bit slimmer for aesthetics, but in practical terms it's about right, putting just enough wood into the palm of my left hand to provide a good grasp on the barrels. The wrist is also thick enough to hold and slim enough to feel good. Standard dimensions are $14^{1}/_{2}$ inches pull to center, the same length to the heel, and 15 inches to the toe. Bend is $1^{1}/_{2}$ inches at the comb and $2^{3}/_{8}$ inches at the heel, with about $^{1}/_{4}$-inch cast-off.

These dimensions, combined with the flat rib, create for me a very flat-shooting gun—which is to say, one that prints about two-thirds of the shot charge above the point of hold and a third below. This means you can pick up the target's line of flight and swing right on it and through for the shot, which is the classic technique that Churchill taught and the best of all methods of game shooting.

The Parker-Hale is a gun to be carried and shot, not one to be squirreled away for fair weather. At 5$\frac{1}{2}$ pounds, the test gun is a pleasure to carry, and though the balance would be better moved a bit farther forward (it balances right on the hinge), the handling is surprisingly good.

Both triggers break cleanly at about 4$\frac{1}{2}$ pounds — a bit heavy for a piece this light but not bad for a field gun. The ejectors are good and reliable.

It performed admirably on the skeet field and at the patterning plate with Winchester AA factory loads, printing dense, even patterns and doing maximal damage to clay targets, which of course is what makes the 28-gauge and its $\frac{3}{4}$-ounce shot charge such a wonderful combination.

This gun has neither floss nor frills. The wood is very plain but quite well fitted; checkering is coarse and not well pointed-up. The barrels aren't struck glassy-smooth (but they also are not chrome-lined, which was Precision Sports' choice and a good one). The frame is nicely filed at the fences but a bit crude at the shoulders and shows some file marks. Engraving is better than you see on most guns of this price.

So, you can get better cosmetics, if you're willing to pay for it. But what this gun does best is handle and shoot. As it happened, the test piece arrived a few days before I left for a week of hunting grouse and woodcock in Minnesota. I carried my old Fox at first, but after some long days a case of incipient tennis elbow set in (more to do with age and too much shooting than the racquet-and-net game I do not play), and it started to interfere with my shooting. I didn't lose any wounded birds, thanks to Tober, but they weren't coming down dead, and that was something to be remedied.

Skeet loads, which means No. 9 shot, are great for woodcock and okay for grouse, but I feel more comfortable firing

No. 7¹/₂ at ruffs. Skeet loads, however, were all I'd brought in 28-gauge. As luck would have it, the local Hardware Hank had a few boxes of Remington Express in 28, all of them filled with No. 6 shot—a bit larger than I wanted, but if you've ever tried to buy 28-gauge shells in the outback, you know it's a matter of taking what you can get and being grateful for finding them at all.

The short version of the rest of the story is that the Fox remained in the cabin for the rest of the week. It took about three flushes before I was accustomed to the weight and the triggers, but from then on the Parker-Hale and I had a hell of a good time together. The little gun handled like a champ; the improved-cylinder and modified chokes provided enough reach to take the reasonable shots as they came, and the cartridges did the rest.

Over the three days I carried it, I fired at eight grouse and killed five, and every one was dead when it hit the ground. Only one was an arm's-length shot. People who've never used one tend to think of a 28-gauge in the same class as a .410, a sort of popgun attitude that the 28 doesn't deserve. Give it shot pellets that are heavy enough, and a 28 will reach out with the best of them. By way of illustration, one more story:

Late one chilly, misty morning when the Minnesota woods smelled sweet as a freshly showered woman, Tober and I decided to walk the trails through some old favorite coverts, some of which had been clearcut the year before and were now full of the regrowth aspen that grouse like so much. We'd moved several birds there the day before. At one edge of the regrowth, the trail forked, and I stopped at the junction to let Tobe know which way I wanted to go. The first grouse came up from the popple shoots not ten feet from me and quartered away across the trail, heading for the spruce thicket on the other side. I dropped it at the edge of trees, about fifteen yards away, opened the gun, and was fumbling in my pocket for another shell when the second bird flushed from the same spot. This one bored away along the edge of the regrowth, staying behind the few trees left along that side of the trail. I got my hand loose, closed the gun, reached for the back trigger, and swung on it just as it cut a hard left across the trail to the spruces. Had everything happened a fraction slower I probably wouldn't have taken the shot, because the bird seemed a long, long way off.

But I did fire, and it went down in a welter of feathers—solidly body-shot, dead as a hammer thirty-seven long paces from where I stood. The 28-bore may not be as versatile as some others, but it's no popgun.

Moments like that lend a certain warmth to your view of any gun, whether it's a London best or a gaspipe. The Parker-Hale is neither; it's a damn good gun that you can buy for not much money and take hunting any time. The more I shot the XXV and the longer-barreled 20-bore I got sometime later, the more impressed I became, until I had to conclude that here is a gun that may well represent the best value in a side-by-side you can find anywhere.

And that made all the sadder the news in 1994 that labor disputes had closed the Ugartechea factory, presumably for good. With the source dried up, Precision Sports had no choice but to drop the line. Likewise Bill Hanus, whose house-brand Birdguns were built in the same shop, to the same basic design.

There has been a renaissance—for Ugartechea and for the Birdguns, at least on a limited basis—but you'll have to do some sleuthing to track down a Parker-Hale version, either left over in some gunshop's inventory of new guns or on the used-gun racks. Either way, it's worth the trouble, and more than worth the money.

CHAPTER THIRTY

An Urge to Reproduce

─────────

That form follows function is axiomatic in the natural world. Natural selection ensures that species are in a continual process of change as they adapt more and more closely to the particular niches they occupy. This ongoing flux unfolds too slowly for us to perceive, but it occurs nonetheless.

Much the same has happened with firearms over the past two hundred years. As technology 'has developed, firearms have grown steadily more efficient in fulfilling the various functions we've devised for them. To an eighteenth-century soldier, for instance, one of today's state-of-the-art military rifles would seem as unimaginably exotic as something from outer space might seem to us. Or imagine what Wyatt Earp would think if you handed him an Uzi . . . There's no shortage of examples; take your pick.

But sporting arms are different—shotguns especially. An 1890s bird hunter would recognize a 1990s game gun instantly, because game guns haven't changed much in a hundred years. In fact, you can take a turn-of-the-century gun—a Holland or a Purdey, Woodward, or Boss, let's say—to a shoot in Britain or Europe today and no one will give it a second look; it's virtually identical to a best London gun that was built last year. If you could hand your great-grandfather a Remington 870, he'd know how it works because chances are he spent some time shooting a Winchester Model 93 or Model 97, perhaps even a Model 12.

Sporting guns represent an evolutionary endpoint. Form follows function only to the extent that function is perfectly fulfilled, and then form remains as it is until either the requirements change or some radically new concept for meeting them comes along. Because game birds and the hunting of them haven't changed, it's no wonder that the sporting gun of a hundred years ago is just as useful now as it ever was.

Time was, if you wanted to use one of the American classics, it had to be an old gun because none were in regular production after the early 1960s, and most had been discontinued long before that. The doubles weren't the only casualties, either: The Winchester Model 12 and the Remington Model 31, arguably the two finest pump guns ever built, were gone as well. Remington closed out the Model 31 in 1949. Winchester kept the Model 12 going till 1980, but in 12-gauge only after December 1963.

None were discontinued because they were bad guns, nor were they obsolete. Changing tastes, rising production costs, and the postwar infatuation with sheer firepower brought the curtain down on most of the doubles. Production costs alone finally did in the repeaters. We missed them all, lamented their passing, wished they could somehow be brought back.

That those old guns are the emblems and artifacts of our hunting traditions is enough to explain why a market for reproductions should exist. Given a yearning to recapture something of the tradition by using a traditional gun, who wouldn't be interested in having a brand-new one? Especially as the older ones grow scarcer, more expensive and, if not more feeble as time goes on, at least more prone to mechanical ills.

How to make new ones available at reasonable cost remained the sticking point until the early 1980s, when Tom Skeuse took the remarkable step of contracting with a Japanese factory to produce Parkers. This was remarkable because, like the weather, the idea had endured much talk with little action. But on the other hand, it made perfect sense; Winchester and Browning and a couple of others had already proven that Japanese technology could turn out high-quality guns at economical prices.

Looking back, it's clear that the Parker Reproduction was a

logical, inevitable step in the process that started with the Winchester 101 and progressed through the Browning Citori and BSS. At the time, however, it stirred some controversy and even some consternation. It brought to life a new age, and new ages always take some getting used to. What was this gun? Was it a Parker, a replica, or what? And where did it fit into our concept of values?

Some, apparently offended by the notion of a traditional American gun manufactured in Japan, dismissed it as a second-rate fake. Others, in a line of reasoning I've always found completely mystifying, declared the Parker Reproduction just fine because it "made the old ones worth more." Still others thought it was the niftiest thing since canned beer.

To me, the Parker Reproduction was a lovely star in a firmament full of promise. I spent several weeks field-testing one of the first production 20-gauges and later did the same thing with the prototype Steel Shot Special—a 12-bore I remember fondly as having one of the best sets of barrels I've ever found on any gun. I could understand—vaguely, anyway—how some hard-core Parker fanatics might sneer, as if the Reproduction might contaminate their purity; closed-mindedness is in the nature of fanaticism about anything. But from my own experience, I couldn't see how anyone willing to take the Reproduction on its own merits could fail to be impressed.

And nothing's happened since to change my mind. The exactitude with which the Reproduction mirrors the original Parker is astonishing. As I said in the first piece I wrote on it, in 1985, it's more clone than copy. If you appreciate Parkers for their quality of craftsmanship and reliability, you have to appreciate the Reproductions for the same reasons. And if you're looking for a gun to shoot, you might even like the Reproductions better; after all, the science of metallurgy did enjoy one or two advances during the forty-year hiatus between the old guns and the new. I suspect the Reproductions, gun for gun, will be heir to fewer mechanical problems just because the steels are better.

PARKER REPRODUCTION
WILLIAM W. HEADRICK

Although factory production shut down at the end of 1988, when the plant owners decided there was more money in making auto parts than guns, the inventory of components was such that new Parker Reproductions remained available for a long time. You probably could still find a few, if you looked hard enough. As late as 1994, you could get new DHE Grades in 12-, 20-, and 28-gauge and A-1 Specials in 12 and 20.

Those A-1 Specials are magnificent. You could have one engraved in the standard pattern (more or less, that is, because virtually no two original A-1 Specials are exactly alike) or you could work out your own custom design. Either way, they were done by Geoffroy Gournet, a young French master engraver trained in Belgium and Italy, and employed by Parker Reproductions for several years. Any style of scroll, *bulino*, or gold inlay—you name it, and he can execute it beautifully.

Successful as the Parker Reproduction was, no one followed suit with Japanese-built Lefevers or Foxes or L.C. Smiths. And wisely so. Even though the market clearly was warming to the idea, it was a relatively small market, and reproductions represented largely unknown territory in a field rife with competition. One success by no means assured another. Moreover, none of the other American classics have quite the same following as Parker, so any others would have been pitched at an even smaller population of potential customers.

But "American classic" describes more than just double guns, and at least one sold much better in the old days than all the doubles put together. Find a gunner older than about forty who's never owned a Model 12 Winchester, and you've found a rare bird. There is no more appropriate gun to be the second-born in the modern reproductions family, and this one came from Browning Arms—introduced in 1989 as the Browning Model 12, a 20-gauge offered in two grades.

Like the Parker Reproduction, it was built in Japan as a virtual clone of the original—the same look, the same feel, and, with one important exception, the same mechanics. You can slam-fire an old Model 12; that is, it'll go off if you hold back the trigger and chamber a round with a smart stroke of the slide. This is the Winchester's one serious mechanical short-coming, and Browning designers cured it by adding a sear-block. For safety's sake, it's definitely an improvement.

With more than two million original Model 12s in existence and most of them still perfectly serviceable, Browning never had any illusions that its version would flood the market. In-stead, the company produced the gun as a limited edition of 12,500 copies—8,500 in Grade I and 4,000 in Grade V—and then followed up in 1990 with a similar number of 28-gauges in the same two grades.

Not surprisingly, factory inventories didn't last long, and now I imagine there are virtually no new ones left in dealers' hands. But having spent some time with one of the 28s on a dove pass in Mexico a few years ago, I can tell you that chas-ing down a used one is worth the trouble. I found shucking and reloading a bit fumblesome at first, though it wasn't the gun's fault that I've spent thirty years addicted to break-actions with two barrels. I did shoot a pump as a kid, though, so I soon quit reaching for the other trigger and began working the slide without having to think about it. From that point on, I had a hell of a good time popping mourning doves as they came sweeping in over the Sonoran grassland, enjoying the slightly muzzle-heavy feel that's typical of a pump. The gun was still fairly new, so the action hadn't yet gone as silky as a Model 12 usually gets, but it was on the way. The whole thing felt like being a kid again.

Browning completed the cycle in 1991 with a reproduction of the Winchester Model 42. Although the action is mechani-cally quite different, the 42 is often thought of as the .410 ver-sion of the Model 12, which is fair enough because it looks like a Model 12 in miniature. Cute little things.

Now I have a bad attitude toward .410s as game guns. Ac-tually, the guns are fine; it's the cartridge I don't like—a patchy-shooting, bird-crippling ballistic abomination. But shooting skeet with a .410 is great fun, especially with a gun that's truly scaled and not just a .410 barrel or two hung on a 20-bore frame. In that, the Model 42 really shines.

The only mechanical weakness in the Winchester 42 that I'm aware of is a tendency of the breechbolt to break at the point where it connects with the action bar. As far as I know, Browning made no changes in the design; but once again, I suspect the newer steel will prove more durable.

That Browning should reproduce Winchester guns may seem odd, but there's a certain symmetry in it because John Browning and Winchester had a long, mutually profitable relationship during the 1880s and '90s. During that time, Winchester bought a total of forty-four different Browning designs, usually to keep them out of the hands of other makers, but the ones the company did manufacture allowed Winchester to dominate the industry. (The marriage ended in 1902 when Winchester president T. G. Bennett refused the opportunity to build the A-5 autoloader because Mr. Browning wanted to collect a royalty instead of selling the design outright. In view of subsequent history, it was not the brightest decision Winchester Repeating Arms ever made.)

Anyway, neither the Model 12 nor the Model 42 is a John Browning design, but both are based on principles he established with what became the Winchester models 93 and 97. And that's close enough to serve the intertwining threads of history.

The notion of producing limited editions added a new wrinkle to the reproductions game, one I wouldn't be surprised to see happen again one day with some other venerable old piece. Meanwhile, though, it's all taken an astonishing, and thoroughly welcome, turn with the rebirth of A.H. Fox.

As there's a whole chapter devoted to the new Fox gun (see page 60), I won't rehearse it here, except to note that it's the first time a high-quality double gun has been in full production in this country in more than a generation. That's something I truly never expected to see again.

And one other important point: The new Foxes are not

reproductions but rather as "original" as those built in Philadelphia or in Utica, New York, under Savage Arms ownership. The other chapter explains why; for the purposes of this one, suffice it to say that we have regained a bit of our manufacturing heritage, that at least one facet of the American gunmaking scene is more filled with promise right now than at any time in nearly forty years. And it all started with an urge to reproduce.

CHAPTER THIRTY-ONE

REMINGTON MODEL 32

The Remington Model 32 was born in the depths of the Great Depression and died ten years later, in the darkest days of World War II. Total production never amounted to more than about six thousand units, and no standard version ever sold for more than $200 retail. Judging only from the stats and the fact that its lifespan coincided almost exactly with the worst economic period in American history, you wouldn't give the gun much chance for fame or fortune.

Fortune did prove elusive, at least during those ten years, but the Model 32 owns considerable fame and distinction. It was the first machine-made over/under built in the United States; it was one of the best over/under guns built anywhere; and in a slightly different incarnation, it still is. The Model 32 is a genuine American classic.

In a world awash with over/unders, it's easy to forget that the stack-barreled gun is a relatively recent phenomenon. Although the form itself dates back to flintlock days, the factory-made breechloading over/under is only about sixty years old. (The first over/unders by Boss, Woodward, and Beesley came along earlier, of course, but they were all bespoke articles, largely hand-built, and not production guns.)

As he so often did, John Browning got there first. Fabrique Nationale was tooling up to produce the Superposed when Browning died, in November 1926. And when the gun finally made its appearance on the American scene in 1931, the gun market responded immediately—in somewhat subdued ways, given the state of our economy then, but enthusiastically nonetheless.

The Model 32 was already aborning, for, like Browning, Remington Arms recognized the over/under as a coming thing. Crawford C. Loomis, one of Remington's most prolific designers and the man who invented the superb Model 31 pump gun, had been working on it since May 1930, and the first patent for the design was issued in March 1931. Five more would follow, the last in July 1936. What they describe is a gun that, if not unique, certainly was unlike most everything seen before.

The most strikingly different feature of the Model 32 is its fastening system. Instead of a top latch, an underbolt, or even a mid-breech bolt—all of which are internal—Loomis put the fastener on the outside of the frame, right up on top, as a sliding breech cover. Linked to a top lever, the cover rides in slots milled into the top of the frame and engages rails on either side of the upper barrel, with bearing surfaces tapered to compensate for wear. Because the top-lever linkage is eccentric, the whole thing travels less than a quarter-inch forward and back. In addition to fastening the action, it also acts as a shroud around the juncture of barrels and frame so the shooter's face is shielded from any gases that might blow back through a pierced primer.

There is some evidence that Loomis adapted the idea from an earlier French design. No one is likely to argue that it's the handsomest system ever built, but there's no question that it works.

The action itself operates on trunnions and notches—true trunnions, in fact, because the studs are on the barrels rather than in the frame—and the Model 32 was the first factory over/under so built. This actioning, now virtually the world standard, not only creates the shallowest possible profile, but also takes advantage of the over/under's inherent superiority in recoil dynamics. Unlike the bores of a side-by-side, which lie on a plane well above the shooter's shoulder, an over/under's barrels—especially the bottom one—align almost level with the heel of the stock. This is particularly true of guns with a trunnion hinge, and it means that over/unders tend to recoil nearly straight backward. Moreover, because the stacked barrels are not liable to the down-flip characteristic of side-by-sides, recoil from the first barrel is less disruptive to the second shot.

Another of the Model 32's novel features (novel at the time, anyway) is the absence of fillets or side ribs. Leaving them off saves an ounce or two and permits slightly thicker-walled barrels for the same balance and weight. More important, open space between the barrels is a definite advantage in target shooting because it helps dissipate heat, which affects a shooter's vision and produces some physical changes in the barrels as well. It's hard to see a target if you're looking through the shimmering mirage of heat waves. And as a barrel heats up from firing, the steel expands; this can change the point of impact.

If heat-expansion were a dire matter, most of the world's great over/unders wouldn't be worth a damn as target guns, but it *can* be a problem, and the Model 32 avoids it by means of a slip-ring barrel hanger. In the prototypes and the first few production guns, the barrels were soldered together at the muzzles. Presently, however, Remington introduced what it called the "Floating Barrel"—a hanger soldered to the top tube that forms a loop around the bottom one, so either barrel can expand and contract without affecting the other.

Single triggers were nothing new in 1932, but truly good ones were rare. The first Superposed guns had two triggers, each of which functioned like a single, but the now-standard Browning trigger was still a few years off. The first Model 32s had double triggers as well. A single was standard for the target models by 1937, and all models had it by the following year.

It's a peach—crisp, light of pull, and designed to shift sears mechanically. A few current guns have better triggers and faster lock times than the old Model 32s, but not many. The selector is on the front end of the trigger itself, so there's not nearly so much chance of jamming as there is with one that operates from the safety thumb-piece.

The Model 32 safety has some niceties of its own. By placing a set-screw in one of three holes in the side of the top tang, you can make it automatic or manual, or disable it altogether. You have to remove the buttstock to do this but, because the stock is attached with a drawbolt, it's not a great chore. The safety system isn't quite as simple as the old-style L.C. Smith three-position safety, but it's just as convenient and, in the disabling feature, more positive, especially for target and pigeon shooting.

The Model 32 came onto the market in March 1932 and was hailed with great acclaim. In the May 1932 issue of *The American Rifleman*, F. C. Ness said, "Its advent marks the beginning of a new era for shotgun enthusiasts because the low price achieved at last places the over-and-under type of gun within reach of the average gunner." Ness was exactly right; in its first year the standard Model 32 sold for $75. A Browning Superposed cost $107.50 at the time. The difference then was far more significant than it is today.

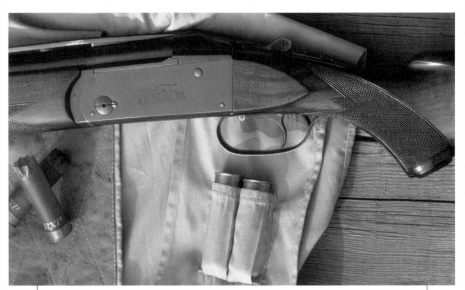

REMINGTON MODEL 32
MICHAEL McINTOSH

Still, it was a small market in a world struggling with economic disaster. No American gunmaker prospered in the 1930s; and though both the Superposed and the Model 32 piqued a lot of interest, actual sales were few. So were the guns' days. After the German army overran Belgium in May 1940, all of the arms factories in Liège, including FN, were immediately converted to the production of military weapons. American makers did the same in 1942. The Superposed came back in 1948; the Model 32 never did.

At least it never came back under its original name nor in the Remington factory. In the late 1940s, the German firm of Heinrich Krieghoff—recently relocated from its old premises in Suhl to new quarters in Ulm—bought manufacturing rights to the Model 32. The gun has gone through some design and name changes, but it's still being built by Krieghoff, still essentially the old Remington, and still one of the best guns in the world.

For its own part, Remington never forgot its accomplishment. In the late '60s, when computer technology opened a new world of gun design and manufacture, Remington assigned designer John Linde and a team of engineers to do what Crawford Loomis had done a generation before: Create an over/under that offered high quality at a reasonable price. They named the result the Model 3200 and introduced it to the market in 1973. It wasn't a $75 gun, but at a base price of $450, it certainly was the equivalent.

The 3200 looks a lot like the Model 32, with the same sliding-cover fastener, separated barrels, and other basic features, but the two are quite different internally. The 3200 is considerably more massive both in the frame and in the barrel breeches. The safety pivots rather than slides, a clever arrangement that some shooters like immensely and others don't. I've never cared for it, but it certainly works.

The lockwork and the trigger were redesigned to achieve a lock time even faster than the Model 32's; pull the trigger of a 3200 and only 1.6 milliseconds elapse before the striker hits the primer. I've fired a few 3200s with triggers that seemed just a wee bit creepy, but only a few. In general, it's one of the best triggers ever.

Like its predecessor, the 3200 was built only in 12-gauge, and it's a heavy devil—nearly 8 pounds even in the lightest field version. The weight turns off most game gunners, but target shooters love the way it dampens recoil.

In the mid-'80s, during the height of my skeet-shooting addiction, the rib on my favorite Superposed came loose, and while it was off being repaired, I spent nearly a whole summer shooting a 3200 on loan from one of my partners. With 1-ounce handloads, 200- or 300-target days were a breeze; $7/8$-ounce loads made it feel like a 28-gauge. And it was the best doubles gun I've ever fired—which is to say the only gun that ever allowed me to post perfect scores in the event where you shoot doubles-only at every station. I was truly sorry to give it back.

While the old Model 32 was about as free of flaws and weaknesses as a gun can be, the 3200 wasn't. For some reason, whether design or execution, the forends have a persistent tendency to crack. I'm told Remington still has a little milling machine in the factory dedicated solely to making new forends, even though the Model 3200 hasn't been in production since 1984.

I don't know how many 3200s were built, but they're fairly easy to find on the used-gun market. They're just as good for trap and skeet as ever, and they make wonderful sporting clays guns.

So do Model 32s, but they're hard to come by. Which isn't surprising for a gun built in such small numbers so long ago. To compound the problem, finding one that hasn't been re-blued, restocked, altered, tinkered with, or outright butchered is more difficult still. In their day they were available in three elaborately engraved high grades—32D Tournament, 32E Expert, 32F Premier—but finding one of those is damn near impossible. Not even Remington knows how many were actually built, and in thirty years of serious fooling with guns I've seen exactly one, a 32E.

But difficult to find or not, if you own a taste for truly fine over/unders and for American classics, a Model 32 is well worth the trouble.

CHAPTER THIRTY-TWO

ANOTHER LOOK AT
L.C. SMITH

It sometimes seems as if the closing years of the twentieth century have become the Age of Reassessment. It seems we've become preoccupied with reevaluating our own past. I suppose it has something to do with the imminence of a new millennium, but whatever the reason, we Americans are now intensely fond of taking new looks at everything from our political motives and presidents to our institutions and cultural heroes—from Manifest Destiny to John Kennedy, from the U.S. Navy to Billy the Kid. Sometimes the intent appears mainly sensational, sometimes even mean. For the most part, though, I think we've simply grown more interested in getting a new perspective on some things we've accepted without much question in the past.

That being the case, consider this: At almost any time in the past hundred years you could ask a shooting man to name the best American guns and almost always get an answer that began, "Well, there's Parker and Smith. . . ." After that, the order might have varied a bit, depending on whom you were talking to, but those two have long been the reigning pair of American gunmaking. It's as if they were a vaudeville team—a suave, polished headliner and a supporter whose contrast filled out the substance of the act. Laurel and Hardy. Abbott and Costello. Burns and Allen. Martin and Lewis. Parker and Smith—or, to use their nicknames, Old Reliable and Elsie.

They weren't really a team, of course. In fact, Parker and Smith were fierce competitors in the gun market. But the metaphor isn't so far-fetched, especially in the notion of contrast.

Actually, the L.C. Smith is in some ways a contrast to virtually every other American gun. The most salient difference is that it's the only true sidelock among the best-known products of the American trade. Dan Lefever's Automatic Hammerless guns do have sideplates, but in the early version (from about 1890 to 1897) only a few lock parts are mounted on the plates, and in the later version all the parts are fastened to the frame. Baker Gun Works built some sidelocks until about 1915, but Bakers never achieved a reputation to equal Smith's.

Because I intend to focus mainly on the virtues and shortcomings of the Smith gun itself, I'll not rehash the details of its production history. Those you can find in the late William Brophy's excellent *L.C. Smith Shotguns* and in the L.C. Smith chapter of my book *Best Guns.* For a basic historical perspective, suffice it to say that Lyman Cornelius Smith was not a gunsmith but rather a businessman whose career in gunmaking began in September 1877 at Syracuse, New York, manufacturing guns designed by his partner, William Henry Baker.

Baker left the company in 1880 and went to Ithaca, where he became one of the founders of what would be Ithaca Gun Company. Although Smith continued to build Baker-patent guns for several years, the L.C. Smith gun as we know it first came on the market May 1, 1884—the brainchild of Alexander T. Brown. The hammerless version, which Brown also designed, appeared in 1886.

In 1890, Smith sold his gun works to the Hunter family of Fulton, New York, and went on to make a fortune manufacturing typewriters. The Hunter Arms Company, through several changes of ownership, continued building L.C. Smith guns until it went bankrupt in April 1945. Marlin bought it a few months later and resumed production under the style L.C. Smith Gun Company. That lasted until January 1949, when the main floor of the old factory collapsed and destroyed most of the machinery. Marlin issued the last L.C. Smith catalog in 1950 to sell off the remaining inventory.

Hammerless Smiths went through three different grading

systems—the first from 1886 till the early 1890s, another from then till 1913, and a third for the remainder of the gun's production history.

The American gun market was brutally competitive during the first decade of this century, and when recessions beset the economy in the early 1910s, gunmakers began looking for ways to lower their manufacturing costs. Fox, for example—recently bankrupt and under new ownership—changed its standard engraving patterns in an effort to reduce the amount of handwork that went into the guns.

The Hunters' approach was more radical. To that point, L.C. Smith frames and sideplates were filed and sculpted in a complex system of arcs and curves. It was handsome but expensive, and it had to go if the guns were to hold their own against the competition. From 1913 on, frames were blockier, lockplates filed to more straightforward shapes. Engraving and checkering were coarser, especially in the lower grades.

Although the changes were significant, they were almost entirely cosmetic, with one important exception. Pre-1913 Smiths have a clever three-position safety system. From the middle, or on-safe, position, you can push the thumb-piece either forward or back. Moved forward, it will automatically click back to on-safe when you operate the top lever; pulled back, it stays off-safe till you manually slide it to the middle. Game shooters tend to like automatic safeties while target shooters don't. With an old-style Smith, you can have it either way.

Otherwise, every hammerless Smith is virtually identical mechanically, and in the mechanics lie the greater share of old Elsie's dimples—and some of her pimples as well.

For one thing, the cocking system is unique, and not just among American guns. Starting with Anson & Deeley's revolutionary means of using leverage from the barrels to arm the locks, levers and pushrods have been the standard approaches to cocking hammerless guns. Alexander Brown chose to use torque instead.

L.C. Smith cocking rods are right where you'd expect them

L.C. SMITH CROWN LONG RANGE
WILLIAM W. HEADRICK

to be—in channels down either side of the action bar. But the exposed ends are in the form of cranklike levers that fit into a milled recess in the forend iron; these cranks rotate as the barrels pivot on the hinge pin, and cams at the inner ends lift the tumblers to where the sears can drop into bent. It's an odd system but surprisingly effective, thanks mainly to the rods being beautifully hardened. In order to work, they have to absorb an ungodly amount of stress, and they do. I'm sure some have died under the strain, but I don't recall ever seeing a Smith with a broken cocking rod—and I've seen a lot of Smiths, some of which have been used to the point of being used up.

I can't really argue that the system is any better than a more conventional approach, only that it works. But it also can be frustrating, because if you trip the locks when the forend is off, you can't put the forend back on without recocking the locks by hand. The factory made a special tool with which to do this, and also to relieve mainspring tension while disassembling the locks, but you have to remove the locks in order to use it.

Actually, you can recock a Smith using pliers or any stout lever—like a screwdriver shaft—without pulling the locks, but if you've never done it, ask someone who has for a demonstration before you try. There's no sense risking damage to a good gun.

If I had to name the single most important feature that makes the L.C. Smith a great gun, it would be the fastener. Alexander Brown wasn't the first to recognize that bolting a gun's action at the top of the standing breech is a sound mechanical theory, but he accomplished this in a way that no one else had done before. The Smith top hook is a cylinder that rotates on a horizontal axis. A slot milled into this forms the actual hook, and the hook fits into a matching slot in the rib extension. As a secondary fastener, the extension has a lip at the rear, which is engaged by a portion of the cylinder.

Company literature referred to this as a "double cross-bolt," and while in most guns the two bearing surfaces are not fitted equally closely, there's no question that the idea works extremely well—well enough that you'll find it copied in the early hammerless Ithacas, in D.M. Lefever guns, and in Ansley Fox's guns built by Philadelphia Arms.

Good as they are in some respects, Smiths are open to criticism in others. It would be nice if the lockwork included intercepting sears, but it doesn't. Jar a Smith lock off the sear with a hard blow, and the gun will fire.

The single trigger, officially known as the Hunter One-Trigger, is possibly the worst of its kind to be used on an American gun. Actually, there were two Smith single triggers; one was patented in 1903 and the other, an improved version, in 1915. Both were designed by Allen E. Lard, of St. Joseph, Missouri. Lard triggers are notable in that they were among the very first manufactured in America, but they are notorious for being complicated and delicate. When they work, they're fine; when they don't, they cause gunsmiths to take up voodoo, coarse language, and strong drink—especially if they've been tinkered with by someone who didn't know what he was doing.

The stocks aren't much better, at least on lower-grade guns. You'll sometimes hear it said that sidelock guns are inherently weak in the stock because wood must be removed to make room for the locks. Not so. In fact, most sidelock stocks are more durable than those on boxlocks. Stocks have to accommodate lockwork no matter where it is, and taking wood out of the sides leaves a larger bearing surface against the frame than if you take it out of the middle, as must be done for a boxlock. Moreover, sideplate locks held together by a transverse pin provide the stock head with lateral support that no boxlock does.

But an L.C. Smith is not your typical sidelock gun. Thanks to the design—and the fact that rough inletting was done by machine—there's less actual bearing surface between wood and steel in a Smith than in a sidelock made on the English pattern. Combine this with a couple of other factors, and an L.C. Smith with a split stock is almost a redundancy.

One culprit is that the lockplates are filed square at the

edges, rather than chamfered slightly toward the inside. Because the inletting is customarily quite tight, the whole surface of the lock edge bears against the wood. When the wood absorbs ambient moisture and swells slightly, the fit is closer still—so recoil turns the lockplates into wedges that drive back against the stock at its thinnest point. Cracks behind the locks show up most often in lower-grade Smiths because the low-grade guns were stocked in American walnut, which is more brittle than European walnut.

You can help prevent this—or keep it from getting worse, if it's already happened—by having a good stockmaker slightly undercut the inletting at the rear of the plates. I've had it done to a couple of my Smiths, and it seems to relieve the pressure enough to keep the stocks intact.

This is a good thing, because some stockmakers demand a premium for putting new wood on an L.C. Smith. I would if I were a stocker. Simply put, it's a bitch of a job, partly because there's so little bearing surface that I'd hate to have to guarantee the work, and partly because whoever designed the wood-to-metal relationship (I assume it was Alexander Brown) arranged things in such a way that one limb of the top-lever spring bears against the wood. Why is beyond me, but there it is. If you're ever tempted to take the stock off your Smith, you'd do well to resist unless you have a dire need for misery in your life. Getting it back on is a bear.

Despite these shortcomings, though, it seems to me that the L.C. Smith truly deserves its reputation as one of America's best guns. No factory-built piece can come off very well judged against a top-quality gun built in England or Europe, but such comparison is an unfair exercise in apples and oranges. Among its peers, the Smith can hold its own. Its lines aren't as pleasing to my eye as those of a Fox or Lefever, but it owns a good measure of slender, handsome grace nonetheless. The high grades are extremely well finished, and if the best Smith engraving isn't quite as good as the best you'll see on a Parker or Lefever, it's still better than most.

For shooting qualities, a steel-barreled Smith in good mechanical order is a delight. In the older guns, stocks usually have more drop than anyone needs, and bending them to better dimensions is tricky because the head has to be specially supported or it's likely to crack. But if you harbor a yen to shoot a real American classic, having the job done by a top-notch professional is worth the expense.

One important part of Elsie's charm is that she's a part of us, part of the halcyon years of American gunmaking. The first really good gun I ever owned was late-production Field Grade 20-bore that somehow got factory-stocked with a gorgeous piece of fiddleback walnut. It was bored a bit too tightly for quail, but it was dandy for pheasants and doves. We spent some good days together, enough of them to make a soft spot in my heart for L.C. Smiths that's never gone away. I've owned quite a few more over the years and wish I still had most of them.

I fancy I know a bit more about guns than I did back then and believe I'm capable of taking a harder-nosed view on what's good and what isn't. Elsie isn't perfect, but no matter how hard I look, she still seems sweet after all these years.

CHAPTER THIRTY-THREE

SYMES & WRIGHT

"The thing about the British sporting gun," Geoffrey Boothroyd said, peering at me over the reading glasses perched on his nose, "is that it's a total anachronism."

"Indeed it is," I agreed, peering back over my own glasses. "It's a relic of horse-and-carriage days, and by all rights it should have gone obsolete seventy-five years ago. But why didn't it?"

"Tradition, for one thing," Geoffrey said. "The tradition of British-style shooting. That, and craftsmanship of the sort one only finds in a handmade object—which in turn leads to a sort of quality that's unmistakable but very difficult to describe."

"It's also a quality that people respond to almost instinctively," David Trevallion said. "Which is a good thing, because otherwise we'd all three be out of work."

We were sitting in Geoffrey's study at the time, he, David, and I—two writers and a gunmaker trained in the finest London tradition. David and I had taken a couple of days out from a footloose tour of the London trade and flown to Glasgow to spend some time with the dean of British gun writers.

Predictably, the conversation that afternoon and evening centered on the English gun trade and the nature of quality—subjects both inexhaustible and inseparable, since the English trade established the standards by which gunmaking quality has been judged for two hundred years. Much of the old trade is now gone, of course, which is just cause for regret. But David and I had in previous days seen firsthand that it isn't all gone, that the splendid anachronism has life in it still, that while the quantity of craftsmanship in the English trade may have withered, old standards of quality have by no means disappeared.

Just a few weeks before our visit with Geoffrey, I had met Peter Symes and looked over some guns from what was then the newest London maker, Symes & Wright. Peter was in his early thirties at the time, a gunmaker since the age of sixteen. That's when he followed his older brother's lead and signed on as an apprentice at Purdey's to learn barrelmaking under the tutelage of George Wood. In 1982, his apprenticeship complete, he hired on with Paul Roberts, whose company, J. Roberts, also owns the old firm of John Rigby. Symes came to the United States in 1984 and spent a year working at Champlin Arms in Enid, Oklahoma.

Back in London, he freelanced for a while as a barrel-maker and then teamed up with finisher Alex Wright, another former Purdey's man, to do repair and restoration work and to build the occasional gun for the trade. Adam Davies, a stocker trained at Purdey's, joined the little company shortly after. Eight months later, seeking better financial security than freelancing could provide, Wright left, and in 1987 Symes and Davies set up a company under the style of Symes & Wright Ltd. The premises amounted to a tiny workshop at 15 Micawber Street, near the City Road in North London.

A year later, with the first three guns in proof and nearing completion, Davies sold his interest, and Symes & Wright moved south of the Thames, to a building at 66 Great Suffolk Street also occupied by Paul Roberts and Rigby's. In March 1991, Symes moved again, to roomier quarters at 8 Monmouth Place. By then, the company had completed nineteen guns and two magazine rifles and was holding orders for ten side-by-sides, eight over/unders, and three double rifles. All but one of the finished guns were sidelock ejector side-by-sides in either Purdey or Holland & Holland style. The other was an over/under made in the Woodward mold.

And in the spring of 1991, one of the side-by-sides came

into my hands as a review piece, a gun built for Michael Krause, who acted as Symes's American agent.

It was Symes & Wright No. 15, a 12-bore game gun of traditional style, a sidelock ejector with two triggers, fitted with a splinter forend, trimly stocked from the fences to the checkered butt—which amounted to a considerable distance, actually. Mike Krause is not a huge man, but he's taller than I, with longer arms, and his stock is 16¼ inches from the front trigger to the center of the butt—a full inch longer than my guns, but more on that presently.

To balance the long stock, Mike asked for a longer forend and rightly chose 30-inch barrels, which he had bored with 2³/₄-inch chambers at one end, improved-cylinder and modified at the other. The barrels are chopper-lump construction, are fitted with a hollow, swamped, game-type rib, and, according to the stamps, were approved by the London Proof House in 1990. (Also according to the stamps, they are proofed to a mean working pressure of 850 BAR. You'll see similar markings on new English guns from now on, because the London and Birmingham Proof Houses went metric at the end of the 1980s. I hate it. Everybody I've talked to hates it. There wasn't a bloody thing wrong with the old system of tons pressure and ounces of shot, but it's gone. At least the damn BAR stamps are out of sight, on a side-by-side gun, anyway.)

Mike chose a Purdey-type action, a self-opener in which the locks cock on closing. Like all self-openers, it's a bit stiff to close, but properly fitted and polished, it's smoother than most. In the notes I made, there is a single word under "Action Working"—silky. Think of how buttery the action of a fine old gun gets after years of use; that's how this one felt, and I have no doubt it felt that way before Mike ever saw it as a finished gun.

While I had it, I put the gun to every test and scrutiny I could think of, short of taking it to pieces, and the closer I looked, the better it looked.

You can learn a lot about how well a set of barrels is made by ringing them. To do so, hang them over your finger by the action hook and then with a little backhand flip, strike the fingernails of your other hand against the tubes. If the solder joints are sound, the whole thing rings with a clear tone. If it doesn't—if the sound is dull and clunky—something's amiss. If a new set of barrels doesn't ring, they weren't soldered properly to begin with; if it's an old set, then the solder has begun to crystallize, and one of the ribs is likely to come loose soon.

The Symes & Wright barrels rang with such a pure, consistent tone that I was able to find it on a piano—a perfect C-sharp (or D-flat, depending on what key you're in). If there weren't enough bad jokes in the world already, I'd call this a well-tuned gun.

Instead, I'll call it a beautifully built gun, and that's no joke. Besides their sweet ring, the barrels show flawless boring and striking, without even the slightest ripple. Wall thickness is about as consistent as wall thickness can be.

A smooth action in a new gun means one of two things: Either a lot of attention went into making it so, or else it wasn't jointed to very close tolerances in the first place. To detect sloppy jointing, or a worn joint in an older gun, take the forend off, hold it by the barrels, and rap the stock from various angles with the heel of your hand. You'll feel some secondary vibration if there's any looseness in the joint, perhaps even hear it rattle.

This does not, however, work very well with a self-opening gun, because spring tension in the opening mechanism holds the barrels tightly against the fasteners even when the forend is off. You can still use the test I just described with a Purdey-style self-opener, but you have to take the locks off first and thereby relieve the tension. Since I don't make a habit of applying screwdrivers to other people's guns, I used an alternative test, which is to remove the forend, open the action just slightly, and flex the barrels from side to side while holding the top lever open. If there's slack in the joint, you'll feel it.

Bottom line in this case is that Gary Hibbert, who actioned the Symes & Wright, did a splendid job. As some further insight on the quality of jointing and breeching, David Trevallion later spent some time shooting Symes & Wright No. 1 at an English shooting grounds in a pouring rain. The breeching was close enough to be watertight. He also mentioned that the stock finish on that gun and on a Symes & Wright over/under he also shot stood up extremely well to three hours in the rain.

I didn't take Mike's gun out in the rain, nor even stick it under the shower, but stockmaker Andy Marshal clearly knows his stuff, too. In keeping with the Purdey-style action, the stock proportions are all Purdey-standard, the wood beautifully fitted and shaped. Maybe another stockmaker could find some flaw

SYMES & WRIGHT
JACK POLLER, SYMES & WRIGHT

in the woodwork, but I couldn't—except perhaps to say that the checkering, which is about 26 lines to the inch, shows just the slightest bit of waviness. I mention this not as a serious criticism but rather as a sign of just how picky I had to get in order to find something even marginally quarrelsome.

In the same vein, I went over every visible metal-to-metal joint with an eight-power glass. At that magnification, it's easy to follow the outlines where the trigger plate and lockplates meet the frame, but they don't look like joints; they look like hairlines scribed with a fine-point graver.

Peter Symes typically has his Purdey-action guns decorated with small scroll and bouquets, and his Holland-type guns with the bolder Holland-style large scroll, often commissioning the work to Rashid el Hadi, a young man who is earning a substantial reputation as an engraver. If the customer prefers some other sort of decoration, custom engraving and inlay are readily available at additional cost.

As a reflection of his fondest hunting experiences, Mike Krause chose a combination of scroll and game birds—pintails on the left lockplate and pheasants on the right, both in ovals outlined with gold carved in a laid-rope design. The birds are engraved in relief, nicely shaped and highly detailed.

For the trigger plate, Mike asked for a *bulino* rendering of his golden retriever, done from a portrait painted by his old friend Eldridge Hardie. The execution is virtually photographic.

As to the trigger guard, Mike says, "While Pete and Rashid and I were discussing the decoration I wanted, Rash noticed my Naval Academy class ring and asked to borrow it. He was a jewelry maker before he started engraving, and the design caught his eye—so much so that when he showed me the sketches for my gun, I found my class ring on the trigger guard. The idea never occurred to me until then, but I liked it, so I agreed. I'm glad he suggested it; it makes the gun even more personal."

And so, you'd think, would a 16$^{1}/_{2}$-inch stock, at least to the point of making the gun difficult for most others to handle. Having found the balance quite lively, the triggers light and crisp, and the ejectors perfectly timed, I was anxious to get onto the clays course but not very optimistic about how well I was going to shoot.

That I shot it as well as I can shoot any gun therefore came as a pleasant surprise. As best I can figure, being conscious of the extra length prompted me to push the gun well forward as I started the swing and mount, which in turn ensured that I was moving it aggressively right from the start. In any event, it was a pure pleasure to shoot.

My shooting chums, most of whom use shorter stocks than I, found the same thing. To a man, they'd mount the gun a couple of times, say, "Boy, that's a long stock," then break a couple of targets and say, "Boy, this thing shoots!" Not that any of us have gone thundering off to have 16-inch stocks put on our guns, but it does suggest that good balance and good triggers contribute more to good shooting than we fully appreciate.

Try as I might, I couldn't find one serious criticism to level against this gun, which is about the only time that happened during my entire tenure as *Shooting Sportsman*'s gun-review editor. Maybe if I'd pulled it to pieces I might have found some inner flaw, but I doubt it. Guns this well made usually are just as good inside as out.

Unfortunately, time and economics were not kind to Symes & Wright; by the mid-'90s orders simply dried up, and the company folded. But not before completing perhaps two dozen-odd guns that are still out there, proving that the London gun remains one of the most valuable anachronisms we could possibly have.

CHAPTER THIRTY-FOUR

WINCHESTER MODEL 21

———————

Winchester's Model 21 is the classic American double gun in its most modern form. All the other great ones—Parker, Fox, L.C. Smith, Lefever, and Ithaca—were designed and first produced before the turn of the century or just after, and except for Fox, their most highly evolved incarnations amount to updated versions of guns developed in the days of black-powder cartridges.

The Model 21 is the Johnny-come-lately of American doubles, and it could hardly have come at a less auspicious time in history. Designed in the late 1920s and put into production in 1929, the first 21s were delivered to warehouse inventory in March 1930. At that moment, the American economy was a shambles, and the world economy would soon be no better off. Winchester Repeating Arms itself was poised on the brink of a deep drain, as imprudent expansion of the manufacturing plant prompted by World War I combined with a series of fixed-price contracts to wreck the old company on the reefs and shoals of the post-war world.

On December 22, 1931, John Olin bought the Winchester assets at the federal courthouse in St. Louis. He and his family were already highly successful manufacturers of powder and brass, and Olin shrewdly reasoned that owning a gun company would place his Western Cartridge Company in a virtually unassailable position, no matter what depths the economy might eventually reach.

Among the diverse products Olin inherited with the Winchester purchase was a new double gun, and it captured his fancy. By taking a supremely hard-nosed approach to reducing the product line, trimming the workforce, and managing for maximum profit, Olin by 1934 had transformed a bankrupt company into one that logged some $17 million in sales. That figure reached almost $30 million in 1937.

And the double gun continued to captivate him. It was the wrong gun at the wrong time for what was fast becoming a non-market, but it fit Olin's concept of what he wanted Winchester to become. (This in itself was somewhat less than realistic; Ned Schwing, whose superb book *Winchester's Finest: The Model 21* was brought out in 1990 by Krause Publications, tells me that Olin considered the English gun trade to be the 21's prime competition.)

And perhaps not so surprising, American shooters began to notice the Model 21 as well.

WINCHESTER MODEL 21 · CUSTOM ENGRAVED
WILLIAM W. HEADRICK

Despite the fact that it eventually became the darling of such influential gun writers as Jack O'Connor and others, the Model 21's chief claim to fame is that it's damn near indestructible, a fact that Olin proved beyond any argument with the famous proof-load destruction test of the 1930s. Taking a Model 21 at random from inventory and bringing together an armload of guns from well-respected European makers, Olin directed Winchester technicians to fire them all with proof-load cartridges until only one was left.

Winchester's proof cartridge was loaded to generate about 16,500 units of chamber pressure, half again more than any load produced by the American ammunition industry. A Purdey digested sixty of them before it broke down, a BSA gun 150, and when the Model 21 was still intact after 2,000 rounds, Olin declared the test conclusive. The gun showed no damage as a result.

Although the whole affair was conclusive only to the extent of proving that a Model 21 is decidedly overbuilt, Winchester made a lot of advertising hay from it, and it was decades before anyone thought to question the comparisons as an exercise in apples and oranges.

Nonetheless, there's no question that a Model 21 is hell for stout, and being overbuilt, which is typical of American guns, doesn't necessarily make for a clumsy, ponderous piece. Short-barreled 12-bore 21s tend to be a bit clubby, but the 16s and 20s are as smooth-handling as any.

The 21 is the only American gun built with chopper-lump barrels and one of the few made anywhere with barrels that interlock with a dovetail joint. The Winchester designers borrowed the idea from Belgian gunmaker Henri Pieper, and the marketing people predictably took pains to point out what a strong system it is. Which is true enough, though you can grow old and gray trying to find a well-made set of conventional chopper-lump barrels that show any likelihood of coming apart.

The fastening system—a single-bite under-bolt—is quite simple and, thanks in part to the fact that the 21 has one of the longest action bars of any side-by-side gun, it is also quite effective. A setscrew in the barrel lump provides means of adjusting the depth to which the bolt enters the bite, thus compensating for wear on the bearing surfaces.

The earliest Model 21s were made with double triggers and extractors. Ejectors and a single trigger soon came available as options and eventually were standard. The ejectors are quite good, and for the most part, so is the trigger. Trigger problems seem to show up most often in Model 21s that have been restocked, especially those restocked by gunsmiths who aren't aware that reducing the distance between the top and bottom tangs can have profound ill effects on the trigger mechanism.

Barrels and frames were made of high-quality chrome-molybdenum steel, and stocks of American walnut. At first, the stocks weren't particularly well shaped. As the story goes, Olin and Frank Parker, of the Parker gun family, were hunting ducks together in the fall of 1934, and Parker remarked that while Olin's Model 21 was a nice gun, the stock looked a lot like a canoe paddle. Olin took the comment to heart, and thereafter the standard 21 stock was slimmer and straighter, the pistol grip more defined, and the whole appearance considerably handsomer.

A beavertail forend was standard among later guns. Though I generally don't care much for beavertails on side-by-sides, the Model 21's is an exception. It's slender enough that it doesn't feel like a two-by-four and still serves the beavertail's function—which is to protect your forward hand as the barrels heat up from firing.

With so much emphasis placed on strength, there is inevitably a trade-off in weight. The Model 21, almost regardless of gauge or configuration, is heavier than it needs to be. You will have a tough time finding a 12-bore that scales less than $7\frac{1}{2}$ pounds, and the really big ones—the trap guns and wildfowlers—often run 8 pounds or more. Even the daintiest (relatively speaking, of course) 20-gauges seldom weigh less than $6\frac{1}{2}$ pounds.

In this, however, the Model 21 is no different from most American guns, and it's just something you'll have to live with if you have a hankering to own one—a hankering for which there is much to be said. It may not be the handsomest of domestic doubles, but you'll have to look a long time to find one more durable or one that better characterizes the last great age of the American factory gun.

PART THREE

SURVEYS

CHAPTER THIRTY-FIVE

BEST BUYS

Of the questions that come my way in a typical year, quite a few go something like: "I'm looking for a new [or better] bird gun, and I have X-number of dollars to spend. What do you recommend?"

A good question, and eminently sensible. It would be nice if price were no object in buying guns. Actually, that's one of the things I have planned for us if I'm ever asked to help design a perfect world. In the meantime, though, price is an object and will likely remain so. Which, of course, makes getting the most for your money an important concern.

The question of value isn't always a simple one, because value can mean different things according to how you approach it. Beyond a certain level of craftsmanship, it's almost impossible to separate the component elements of a fine gun; materials, fit, finish, function, and decoration all combine to create something greater than the sum of parts.

On the other hand, this doesn't necessarily apply to guns of more modest cost. There, value is easier to define in practical terms, and therefore easier to correlate with a price tag.

In 1991, with this idea in mind, I departed from the usual approach to my *Shooting Sportsman* gun-review column and, instead of focusing on a single gun, surveyed a number of guns in various price ranges. Some had been subjects of earlier columns, others were to be covered in future ones, and yet others never got reviewed, period; but all of them seemed to me good values—by which I mean they are guns whose intrinsic merits could justify prices higher than their actual cost.

Times have changed since that piece appeared in print.

Some guns that were then available new are no longer in production, a few new models have come on the scene, and for the most part, prices have gone up a little or a lot. What follows here is a full-scale update—because the question of value is every bit as important now as then.

And two points still apply: There are guns I don't mention here, but you shouldn't take that as condemnation by omission. The ones I do mention are the ones I'm most familiar with, ones I know for certain to be good buys. And some of them are available in higher-priced versions than the ones I talk about. The higher prices are mainly matters of better wood and more, or better, decoration. Here, I'll focus on the lowest-priced models or grades and on the intrinsic quality of the gun itself. You'll get the same quality—indeed, the same gun—should you decide to spend more on cosmetics.

Under $1,000

Sometimes it seems as if you can't buy anything for less than a grand these days, much less a *good* gun. The operative word here is good. You can find a lot of guns available for a few hundred dollars apiece, but many of them are poorly assembled from second-rate materials glossed over with showy decoration that creates an illusion of quality. Underneath, you often get badly bored and regulated barrels, clumsy stocks, triggers rough as concrete and hard as stone, ejectors that don't work right, and parts that wear out or break after less than a season's use.

The same is true of some more-expensive guns as well, but the problem seems most acute in the lower price range. Cheap or dear, beauty is as beauty does, and a gun that doesn't is too expensive at any price.

Fortunately, there are still some real winners in the crowd, guns in which the greater portion of production costs clearly has been spent where it really counts.

The SKB Model 505, for instance—a plain, well-made over/under that comes in both 12- and 20-gauge. No frills, just good stuff.

Same is true of Lanber over/unders. Made in the most technologically sophisticated gun factory in Spain, Lanber guns are exceptional values.

Marocchi's Avanza is another good one. Lightweight and nimble in the hands, you can have it as a 12 or a 20.

The Ugartechea boxlocks that were until recently imported under the Parker-Hale marque have long seemed to me the world's best value in a side-by-side. You can still get them in small bores as Bill Hanus Birdguns; otherwise, they belong almost entirely to the secondary market—and they're still great values. (As its economic recovery continues, Ugartechea is once again turning out boxlocks, this time under its own name. They are well finished, stocked with good wood, and sell for $1,375 to $2,010. Aspen Outfitting Company is the source.)

If you're into autoloaders, a couple of Benelli models sell for less than $1,000, as do most of the Berettas, Browning's Gold series, and the venerable A-5. For pumps, there are a whole slew of models from Remington, Mossberg, and Browning, and they're all good, reliable guns.

$1,000–$1,500

Fluctuations in domestic and international economics have conspired in recent years to move some guns out of the high end of the previous category and into this one. They were good buys before, and still are.

In some ways, this price bracket is a watershed; it's where you can expect to find more attention paid to fit and finish. Not that you're likely to find much meticulous hand-work, and certainly no high-quality hand engraving, but you will see somewhat better wood and find evidence of more time spent on details. Still, true value resides in function.

Here's where you find the lower-grade Browning Citoris and Berettas, and Ruger's Red Label. They're all quite different from one another mechanically, but they don't leave much to quarrel with in the quality of materials or workmanship or durability. For function and reliability, you simply can't go wrong buying a Browning, a Beretta, or a Ruger.

As 12-bores, neither Browning nor Ruger is any lightweight. A 12-gauge Ruger, in fact, is entirely too heavy for an upland gun—unless you're about six-foot-five and lift refrigerators for profit or pleasure—but it's a dandy wildfowler. If you're an uplander, you'll like the 20-bore Red Label, and the new 28-gauge version is the only factory over/under in the world available on a true 28-gauge frame at a selling price of less than $3,000.

Most of the SKB over/unders sell in this price range, as does the Tikka Model 512S. Shooters with a bit of gray in their hair will remember the Valmet—built in Finland—as a particularly good gun at a relatively low price. Several years back, the Finnish firms of Sako, Valmet, and Tikka merged to form a single company now known simply as Sako. The old Valmet over/under is now marketed under the Tikka name, and so far as I can see, that's about the only change in it. It's now built in Italy rather than Finland, but the design, which uses a sliding-shroud fastener à la Remington 32 and Krieghoff, appears to be the same.

Most grades of Weatherby's Orion sell here, too, and they're very well worth consideration.

$1,500–$2,000

This range offers more to choose among in terms of decoration and detail. You still won't find much hand engraving, but you will notice more intricately filed frames, handsomer wood, better checkering—in sum, more attention to aesthetics.

This is fine, so long as it isn't done at the expense of function. Triggers may still be somewhat heavy, but they should be crisp and consistent. Any gun in this price range ought to have ejectors, and it goes without saying that they should work properly.

Thanks to economic changes, there aren't as many new guns available in this range as there once were, but some that are offer exceptional value. And to my thinking, the Marocchi Conquista is the best of all.

The Conquista is successor to the superb Marocchi Contrast and is in some ways a better gun. It's built in 12-bore only, in Sporting, Light Sporting, Skeet, Trap, and Lady Sport models, all of which sell for less than $2,000 in Grade I. In terms of mechanics and function, you can spend a lot more and get less.

Most of Beretta's 686-series guns sell in this range, and they're typical Beretta quality, which amounts to 'nough said.

Bernardelli's Roma series begins here, with the Roma 3. They aren't the cheapest Bernardellis, but the Roma guns offer decidedly good value in the way they combine reliable function with a handsome look. These are boxlocks fitted with decorative sideplates, and the amount and quality of decoration grows progressively greater up to Roma 9; so, of course, does the price.

$2,000–$3,000

Here you are fully justified in getting picky about such things as wood-to-metal and metal-to-metal fit. Don't expect micro-hairline joints everywhere, but for this kind of money, the fit should be very close. Any gap of more than a thousandth or two is unacceptable, and there should not be many gaps at all.

Those that meet all the criteria include Beretta's 682 Gold and 687 Silver Pigeon, the mid-grade Brownings, Weatherby's Athena in grades IV and V, and the B. Rizzini over/unders.

$3,000–$4,000

These are in some important ways magic numbers, because they represent the price range of the less-expensive sidelock guns offered by some of the best Spanish makers, notably AyA and Arrieta. As I've gone on at length elsewhere in this book about what exceptional values these guns represent and about the unique niche they occupy, I won't repeat it now. Suffice it to say that this is where high-quality Spanish sidelocks built to order begin.

It's also the price range in which you'll find the high-grade boxlock over/unders from Browning and Beretta.

And I suspect it's about the practical ceiling for those of us who buy guns on limited budgets. Beyond this, quality tends to speak for itself.

CHAPTER THIRTY-SIX

GUNS FOR THE GAME

A new class of guns has come along about once each generation since the turn of the century. Each time, a target game has been the catalyst, and each time form has followed function.

First came the evolution of trap shooting, from live pigeons to clay targets. Pigeon shooting at the traps was a two-shot affair, and still is, but the clay-target form allows only one. Pigeons offer infinite variety in angle and elevation; targets always describe an arc, rising then falling. And so a new gun evolved as well—a break-action single-shot with a long barrel for a smooth swing and precise pointing, a high-combed stock for some built-in lead on a climbing target. Dan Lefever's single trap gun came first, in 1905. The Ithaca Knick, which appeared in 1922, was the last new one till the 1960s. Between-times, all of the great American gunmakers got involved—Baker, Ithaca, L.C. Smith, Parker, and Fox.

As formal trap shooting grew progressively less relevant to game shooting, skeet came on the scene. The standard layout for a skeet field was first published in 1926. Within ten years, more than 1,500 fields existed nationwide, and every gunmaker in America offered at least one gun tailored to the game—short-barreled, quick-handling, stocked to accommodate crossing shots. Adjustable chokes, the likes of Poly and Cutts, became all the rage—less for their effect on patterns than for their ability to lessen muzzle-jump.

Skeet brought a renaissance to shooting in America and lent new vitality to both the gun and ammunition industries. This spilled over to the benefit of peripheral industries as well, those supplying everything from shooting glasses and hearing protectors to cartridge bags and clothing.

By the late 1970s, skeet in its turn was growing moribund, victimized by a mania for high scores that transformed a once-bright, exciting game into a monotonous exercise in endurance. Enter sporting clays, stage south; in 1984, Bryan Bilinski, then manager of the Orvis shop in Houston, set up the first true sporting clays course in the United States. Now, I doubt anyone knows exactly how many there are in the country, but the game's growth in popularity has surpassed even what happened with skeet in the 1930s. If we broaden the view to take in all the accessories and accoutrements, as well as the guns and cartridges and traps, it seems fair to say that no target game has ever had a more widespread revitalizing effect upon shooting in America.

And true to precedent, a new class of guns has evolved along with the game.

By its historical lights, sporting clays was meant to be shot with game guns. The whole idea, as it originated with the London gun trade, was to provide shooters a means of sharpening their skills on birdlike targets. That still is the idea, basically, and any clays course that cannot be adequately shot with a bird gun isn't much of a course.

But so fascinating a game inevitably becomes appealing for its own sake, and this, as it was for trap and skeet, is the germ from which new guns grow. The old axiom about "horses for courses" applied. Obviously, you can shoot any shotgun game with anything that fires a shotshell; whether you shoot it well is another matter. You'll break more skeet targets with a skeet gun than with a trap gun and vice versa. Since sporting clays is in some ways a synthesis of the two—offering the distances of trap and the varied angles of skeet, all in greater abundance—a clays gun clearly cannot be quite so specialized as are the guns tailored for the other games. In fact, a good clays gun is suited about equally well for all. It's not only the proverbial Jack-of-all-trades, but it can be master of all as well.

You don't have to browse far among the clays guns on the market to see that they're essentially more alike than different. The mechanics vary, but the concepts by and large do not. Most important, the features given the greatest emphasis tend to be those that exert the greatest influence on effective shooting, no matter what the target might be.

Although these concepts apply to any gun of any form, the typical sporting clays piece of the moment is a 12-gauge over/under. The boring is mostly a matter of efficiency, since no modern gauge can match the splendid versatility of the 12 nor handle the standard $1^1/_8$-ounce target load so well.

You can effectively shoot just about any clays course with a 16 or 20, and most with a 28. I don't know of any maker that builds clays guns in 16-bore, but quite a few offer 20s.

That the typical clays gun is an over/under also has to do with efficiency but of a sort less easy to quantify. I shoot better at targets with an over/under and better at game with a side-by-side; so does everyone I know who uses both types of gun. I have no ultimate explanation for this. I believe it has something to do with the interrelationships among our hands and our eyes, and also with our ability to see targets from certain angles, but this certainly isn't the whole story. What I know for sure is that an over/under allows me to shoot small targets just a bit more precisely and more consistently than a side-by-side does.

There's no reason why you shouldn't shoot clays with a side-by if that's your fancy, but if you go looking for a gun specific to the game, what you find will be an over/under—unless you opt for an autoloader from Beretta, Browning, or Remington.

One thing you'll notice is that clays guns have brought long barrels back into vogue. Twenty-eight inches or thereabouts is the minimum; 30-inch tubes are common, and a few makers offer clays guns with 32-inch barrels. The reason behind the length is both very simple and very good—in a word, smoothness. In sporting clays, you aren't allowed to pre-mount the gun or even move it from the ready position until you see the target, which means that a clays gun has to be dynamic and handle well. The short-barrel fad, which took hold in this country after World War II, has in my view done more harm to effective shooting than anything else. It created a whole class of fast-starting, quick-stopping, whippy little guns whose handling quality is so hopelessly wretched that they're all but uncontrollable.

If I seem to feel strongly about this, it's for good reason. Like nearly everybody else, I bought into the rubbish that short barrels and muzzle-light balance make a proper bird gun and consequently spent about twenty years struggling to shoot the damn things with any kind of consistency. It was not fun, and I eventually learned better, but too many shooters are still caught in the same snare.

In the hands of all but a few, a muzzle-light gun is a pandemonium of jerks, twitches, wobbles, and pokes waiting to happen. It's all but useless against game birds and even worse for targets. Clay targets do not change course abruptly, and the more smoothly you can trace their flight-lines with your gun barrels, the more you'll break. This means having enough weight in your forward hand to lend optimum control, and the way to get that weight in a factory gun is through longer barrels.

The same concept applies to game guns. Stubby, light-nosed little wands look nice in the gun cabinet and are pleasant to carry around. So is a billiard cue—and it's about as useful for good, consistent shooting. With any luck, the concepts of weight and balance as applied to clays guns will impress enough shooters that the factories will get the message and start building better-handling bird guns.

Although I don't know all the reasons why the over/under is a more efficient target gun, I do know that it has nothing to do with the fabled "single sighting plane," which is one of the oldest rations of sheer hogwash in gundom. No gun has more than one "sighting plane," regardless of how many barrels it has or how they're arranged, and you don't "sight" a shotgun anyway; you just point it. But this is not to say that ribs are unimportant, and rib design is one thing that often sets clays guns apart.

The more highly refined pieces typically wear ribs a bit wider than those you'll find on game guns; 12 millimeters is a standard. Exactly what this does for target shooting, I'm not sure. Some awfully good clay shots tell me it makes a difference for them. From my own experience, I can only say I don't notice that a wider rib lets me break any more targets, nor any fewer, than a game-type rib.

Some makers—such as Beretta, Krieghoff, and Antonio Zoli—offer tapered ribs. These typically are wider at the breech than at the muzzle. The thinking seems to be that the taper subtly concentrates a shooter's vision, much on the order of looking down a pair of railroad tracks converging toward infinity.

While I'm not convinced that width is especially significant in rib design, height is something else again. The traditional low rib looks better to me, but I seem to break more targets with a high-rib gun. My old Marocchi Contrast, which was set up for International skeet, has a rib that stands a full half-inch above the top barrel. When I do my part, it's sheer death on sporting clays.

Like clays, International skeet is a low-gun game that often leaves only a narrow time-window in which to swing, mount, and shoot. You don't have to lift a high-rib gun quite as far to bring it to your eye and shoulder, which promotes an economy of motion that means a few milliseconds' edge in being quick without rushing. Moreover, being able to mount the gunbutt a tad lower on your shoulder makes recoil easier to manage, especially when you're shooting targets in pairs. Not all makers offer high ribs, but some of the best ones do—Beretta, Browning, and Perazzi, for instance. How high depends on the model and maker, but any rib taller than normal is worth considering.

A couple of other points about barrels. Just as skeet shooters long ago found that cage-type variable chokes help control recoil, so clay shooters are enjoying the virtues of ported barrels. Porting amounts to a series of holes in the barrel walls near the muzzle, positioned so escaping gas counteracts the forces that drive the muzzles upward. Eliminating a degree of muzzle-jump is a definite advantage for the second shot at pairs. A few makers offer factory-ported barrels, and most custom barrel shops can port any gun. This, too, is worth considering—though you should also be aware that porting directs a certain amount of muzzle-blast sideways and may not endear you to other shooters nearby.

Despite the fact that modern ammunition has made choke-boring all but obsolete, you'll have a hard time finding a new clays gun that doesn't have screw-in choke tubes, and an equally hard time finding serious clay shooters who don't fuss over which tube is the magic ticket for every field. If you need something to fret about, I suppose chokes are as good as anything; if you don't, stick in the most open tubes you have and forget about them.

Some makers treat their clays-model guns to some extra attention inside the barrels as well—overboring, longer forcing cones, and such—all in aid of achieving optimally dense, even patterns. Custom barrel shops can perform this sort of fine-tuning, but as factory work, it's typically available only in the higher price ranges. Browning and Ruger are the exceptions, offering overbored barrels at more modest prices.

Looking at the other end, you'll find clays guns stocked to standard field dimensions. Because clays courses include rising, falling, and crossing targets in about equal numbers, you're best served by a flat-shooting gun, one that puts the shot right where you look, without much built-in elevation.

The typical clays gun is also stocked with a pistol-grip, which is appropriate for the single trigger. And it may have a palm-swell besides; some shooters like them, others don't. I rather like the feel of one, myself.

Most clays guns also have moveable triggers that you can

slide forward or back to find the reach most comfortable for the size of your hand. Functionally, target guns have always had the best triggers among factory pieces, and clays guns are no exception, especially those from such makers as Beretta, Browning, Krieghoff, Marocchi, and Perazzi. Some are adjustable for weight of pull; all are crisp and smooth and light, and if you shoot one for a while, you'll never again be satisfied with anything less.

As I said at the start, the evolution of guns, like the evolution of everything else, is a matter of form adapting to function. Sporting clays being the wonderfully varied game it is, the guns that serve it best are in many ways the ideal of what any gun should be—dynamic, well-balanced, highly controllable, mechanically excellent. Like most target guns, they tend to be heavier than their counterparts built for game shooting, which is fine because the weight helps dampen recoil. A shooter who likes over/unders and doesn't find a $7^1/_2$- or 8-pound piece burdensome to carry afield would be hard-pressed to find a better factory-built gun for hunting. And anyone even moderately serious about shooting sporting clays could scarcely do better at all.

A P P E N D I X

SOURCES

―――――――――――

SOME OF THE GUNS REVIEWED IN THIS BOOK ARE EASY TO FIND, OTHERS ARE MORE DIFFICULT. THE LARGER COMPANIES LIKE BERETTA AND BROWNING AND RUGER HAVE EXTENSIVE DEALER PROGRAMS, AND THE CHANCES ARE YOU WON'T HAVE TO GO FAR TO FIND A DEALER NO MATTER WHERE YOU LIVE. MOST OF THE OTHERS ARE SERVED BY MUCH SMALLER SYSTEMS THAT MAY INCLUDE ONLY A SINGLE IMPORTER AND A VERY LIMITED NUMBER OF DEALERS; A LETTER OR PHONE CALL CAN USUALLY TURN UP CATALOGS, PRICE LISTS, AND OTHER INFORMATION.

BUT THE GUN BUSINESS BEING WHAT IT IS, SOURCES CAN CHANGE ALMOST OVERNIGHT AS ONE IMPORTER DECIDES TO DROP A CERTAIN LINE DUE TO LOW SALES; ANOTHER IMPORTER MAY OR MAY NOT STEP IN TO FILL THE VOID. THE FOLLOWING LIST IS CURRENT AT PUBLICATION TIME, BUT THERE'S NO TELLING HOW LONG IT WILL REMAIN SO.

FOR THOSE GUNS NO LONGER IN PRODUCTION, DEALERS ACTIVE IN THE SECONDARY MARKET ARE THE BEST SOURCES. YOU CAN FIND THEM THROUGH ADS IN THE SPORTING MAGAZINES LIKE *SHOOTING SPORTSMAN* AND IN PUBLICATIONS SUCH AS *THE GUN LIST*.

ARRIETA

THE PRIMARY ARRIETA IMPORTER IS:

Jack J. Jansma
0-1845 West Leonard Road
Grand Rapids, Michigan
49544-9610
616-677-1980
fax 616-677-1986

ARRIETA DEALERS INCLUDE:

Orvis
Historic Route 7A
Manchester, Vermont 05254
802-362-2580
fax 802-362-3525

Quality Arms
P.O. Box 19477
Houston, Texas 77224
713-870-8377
fax 713-870-8524

New England Arms Company
Box 278, Lawrence Lane
Kittery Point, Maine 03905
207-439-0593
fax 207-439-6726

Aguirre y Aranzabal–AyA

IMPORTERS AND DEALERS:

Fieldsport Ltd.
3313 W. South Airport Road
Traverse City, Michigan
49684
616-933-0767
fax 616-933-0768

British Game Guns
P.O. Box 5795
Kent, Washington 98064-5795
206-859-5164
fax 206-781-1233

John F. Rowe
2501 Rockwood Road
Enid, Oklahoma 73703
405-233-5942
fax 405-233-4038

**New England
Custom Gun Ltd.**
438 Willow Brook Road
RR2, Box 122W
West Lebanon, New
Hampshire 03784
603-469-3450
fax 603-469-3471

Armes de Chasse
P.O. Box 86
Hertford, North Carolina
27944
919-426-2245
fax 919-426-1557

Beretta

Beretta U.S.A. Corp.
17601 Beretta Drive
Accokeek, Maryland 20607
310-283-2191
fax 301-375-7677

Bernardelli

Armsport, Inc.
3590 NW 49th Street
(P.O. Box 523066)
Miami, Florida 33142
305-635-7850
fax 305-633-2877

Bertuzzi

**New England
Arms Company**
Box 278, Lawrence Lane
Kittery Point, Maine 03905
207-439-0593
fax 207-439-6726

Browning

Browning
Route One
Morgan, Utah 84050
801-876-2711
fax 801-876-3331

A.H. Fox

**Connecticut Shotgun
Manufacturing Company**
P.O. Box 1692
New Britain, Connecticut
06051-1692

203-255-6581

fax 203-832-8707

GARBI

**William Larkin Moore
& Company**

31360 Via Colinas, No. 109

Westlake Village, California
91361

818-889-4160

fax 818-889-1986

AND

8727 Via de Commercio,
Suite A

Scottsdale, Arizona 85258

602-951-8913

fax 602-951-3677

The Hunter Collection

3000-D Zelda Road

Montgomery, Alabama 36106

334-244-9586

fax 334-270-4134

HOLLAND & HOLLAND

Holland & Holland Ltd.

50 East 57th Street

New York, NY 10022

212-752-7755

fax 212-752-6805

STEVEN DODD HUGHES CUSTOM GUNS

Steven Dodd Hughes

P.O. Box 545

Livingston, Montana 59047

406-222-9377

KRIEGHOFF

Krieghoff International, Inc.

P.O. Box 549

Ottsville, Pennsylvania 18942

610-847-5173

fax 610-847-8691

LANBER

ITC International

720 Cumberland Point Drive,
Suite 5

Marietta, Georgia 30067

770-858-0048

fax 770-858-0051

MAROCCHI

Precision Sales International

P.O. Box 1776

Westfield, Massachusetts
01086

413-562-5055

fax 413-562-5056

MERKEL

GSI, Inc.

Box 129

Trussville, Alabama 35173

205-655-8299

fax 205-655-7078

PERAZZI

Perazzi U.S.A.

1207 S. Shamrock Avenue

Monrovia, California 91016

818-303-0068

fax 818-303-2081

B. RIZZINI

William Larkin Moore
& Company
31360 Via Colinas, No. 109
Westlake Village, California
91361
818-889-4160
fax 818-889-1986
AND
8727 Via de Commercio,
Suite A
Scottsdale, Arizona 85258
602-951-8913
fax 602-951-3677

The Hunter Collection
3000-D Zelda Road
Montgomery, Alabama 36106
334-244-9586
fax 334-270-4134

J&L RUTTEN

Labanu, Inc.
2201-F Fifth Avenue
Ronkonkoma, New York
11779
516-467-6197

UGARTECHEA

Aspen Outfitting Company
315 East Dean
Aspen, Colorado 81611
970-925-3406
fax 970-920-3706

Bill Hanus Birdguns
P.O. Box 533
Newport, Oregon 97356
541-265-7433

WEATHERBY

Weatherby, Inc.
3100 El Camino Real
Atascadero, California 93422
805-466-1767
fax 805-466-2527

GLOSSARY

ANSON & DEELEY ACTION: The original boxlock action, patented in 1875. The lock parts are fastened to the frame rather than mounted on removable sideplates, and the locks are cocked by leverage from the barrels when the action is opened.

ANSON LATCH: A forend fastener invented by William Anson in 1872, comprising a push-rod that extends out from the forend tip. It became a standard feature on English and European guns, especially side-by-sides. See *Deeley latch.*

BEND: The British term for what's known in America as the "drop" of a stock—the distance from the top of the barrel or rib to the comb of the stock.

BROACH: A cutting tool used to shape an inner surface; also, a tool used to slightly score metal surfaces, either for decoration or to help the surface retain oil.

BULINO: An engraving technique, developed in Italy, in which very fine lines are cut to create a shaded, three-dimensional effect. Done by a master, *bulino* can be almost photographic in its realism and detail. Also called "banknote" engraving, the term *bulino* derives from the Italian word for the engraving tool used in this sort of work.

CAST: The dimension of a gunstock in which the center of the butt is offset, right or left, from the centerline of the barrel or rib. A stock bent to the right, for a right-handed shooter, is said to be cast-off; bent to the left, it is cast-on.

CHOPPER-LUMP BARRELS: Barrels of a side-by-side gun in which half the barrel lump is an integral part of each tube, so called because a barrel with a half-lump resembles a chopping tool. Chopper lumps were first devised in the 1880s and are customarily used on best-quality guns.

DEELEY LATCH: A forend latch, co-patented in 1873 by John Deeley and James Edge, comprising a finger-lever mounted in a steel housing that is inletted in the forend wood. Along with the Anson latch, it is a world standard. It is sometimes called a Deeley & Edge latch.

DOVETAIL LUMP: In a side-by-side gun, a barrel lump that is milled as a separate part and fitted between the barrels in dovetail fashion.

DROP: See *Bend.*

DROP POINTS: Small, teardrop-shaped panels on a stock, located just behind the lockplates of a sidelock gun; occasionally seen on boxlocks, as well. Purely decorative, drop points are traditional features of best-quality guns.

ENGLISH SCROLL: A style of engraving featuring small, circular, scroll-like patterns. Derived from standard English patterns of jewelry engraving, scroll was first applied to guns in the 1870s and has since become a world-standard style of decoration. There are two basic forms—small and large. Small scroll is often combined with floral patterns and is sometimes called rose-and-scroll or bouquet-and-scroll engraving. Large scroll is bolder, more deeply cut, and shaded.

FENCES: Originally a steel barrier behind the priming pan of a flintlock or the nipple of a percussion lock, meant to shield the shooter from bits of burning powder or flying shards of an exploded percussion cap. With the advent of breechloaders, the term was applied to a gun frame's rounded bosses, which seal the barrel breeches when the action is closed.

FILE-MATTING: A technique of filing fine, crosshatched lines on the top of a rib to create a nonreflective surface.

FURNITURE: The term originally used to denote the various small metal parts of a flintlock or caplock gun—escutcheons, patch-box, forend tip, ramrod pipes, butt-plate, and so on. The forend tip, forend latch, trigger plate, and triggers of a breechloader are still sometimes called the furniture.

GREENER CROSS-BOLT: A fastening system for break-action guns invented by W.W. Greener. It comprises a transverse bolt, located at the top of the frame, that engages a lump extending from the breech-end of the barrels.

GRIP: The portion of a stock the shooter grasps with his trigger hand. Also called the "wrist" or, in England, the "hand."

HEAD: The portion of a stock that meets the frame. A solid fit between wood and metal is crucial. Fitting the head, a process called "heading-up," is the first step in making a gunstock.

HEEL: In America, the top rear-end of a gunstock. In England, this is called the "bump." There, the "heel" is the entire flat surface at the rear, what we call the "butt."

HEEL AND TOE PIECES: Small steel plates inletted at the heel and toe of a stock, partly for decoration, partly to protect the wood against chipping.

HOLLAND & HOLLAND ACTION: An action invented in the 1890s as the Holland & Holland Royal sidelock gun. The mechanics of the cocking system and lockwork have now become virtually the world standard for side-by-side sidelock guns.

HOLLOW RIB: A rib whose upper surface is concave in cross section.

INTERCEPTING SEARS: A secondary sear in a sideplate lock, meant to keep the tumbler, or hammer, from falling if the main sear is tripped by accident, such as being jarred off if the gun is dropped. Also called "safety sears."

INVESTMENT CASTING: The process of making metal parts, such as gun frames, by flowing molten steel into a mold. If the mold is properly made and gated, the casting is uniformly dense and free of voids or other internal flaws.

Lock plate: The steel plate on which the working parts of a sideplate lock are mounted.

Luggers: English term for the extractors of a break-action gun.

Pointing up: The process of cutting or filing checkering so that the diamonds come to a point on their tops.

Pull: The practical length of a stock, measured from the trigger (the front one, if there are two) to the center of the butt.

Purdey action: A self-opening action invented in 1879 by Frederick Beesley, who sold the rights to James Purdey & Sons the following year. It has been a Purdey signature ever since. It is unique in that the mainsprings of the locks force the action open when the fastening bolt is withdrawn and also cock the locks as the action is closed.

Purdey bolt: A sliding underbolt fastener for a break-open action, invented and patented by James Purdey the Younger in 1863. The bolt has two bearing surfaces that engage notches—"bites," in England—in the barrel lump. The system works on any side-by-side gun, sidelock or boxlock, and after the patent protection expired in 1877, the Purdey bolt was adopted by gunmakers worldwide.

Rebounding locks: Locks in which the tumblers, or hammers, rebound slightly after striking the firing pins. This type of lock was perfected in the 1860s by English lockmaker John Stanton. Although originally designed for exposed-hammer locks, the same system works equally well with so-called hammerless locks.

Round body: A gun frame whose bottom edges are rounded to reduce weight and lend a slimmer appearance. Not to be confused with "round action," which specifically denotes guns, built by John Dickson and others, made with the lockwork mounted on the trigger plate.

Standing breech: On a break-action gun, the vertical surface of the frame, against which the barrel breeches rest when the action is closed.

Strikers: Firing pins.

Striking: The process of shaping and smoothing the exterior of a gun barrel, done with a special, filelike tool.

Style: A designation or title, such as a company's official name.

Swamped rib: A rib with a concave profile, one that essentially follows the taper of the barrels from end to end.

Toe: The bottom rear-end tip of a stock.

Trigger plate: In a break-action gun, the steel plate to which the triggers are attached; the front end is mortised into the bottom of the frame, and the rear end forms the bottom tang.

Trunnions: Studs on the bottom barrel of an over/under that fit into notches in the frame to form the action hinge. In some guns, the studs are on the frame and the notches on the barrel.

Tumblers: The hammers of a so-called hammerless gun.

INDEX